Lecture Notes in Computer Science 7516

Commenced Publication in 1973
Founding and Former Series Editors:
Gerhard Goos, Juris Hartmanis, and Jan van Leeuwen

T0232345

Stefan Göbel   Wolfgang Müller
Bodo Urban   Josef Wiemeyer (Eds.)

E-Learning and Games for Training, Education, Health and Sports

7th International Conference, Edutainment 2012
and 3rd International Conference, GameDays 2012
Darmstadt, Germany, September 18-20, 2012
Proceedings

 Springer

Volume Editors

Stefan Göbel
Technische Universität Darmstadt
Multimedia Communications Lab – KOM
Rundeturmstr. 10, 64283 Darmstadt, Germany
E-mail: stefan.goebel@kom.tu-darmstadt.de

Wolfgang Müller
University of Education, Weingarten
Media Education and Visualization Group
Leibnitzstr. 3, 88250 Weingarten, Germany
E-mail: mueller@md-phw.de

Bodo Urban
Fraunhofer Institut für Graphische Datenverarbeitung IGD
Joachim-Jungius-Str. 11, 18059 Rostock, Germany
E-mail: bodo.urban@igd-r.fraunhofer.de

Josef Wiemeyer
Technische Universität Darmstadt
Human Sciences, Sport Science
Magdalenenstr. 27, 64289 Darmstadt, Germany
E-mail: wiemeyer@sport.tu-darmstadt.de

ISSN 0302-9743   e-ISSN 1611-3349
ISBN 978-3-642-33465-8   e-ISBN 978-3-642-33466-5
DOI 10.1007/978-3-642-33466-5
Springer Heidelberg Dordrecht London New York

Library of Congress Control Number: 2012946630

CR Subject Classification (1998): K.8.0, K.3.1, I.3.7, H.5.1-3, H.4.1-3, I.2.9-10, I.2.6,
H.5.1

LNCS Sublibrary: SL 3 – Information Systems and Application, incl. Internet/Web
and HCI

Typesetting: Camera-ready by author, data conversion by Scientific Publishing Services, Chennai, India

Printed on acid-free paper

Springer is part of Springer Science+Business Media (www.springer.com)

Preface

The GameDays were established in 2005 as a "science meets business" workshop in the field of serious games, taking place on an annual basis in Darmstadt, Germany. The principle aim is to bring together academia and industry and to discuss the current trends, grand challenges, and potentials of serious games for different application domains. Since 2010, the academic part has been emphasized resulting in the first International Conference on Serious Games for Sports and Health. In 2011, the GameDays spectrum of topics was broadened and the different facets, methods, concepts, and effects of game-based learning and training have been covered since then.

Similarly, the Edutainment conference provides an international forum for researchers and practitioners in various disciplines to share and exchange experiences in the emerging research area combining education and entertainment. Edutainment 2012 kept its tradition as a major international conference, facilitating the international exchange of the state of the art in academic research and practice. The conference covered all aspects of pedagogical principles, designs, and technological issues for education and entertainment.

The organizers of the GameDays series highly appreciated the request by the Edutainment initiators to bring Edutainment 2012 to Europe and to combine it with GameDays 2012. A joint Editorial Board and Program Committee were set up to cover both areas. All scientific papers were reviewed by 4 reviewers on average; the overall acceptance rate was 50%. Authors originated from 18 countries all over the world, among others Australia, China, Hong Kong, Japan, Singapore, Taiwan, and the United States, as well as Germany and different European countries.

The topics of the papers cover the fields of (game-based) training, teaching and learning, emerging learning and gaming technologies, authoring tools and mechanisms, and serious games for health. Further, two workshops were offered in the context of authoring tools for the creation of serious games and edutainment applications (StoryTec) and the selection of appropriate virtual environments for teaching and learning purposes (Vicero). Practical demonstrations of systems (e.g., tools or interactive installations) and applications (games, learning environments) – ranging from ideas and concepts (posters) to prototypes and commercially available products – were provided within the exhibition space throughout the three conference days. There were more than 30 exhibits altogether.

The editors would like to thank all PC members for their tremendous work and all institutions, associations, and companies for supporting and sponsoring the Edutainment and GameDays 2012 conference: Technische Universität Darmstadt (Multimedia Communications Lab – KOM, Institute for Sport Science, Graduate School Topology of Technology and Forum for Interdisciplinary

Research – FIF), Fraunhofer Institute for Computer Graphics, Hessen-IT, German Association of Computer Science, German Chapter of the ACM, G.A.M.E. (German game developers association), BIU (German association for the interactive entertainment industry), VDE/ITG Association for Electrical, Electronic and Information Technologies, Darmstadt Marketing, KTX Software Development, and Springer.

Special thanks goes to Springer for publishing the proceedings of the Edutainment conference series in LNCS since its beginning in 2006, to Hessen-IT for supporting the GameDays since its early days in 2005, and to the Forum for Interdisciplinary Research (FiF) for bundling and supporting the wide range of serious games research activities at the Technische Universität Darmstadt (TU Darmstadt). The forum offers space for topics, problems, and projects too broad to fit within the framework of a single discipline. It proved to be the perfect partner for expanding the various serious games research efforts and consolidating the network of serious games researchers at the TU Darmstadt. The disciplines involved in the FiF Serious Games Research Group range from computer science, bioinformatics, and civil engineering to mathematics, sports science, and psychology. Further information about the interdisciplinary research in serious games at TU Darmstadt is available at www.fif.tu-darmstadt.de.

Further information about the joint conference on E-Learning and Games for Training, Education, Health, and Sports is available on the conference website: http://www.edutainment2012.de, http://www.gamedays2012.de

July 2012   Stefan Göbel
                                                                          Wolfgang Müller
                                                                             Bodo Urban
                                                                          Josef Wiemeyer

Conference Co-chairs and Program Committee

Conference Co-chairs

Stefan Göbel	Technische Universität Darmstadt, Germany
Josef Wiemeyer	Technische Universität Darmstadt, Germany
Tom Gedeon	Australian National University, Australia
Wolfgang Müller	PH Weingarten, Germany
Zhigeng Pan	Hangzhou Normal University, Hangzhou, China
Bodo Urban	Fraunhofer Institute for Computer Graphics, Rostock, Germany
Kevin Wong	Murdoch University, Australia

Program Committee

Thomas Baranowski	Baylor College of Medicine, Houston, TX, USA
Gerald Bieber	Fraunhofer Institute for Computer Graphics, Rostock, Germany
Linda Breitlauch'	Mediadesign Hochschule, Düsseldorf, Germany
Maiga Chang	Athabasca University, Canada
Owen Conlan	Trinity College, Dublin, Ireland
Karin Coninx	Hasselt University, Belgium
Holger Diener	Fraunhofer Institute for Computer Graphics, Rostock, Germany
Ralf Dörner	RheinMain University of Applied Sciences, Wiesbaden, Germany
Abdulmotaleb El Saddik	University of Ottawa, Canada
Patrick Felicia	Waterford Institute of Technology, Ireland
Paul Grimm	University for Applied Sciences Fulda, Germany
Peter A. Henning	Karlsruhe University of Applied Sciences, Germany
Markus Herkersdorf	TriCAT GmbH, Germany
M. Shamim Hossain	King Saud University, Kingdom of Saudi Arabia
Jun Hu	Eindhoven University of Technology, The Netherlands
Ido Iurgel	Center for Computer Graphics, Minho, Portugal
Pamela Kato	University Medical Center Utrecht, The Netherlands
Fares Kayali	TU Vienna, Austria
Michael Kickmeier-Rust	TU Graz, Austria

Game Science – State of the Art in Game Research and Teaching Games at University

Noah Wardrip-Fruin

University of California, Santa Cruz, CA 95064, United States
nwf@soe.ucsc.edu

Abstract. Computer games have made amazing strides in the past 50 years — thanks to work in universities, national labs, and industry. We now see powerful games being made for entertainment, education, fitness, and other purposes. But we also see fundamental limitations in the technology and design approaches used to make today's games. These limitations have caused AAA team sizes to balloon, have walled designers off from much of the computational power of game technologies, and have made it impossible to integrate the things that matter most in other media into gameplay (including language, social state, storytelling, and more). This limits how much games can matter — and what they can teach us. At the University of California, Santa Cruz we are addressing these challenges directly, bringing computer science research into collaboration with game design and insights from the humanities and arts. We call our approach "Computational Media." This talk outlines our motivations, our approach, and a selection of our current projects.

Engage! Inspire! Through Digital Experiences

Wolfgang Müller-Wittig

Fraunhofer IDM@NTU,
Nanyang Technological University, Singapore
`wolfgang.mueller-wittig@fraunhofer.sg`

Abstract. Advances in computer graphics make the creation of realistic interactive virtual and augmented learning environments possible, enabling us to enjoy a whole ambience of new experiences. The effectiveness of education through such virtual means is well captured in this Chinese proverb: I hear - I forget, I see - I remember, I experience - I understand. With highly interactive visual real-time systems, users are submerged in simulated real worlds, where they can visualize complex data and processes in a realistic sensory environment. Apart from science centers, theme parks or museums where topics can be successfully transferred through attractive exhibits using highly interactive virtual and augmented worlds, these technologies are currently entering more and more the classroom offering new digital experiences which are complementary to existing educational approaches. Augmented reality in a classroom of young learners turns the usual learning space of tables, chairs and walls into a rich educational experience. Such interfaces can be either single-user or for multi-users. The single-user is able to interact with the environment, garner information, etc. In collaborative environments, we see the addition of social skills, group dynamics and teamwork towards a shared purpose. With edutainment scaling new heights, the common person is always looking for more interaction, more information in the real world context, at his fingertips and at an instant, and Augmented Reality is able to do this. And all without a keyboard!

Playware – Effects of Playful Training with Modular Playware

Henrik Hautop Lund

Center for Playware, Technical University of Denmark
Building 325, 2800 Kgs. Lyngby, Denmark
hhl@elektro.dtu.dk

Abstract. Playware is intelligent hardware and software that creates play. On particular example of such playware is modular interactive tiles that can provide playful training. The playful aspect of the modular interactive tiles motivates e.g. elderly to exercise, and thereby provides an opportunity for maintenance and rehabilitation of functional abilities amongst elderly people. Hence, the modular tiles are used both for prevention and for rehabilitation. The simple set up and adjustment to individual intervention and individual capabilities facilitates the use of the modular tiles both in institutions and in private homes. Hence, the technology can potentially be used to make a continuous flow for patients, in which training with modular tiles can take place in hospital, in training, rehab, and care institutions, and as home training in the private home, where the intervention and the effect is documented. Tests with the modular interactive tiles amongst elderly show that training with the modular tiles has a large effect on the functional abilities of the elderly. The tests of effect show that training with the modular tiles provides improvements on a broad range of abilities including mobility, agility, balancing, strength and endurance. The training improves the abilities of the elderly in many areas of high importance for activities of daily living, in contrast to several other forms of training and exercise, which typically only improve a subpart of these abilities. With the studies of effect amongst elderly, it is shown that playful training with the modular interactive tiles can give such significant effects with substantial less training sessions than what is needed with more traditional training. Indeed, significant improvement are obtained on all test parameters after just 9 training sessions, whereas research show that other training methods typically use at least 25 training sessions. In relation to groups in risk of loss of functional mobility, the tests show that 56At the same time, another test of effect shows that elderly training on the modular tiles improve their dynamic balance ability, whereas elderly in a control group who continue their normal daily activity with no training on modular tiles, decrease their dynamic balance ability. Even though the elderly start at the same level, with a statistical significant increase in balancing ability those elderly training on the tiles are transferred outside the risk group for falls, whereas those not training on the tiles remain at risk of falling.

The Body in Digital Games

Florian 'Floyd' Mueller

RMIT University, Bldg. 9.1.27, 124 LaTrobe St,
Melbourne, VIC 3000, Australia
floyd@floydmueller.com

Abstract. Playing with computers mostly means focusing on the mind, rather than the body. However, sports teaches us how powerful experiences can be if the body is involved. In consequence, I propose to see the body as a design opportunity to enhance the digital play experience. I argue that this can be achieved by framing the body's limitations as challenges that can facilitate bodily play, as inspired by sports. As such, I propose to put the human body into the center of the digital play experience. I illustrate this thinking by presenting recent work from the Exertion Games Lab, including a flying robot as jogging companion, games for commuters on public transport, interactive bicycle helmets, exercise gym equipment that incorporates computer gaming, and interactive basketball hoops.

Acquisition of Nutritional Knowledge Using Footgaming in the Classroom Setting

Robin Mellecker, Lisa Witherspoon, and Tom Watterson

Institute of Human Performance, The University of Hong Kong
robmel@hku.hk

Abstract. The increasing trend in childhood obesity coupled with decreasing levels of academic achievement have given rise to the introduction of innovative technology, which offers physical activity elements together with healthy lifestyle learning objectives. In this preliminary study, we aimed to determine whether participation in Footgaming in the classroom setting would result in learning healthy, nutritional concepts. The experiences of student participation in the academic classroom and teachers perceptions of using active gaming in the academic classroom were also reported in self report journals. A total of 57 students (grades 3rd-5th) played nutritional games on the computer utilizing their feet to control mouse functions on a Footgaming pad. Nutritional knowledge was assessed at baseline and following 10 weeks of Footgaming in the classroom. These preliminary findings suggest that children can learn nutritional concepts using active video games in the classroom setting. Further qualitative analysis revealed that both teachers and students valued the educational experience received from playing the nutritional games. Although preliminary, these findings are an important step in improving the understanding of the influence of physical activity based technologies in the classroom setting.

Table of Contents

Emerging Learning and Gaming Technologies

Authoring Tools and Mechanisms

Serious Games for Health

Workshops

Collaborative Virtual Environments for Training: A Unified Interaction Model for Real Humans and Virtual Humans

Andrés Saraos Luna, Valérie Gouranton, and Bruno Arnaldi

Université Européenne de Bretagne, France INSA, Inria, Irisa, UMR CNRS 6074,
F-35708 RENNES
{andres.saraos_luna,valerie.gouranton,bruno.arnaldi}@irisa.fr

Abstract. Our work ponders on collaborative interactions in Collaborative Virtual Environments for Training, with an emphasis on collaborative interactions between Real Humans and Virtual Humans working as a team. We put forward a new model of collaborative interaction and a set of tools that describes and defines such interactions.

1 Introduction

The use of virtual reality for training offer many assets: low cost and low risk, no need for physical and often costly equipment, possibility of various degree of teamwork [7]. In Collaborative Virtual Environments for Training (CVET), a group learn and practice the completion of a task as a team using all the assets provided by virtual reality. Depending on the system, the task can be extensively defined in a scenario or be defined as a global goal to pursue. Teammates can work together even though they are not physically in the same place using network, the task can be repeated as many times as necessary. The collaborative actions between teammates range from planning their next actions together to collaboratively manipulating objects, to remove a heavy piece of machinery for instance.

Moreover, teammates can either be human beings or computer generated agents. Teamwork between human beings and autonomous agents has been for some time a subject of interest [6]. Agents can be used in a variety of ways in this context. As collaborators, they share a common goal with their teammates and work towards its achievement. As troublemakers, they will try to interfere with the accomplishment of the task forcing its teammates to find alternate solutions or to deal with the additional issues. As teachers and guides, they can provide contextual help whenever they're needed. The different roles that agents can play in a team can be sorted in two main groups [26]:

- the role of an equal team member.
- the role of assistants to either the team as a whole or an individual team member,

S. Göbel et al. (Eds.): Edutainment 2012/GameDays 2012, LNCS 7516, pp. 1–12, 2012.

In CVETs all team members are on the same ground, working towards the same goal. CVETs therefore focuses on the first case.

Main Results. Our work concentrates on collaborative interaction in CVETs with a focus on collaborative interactions, more precisely collaborative manipulation of objects, between Real Humans (RH) and Virtual Humans (VH) working as a team. We propose a new collaborative interaction model and from it construct a set of tools to describe and define such collaborative interactions.

Organization. In section 2 we investigate related works. Throughout section 3 we present the collaborative interaction model constituting our contribution all the way to a demonstrator. Finally, we conclude in section 4.

2   Related Work

An overview on existing CVETS is presented in section 2.1 leading to an analysis on two points: the collaborative interactions offered to RHs and VHs, and the level of teamwork achieved. We then look at how behavior and interactions between objects can be described in section 2.2, and how collaborative interaction in virtual environments has been handled in previous works in section 2.3.

2.1   CVETs

In this section, we focus on CVET applications that emphasize on collaborative training and look at their interaction capability and the way RHs can interact with VHs. Three different collaboration levels in virtual environments have been identified [18]:

1. Awareness of team members' presence in the virtual space and communication between them.
2. Individual interaction of each user with objects in their environment.
3. Collaborative and codependent interaction of various users with the same object.

Scarcely any CVET implements level 3 collaboration. In the COVET [21] application, users learn collaboratively by looking, communicating and thus assisting one of the trainees who is the only one able to interact with the world. This is also the way most medical training applications implement collaboration [4], with one teacher performing the medical operation while students can switch viewpoints and communicate to learn the procedure. One exception is the CyberMed/CybCollaboration framework [25] that authorizes concurrent inputs from various users to the same object, although the only known application of the framework does not seem to use this asset. All these applications share another common point: none of them offer to interact with VH, thus not providing any collaborative teamwork with virtual users.

The Dugdale's fire training simulation [10] stops at the second level of collaboration and was aimed to support collaboration between RH and VH. However, the demonstrator was implemented using only RH and succeeding works focused on agent-only collaborative work for emergency management [12].

The MASCARET model implemented in the SecureVI fire-training application [23], proposes a framework for designing pedagogical software with team training. The model supports interaction through their "interaction network" where a source agent and a target agent exchange information about the interaction. Although this model seems to support collaborative input, it is not explicitly addressed and not implemented in the SecureVI software.

We note that the collaborative work is often viewed as one user interacting with the virtual environment while the other users can share his view, feedback and/or actions. Even though some models state to authorize joint manipulations of objects, it is scarcely addressed and even less so implemented.

2.2   Interaction Description

The research in behavioral animation can be narrowed down to 3 approaches [9], stimulus response systems, rules systems and state machines. In stimulus response systems, each stimulus evolves through a grid of interconnected nodes to generate a behavior from the system, as done with the SCA network [16] to control the behavioral animation of a VH. Although these networks offer responsive and reusable behaviors, the underlying mechanisms produce behavior with low-level of both abstraction and control.

Rules systems approaches like Reynolds' flock of birds [24] or Blumberg's dog modelization [3] propose to assign simple rules to model behavior. Complex group behavior emerges from the rules defined for each entity. This gives us a high level of abstraction to describe entities' behavior but low re-usability as the rules are designed for each system. As the environment becomes more complex and the number of rules increases, run-time is slowed thus making it difficult to use in an interactive context.

Although simple state machines are deemed impractical to describe complex behaviors [17], hierarchical and parallel-state machines like the HPTS language [8] allow a precise tuning of behavior while maintaining re-usability. However the process of designing complex automata can be long and tedious.

The Simulation and Training Object-Relation Model (STORM) [19] is an hybrid method built from the state machine family and aims to regroup the properties of existing methods in one model in order to obtain a generic and reusable solution. STORM is composed of two parts : a behavioral model to easily describe reusable objects, and an interaction engine which defines a standard process that allows objects to interact with potentially unknown objects. The capacities are designed as to be pluggable into any existing STORM object with few parameters to configure. Any object can then be enhanced with existing capacities, allowing the description of behavioral objects in a generic and reusable way.

The main drawback of the existing approaches is that collaborative manipulations are not explicitly taken into account by the existing techniques, which makes the description of collaborative interactions between users difficult.

2.3 Collaborative Interaction

Interaction methods for individual users serve as a ground base for collaborative techniques. We only consider virtual hand and virtual pointers technique as they prove to be more suitable for a collaborative setting [2]. However, these techniques need to be re-factored for collaborative usage.

A first approach is to restrain users to different degrees of freedom to interact with the object [22]. If one user modifies an object's orientation, this parameter becomes unavailable to a second user who would only be able to alter the object's position in space. As such, it is still possible to use single user techniques for users with different points of view in the environment. The main drawback is that it hurts the credibility of the interaction as real world interactions are not cleanly disjoined in this way.

We thus consider interaction techniques allowing concurrent access to the same properties of an object. A variety of techniques exists: by averaging forces applied to objects via multiple virtual hands, virtual 3D cursors or variations of the virtual ray metaphor. One of the main issues of such techniques is the feedback given to the users in return of the actions, both theirs and their teammates'. Without force feedback, it can be difficult to offer the users a proper one.

An interaction as a bidirectional communication between two objects, named tool and interactive object [13][1]. The tool sends commands and parameters to an interactive object that is responsible for the treatment of the commands. Pluggable extensions to objects convey the ability to interact or be interacted upon, with no prior knowledge of the available parameters needed to initiate the control. When various tools control the same parameters of a single interactive object, the latter deals with concurrent inputs as he sees fit and the sends feedback of the final result to the connected tools. The extension mechanism makes it generic enough to be adapted on existing models although the presented implementation depends heavily on the OpenMask [1] platform.

We raise one main common issue amongst all the presented works: none of them seems to consider VHs as users of the interaction methods. It is always assumed that a human being is the source of interaction, and as such the methods may need some tuning to allow virtual users.

2.4 Synthesis

To conclude this state of the art, let us underline the key points of our analysis:

1. Interactions between objects in the virtual world can be described in a generic way, but the available models don't take *collaborative manipulation* into account.
2. Objects of the environment can be controlled by human beings, single-handedly or collaboratively. Virtual humans are not considered as potential *users* by the exposed methods of interaction.

---

[1] COllaboRative Virtual Environment for Technical Training and Experiment, http://corvette.irisa.fr/

3. *Collaboration between Real Humans and Virtual Humans* is scarcely addressed in existing CVETs, and even less so when considering collaborative manipulation of an object by users of different nature.

3   Unified Interaction Model for Real Humans and Virtual Humans

After a quick overview of our objectives (section 3.1) and a presentation of our experimental use case (section 3.2), we define a new collaborative interaction model, named **Collaborative-STORM** (C-STORM), based on the STORM model (section 3.3). C-STORM collaborative objects can be manipulated from multiple sources, thus achieving a level 3 collaborative interaction. We then use this model as a ground base to define the **Interaction Mediator** (InterMed) (section 3.4), an entity connecting the user, real or virtual, to the virtual environment. The InterMed is an inhabitant of the virtual world and as such is able to perceive and interact with its environment. We finally expose an implementation of these concepts in a demonstrator (section 3.5).

3.1   Overview

The construction of our novel collaborative manipulation model aims for the following objectives:

1. *The construction* of a model capable of describing generic collaborative interactions and behaviors.
2. *The unification* of Virtual Humans and Real Humans as interactors and users of the CVET.
3. *The implementation* of those collaborative methods in a CVET.

Connecting RHs and VHs to the virtual world through a mediator offers a number of benefits. From a software engineering point of view, it greatly simplifies the design process. All the actions are performed by the InterMed, regardless of the nature of the commanding user and thus only need to be defined as such. From a behavioral point of view, VHs interacting through the C-STORM model make no difference between RHs and VHs as everyone is embodied by an InterMed. Interactions between users in the virtual world are consequently abstract from the nature of the user. From a usage point of view, RH using the system can collaborate with the other teammates in the virtual world while being unaware of their real nature without impeding their task.

3.2   Experimental Use Case

Throughout our contribution section, we provide examples extracted from our experimental use case. It provides a collaborative setting in which various people have to build a small piece of furniture. Some steps can be carried out by one person and some others need two or more people to collaboratively interact. Some knowledge concerning the handling of various tools (screwdriver, hammer...) is needed. The key step in which we will focus for our examples is the screwing process, where one user needs to take control of a screwdriver in order to screw some pieces of furniture together.

3.3   The Collaborative-STORM Model

The **Collaborative-STORM** model takes advantage of the perks of the STORM model and constructs upon it to address its lack of description of collaborative manipulation of one object by various users. C-STORM displays new capacities that will give C-STORM objects the ability to control other objects, and to share this control with multiple other sources. This mechanism allows users, who are considered as objects, to share the control of an object, thus achieving *collaborative manipulation*. A small example of how STORM connects objects through relations is provided in Fig1.

Two new capacities are introduced by the C-STORM model: the **Interactor** capacity and the **Interactive Object** capacity. The Interactor capacity grants C-STORM objects the ability to take control of objects disclosing the Interactive Object capacity. The latter offers a list of controllable parameters and treats the commands it receives. This mechanism grants users the aptitude to take control of objects in the virtual environment. From now on, we will refer to objects enhanced with the according capacity as *interactors* and *interactive objects*.

The control mechanism is encapsulated in a dedicated relation. The **Collaborative Interaction Protocol Relation** (CIPR) connects Interactor and Interactive Object capacities, as illustrated in Fig. 2. The CIPR opens a communication channel between interactors and interactive objects. Through this channel, they play out a protocol that determines the terms of the control contract between them. Once the connection is established, the **Control Relation** (CR) takes over. CR is a sub-relation contained in the CIPR. It delivers all parameters, commands and feedback sent from one object to the other, as long as no ending signal is received from within the CIPR.

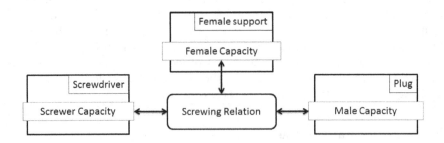

Fig. 1. Example: a STORM Relation: behavioral objects linked together

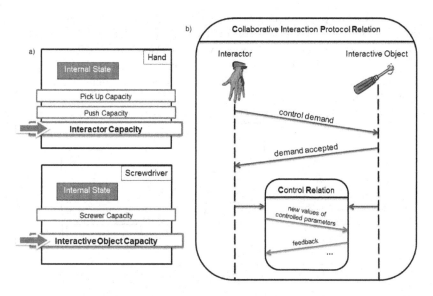

Fig. 2. a) Two C-STORM objects with the Interactor and Interactive Object capacities.
b) The CIPR plays out the communication protocol between 2 C-STORM objects, then
the CR conveys the different signals and commands from one object to the other

The control protocol can be split into the following steps:

- The interactor initiates contact, asking for a control authorization and the parameters available to him.
- The interactive object considers the demand. If it is accepted, a clearance is sent along the parameters it offers for modification.
- The CIPR inititates the CR, which will serve as a transmission channel for new parameters values.
- When the CIPR receives an ending signal, the control is terminated.

Each interactive object can accept multiple connections from multiple interactors. The way concurrent inputs are evaluated is parameter dependant and is handled internally by the interactive object. In the same way, interactors can be connected to various interactive objects and consequently control several objects simultaneously.

C-STORM objects effectively achieve *collaborative manipulation* through the Interactor and Interactive Object capacities. Collaborative objects can be constructed directly from existing objects thanks to the capacity mechanism, facilitating the design process and offering *reusable collaborative behaviors*.

Example. We modelize a sequence extracted from our use case presented is section 3.2, illustrated in Fig.3. To build the piece of furniture, it is required to screw a few pieces together. To do so, we use a Screwing Relation that connects a screwdriver with the Screwer capacity, a female support with a Female capacity and a plug with a Male capacity. The screwdriver and the male plug need to be put in a certain position in order to proceed with the Screwing Relation. Interactor capacities are connected to the screwer tool and the male plug through CRs. This allows the interactors to modify the position and orientation in space of the objects they control. Once the screwdriver and the male plug are in a certain area of effect defined in the Screwing relation, the behavior associated with the relation can proceed.

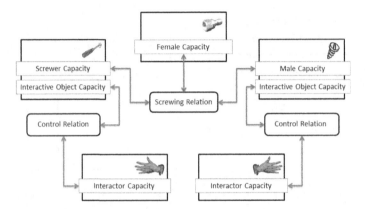

Fig. 3. The screwing relation example, two hands controlling the screwdriver and the screw thanks to Control Relations

3.4 The Interaction Mediator

Using the C-STORM model defined in the previous section, we construct a unified interaction model for both RHs and VHs by introducing a new C-STORM object, the **Interaction Mediator**. This new tool allows us to define a unified model of interaction for RHs and VHs.

Concept. We define in the term **users** either real or virtual humans involved in the teamwork. This decision arises from the role VHs play in the team. As they assume the role of an equal team member, we propose that they share the same characteristics. We thus choose to dissociate the users from the interactive actions within the virtual world. Users are considered as living outside the virtual environment; as such, they can't interact directly with objects in the environment and don't have knowledge about the objects either. They are independant of any kind of embodiment in the virtual world.

We thus have on the one hand objects in the virtual environment that can interact with each other, and on the other hand users that cannot alter the environment. We introduce a specific object of the environment, *a mediator* closing the bridge between the users and the virtual world.

This mediator is more than a simple embodiment though. It is an entity living in the virtual space, capable of perceiving the objects surrounding it and storing all the perceived data into its knowledge base. Unlike the users, the mediator can thus perceive the virtual environment and as an object it can interact with other objects. However, being deprived of any kind of decision process it will never initiate interactions on its own.

Users, either real or virtual, can consequently connect to a mediator to interact with the virtual world through the mediator's interaction capabilities and use its knowledge to aid their decision process. Mediators serve as a *gateway* unifying the interaction commands sent by the users, and relaying the knowledge acquired from within the virtual world. We will refer to this mediator as an **Interaction Mediator** (InterMed) as illustrated in Fig.4.

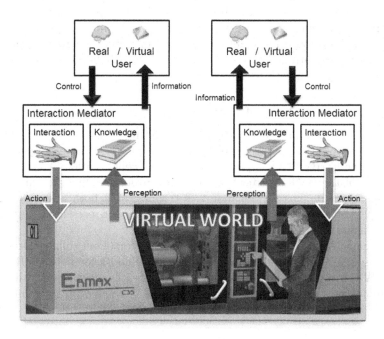

Fig. 4. The InterMed, a mediator between the users and the virtual world

Model. Having defined our user notion and its connection to the virtual world, we integrate the concept into our C-STORM model. Our key concept, the InterMed, is constructed as a special C-STORM object. As stated before, users control InterMeds to interact with the virtual world. Translated in our modelization, this means users are represented as interactors that can take control of InterMeds, through the CIPR relation described in section 3.1. The user is embedded in a C-STORM object that transmits his commands to the connected InterMed. As such, it needs a list of the parameters and commands it can convey, encapsulated in a dedicated activity. The data is then transmitted through the Interaction capacity to the controlled InterMed.

The InterMed can perceive and interact with other objects, and receives control inputs from the connected user. The interaction mechanism is assured by the Interactive Object and Interactor capacities to let users control the InterMed and to let the InterMed interact collaboratively with other objects. The perceptive capabilities of the InterMed are encapsulated in a new capacity, the Perceptive capacity. It grants the ability to perceive the environment via various perceptive channels. All the capacities of the InterMed can be adjusted by the designer at will. Any type of InterMed can be designed by fine tuning its capacities, from a floating eye to a full-fledged humanoid. The awareness of the Perceptive Puppet fully depends on the implementation of its Perceptive capacity.

This model follows our concept key points: users interact with the virtual world by controlling InterMeds. The knowledge acquired by the InterMed through its perceptive channel is available for the user that controls it, allowing informed decision making. InterMeds can interact alone or collaboratively thanks to the C-STORM mechanisms described in section 3.3. Consequently, as InterMeds can be controlled by either a RH or a VH, collaborative manipulation occurs seamlessly even with users of different nature.

3.5   Validation: A Proof of Concept

We demonstrate our InterMed concept by implementing the model described in section 3.3 in our experimental platform. This platform is developed in the context of the CORVETTE [1] project, a Research collaboration. The project is a follow-up of the GVT [2] project, a VR platform for building virtual training environments, that aims for collaborative training with both real and virtual humans [20][14][15]. The CORVETTE project has been presented during the LAVAL Virtual 2012 event [3].

The demonstrator serves as an early implementation of our collaborative tools in an existing CVETs, a first step to full-fledged collaboration between RHs and VHs in CVETs and this paper does not aim at a full explanation of our validation. Our demonstrator (Fig.5) allows for a VH and RH to collaboratively manipulate a piece of furniture. Each user is embodied by an InterMed.

Fig. 5. Left: Our demonstrator in action, with two humanoid InterMeds collaboratively manipulating a piece of furniture. Right: The CORVETTE project as exposed in the LAVAL Virtual 2012 event.

---

[2] Generic Virtual Training, https://www.gvt-nexter.fr/

[3] http://www.laval-virtual.org/

4   Conclusion

The analysis of existing work highlighted various gaps in collaborative training between Real Humans and Virtual Humans in Collaborative Virtual Environments for Training. A new model of collaborative interaction was needed in order to easily describe and integrate collaborative actions between RHs and VHs in CVETs. Throughout this paper, we presented:

1. **Collaborative-STORM**, a generic collaborative model of interaction between objects.
2. **The Interaction Mediator**, a specific C-STORM object serving as a gateway between users either real or virtual and the virtual environment.
3. **A demonstrator** showcasing an implementation of our concepts in an existing CVET platform, the GVT project.

These contributions successfully address the identified needs. Moreover, the work hereby presented opens doors to many upgrades: pushing forward with our unified model to propose an effective interchangeability between users during teamwork, proposing various profiles of InterMeds by altering or improving their capacities or even considering mutual control of an InterMed by various users. The presented work and its subsequent follow ups could also be considered in a gaming context, although it is not the focus of this paper.

Acknowledgments. This work was supported by the French Research National Agency project named CORVETTE (ANR-10-CONTINT-CORD-012).

References

1. Aguerreche, L., Duval, T., Arnaldi, B.: A description of a dialog to enable interaction between interaction tools and 3D objects in collaborative virtual environments. In: VRIC 2009, pp. 63–73 (2009)
2. Aguerreche, L., Duval, T., Lécuyer, A.: Comparison of Three Interactive Techniques for Collaborative Manipulation of Objects in Virtual Reality. CGI 2010 Computer Graphics International (2010)
3. Blumberg, B., Todd, P., Maes, P.: No bad dogs: Ethological lessons for learning in hamsterdam, pp. 295–304 (1996)
4. Boulanger, P., Wu, G., Bischof, W.F., Yang, X.D.: Hapto-audio-visual environments for collaborative training of ophthalmic surgery over optical network. In: IEEE International Workshop on Haptic Audio Visual Environments and their Applications, HAVE 2006, pp. 21–26 (2006)
5. Bowman, D., Kruijff, E., LaViola, J., Poupyrev, I.: 3D User Interfaces: Theory and Practice. Addison-Wesley (2005) ISBN 0-201-75867-9
6. Christoffersen, K., Woods, D.D.: How to make automated systems team players. In: Advances in Human Performance and Cognitive Engineering Research, pp. 1–12 (2002)
7. Cobb, S., D'Cruz, M., Day, A., David, P., Gardeux, F., van de Broek, E.L., van de Voort, M.C., Meijer, F., Izkara, J.L., Mavrikios, D.: How is VR used to support training in industry? In: The Intuition Network of Excellence Working Group on Education and Training in VRIC 2008, pp. 75–83 (2008)

8. Donikian, S.: HPTS: a behaviour modelling language for autonomous agents. In: Proceedings of the Fifth International Conference on Autonomous Agents, pp. 401–408 (2001)
9. Donikian, S.: Modelling, control and animation of autonomous virtual agents evolving in structured and informed environments Habilitation to supervise research in computer science, University of Rennes 1 (2004)
10. Dugdale, J., Pavard, B., Pallamin, N., El Jed, M.: Emergency fire incident training in a virtual world. In: Proceedings ISCRAM 2004 (2004)
11. Dugdale, J., Darcy, S., Pavard, B.: Engineering effective cooperation and communication: a bottom-up approach, pp. 58–65 (2006)
12. Dugdale, J., Bellamine-Ben Saoud, N., Pavard, B., Pallamin, N.: Simulation and Emergency Management, p. 229 (2009)
13. Duval, T., Le Tenier, C.: 3D Collaborative interactions within virtual environments with OpenMASK for technical objects exploitation. Mécanique & Industries, 767–797 (2004)
14. Gerbaud, S., Mollet, N., Arnaldi, B.: Virtual Environments for Training: From Individual Learning to Collaboration with Humanoids. In: Hui, K.-C., Pan, Z., Chung, R.C.-K., Wang, C.C.L., Jin, X., Göbel, S., Li, E.C.-L. (eds.) Edutainment 2007. LNCS, vol. 4469, pp. 116–127. Springer, Heidelberg (2007)
15. Gerbaud, S., Gouranton, V., Arnaldi, B.: Adaptation in Collaborative Virtual Environments for Training. In: Chang, M., Kuo, R., Kinshuk, Chen, G.-D., Hirose, M. (eds.) Edutainment 2009. LNCS, vol. 5670, pp. 316–327. Springer, Heidelberg (2009)
16. Granieri, J.P., Becket, W., Reich, B.D., Crabtree, J., Badler, N.I.: Behavioral control for real-time simulated human agents. In: SI3D 1995, pp. 173–180. ACM Press (1995)
17. Kallmann, M., Thalmann, D.: Modeling Objects for Interaction Tasks. In: Proc. Eurographics Workshop on Animation and Simulation, pp. 73–86 (1998)
18. Margery, D., Arnaldi, B., Plouzeau, N.: A general framework for cooperative manipulation in virtual environments. Virtual Environments 99, 169–178 (1999)
19. Mollet, N., Gerbaud, S., Arnaldi, B.: STORM: a Generic Interaction and Behavioral Model for 3D Objects and Humanoids in a Virtual Environment. In: IPT-EGVE the 13th Eurographics Symposium on Virtual Environments, pp. 95–100 (2007)
20. Mollet, N., Gerbaud, S., Arnaldi, B.: An Operational VR Platform for Building Virtual Training Environments. In: Hui, K.-c., Pan, Z., Chung, R.C.-k., Wang, C.C.L., Jin, X., Göbel, S., Li, E.C.-L. (eds.) Edutainment 2007. LNCS, vol. 4469, pp. 140–151. Springer, Heidelberg (2007)
21. Oliveira, J.C., Hosseini, S., Shirmohammadi, M., Cordea, M., Petriu, N.D., Petriu, E., Georganas, D.C.: Virtual theater for industrial training: A collaborative virtual environment (2000)
22. Pinho, M.S., Bowman, D.A., Freitas, C.M.D.S.: Cooperative Object Manipulation in Immersive Virtual Environments. In: Proceedings of the ACM Symposium on Virtual Reality Software and Technology, Hong Kong, China, pp. 171–178 (2002)
23. Querrec, R., Buche, C., Maffre, E., Chevaillier, P.: SécuRévi : virtual environments for fire-fighting training. In: Proceedings of the 5th Virtual Reality International Conference, VRIC 2003 (2003); Computer Graphics Forum, 41–52 (1998)
24. Reynolds, C.W.: Flocks, herds, and schools: A distributed behavioral model. Computer Graphics 21(4), 25–34 (1987)
25. Sales, B.R.A., Machado, L.S., Moraes, R.M.: Interactive collaboration for virtual reality systems related to medical education and training. In: 6th Int. Conf. on Tech. and Medical Sciences, Porto (2010)
26. Sycara, K., Sukthankar, G.: Literature Review of Teamwork Models Robotics Institute (2006)

Developing a Situated Virtual Reality Simulation for Telerobotic Control and Training

Tom Gedeon, Dingyun Zhu, and Stephane Bersot

Research School of Computer Science, College of Engineering and Computer Science,
The Australian National University, Canberra, ACT 0200, Australia
{tom.gedeon,dingyun.zhu}@anu.edu.au, stephane.besot@gmail.com

Abstract. In this paper, we present the development of a situated virtual reality simulation for control and training in a telerobotic mining setting. The original research scenario is derived from a real-world rock breaking task in mining teleoperation. With the intention of having better situational awareness and user control model for this application, we simulate the entire setting in a 3D Virtual Reality (VR) environment. Therefore, users are able to obtain more information (e.g. depth information) and feedback from the remote environment in this simulation than only working with real video streams from the remote camera(s). In addition, the concept of natural interaction has been applied in building more intuitive user control interfaces than conventional manual modes. Both human eye gaze and head movements have been used to develop natural and interactive viewpoint control models for users to complete the teleoperation task. By using such a 3D simulation, training in the complex teletotobic control process can be effectively carried out with the capability of changing visual and control conditions easily. A user study has also been conducted as the preliminary evaluation of the simulation. Encouraging feedback has been provided by the experimental participants regarding task learning, which suggests the effectiveness of using the simulation.

Keywords: situated virtual reality, simulation, training, telerobotic control, teleoperation, 3D models, natural interaction, eye tracking, head tracking.

1 Introduction

Virtual Reality (VR) environments have been used extensively in a variety of fields, such as video games [13], industrial applications [1], medical simulations [4], education and training [9], and so on. VR environments are commonly recognized as computer-based simulations through which users can interact with virtual objects or stimuli that are modeled from the real world. Using such environments offers users numerous advantages and benefits such as being immersive, interactive and cost-effective.

There has been much research and development work regarding using virtual reality techniques to construct simulations for different types of teleoperation applications. Conducting effective training to improve user performance is the common motivation

S. Göbel et al. (Eds.): Edutainment 2012/GameDays 2012, LNCS 7516, pp. 13–22, 2012.
© Springer-Verlag Berlin Heidelberg 2012

of building VR based simulations. In this research, we developed a virtual reality simulation which is able to connect to the modeled setting in the real world. By connection to the modeled setting, we mean the interaction between the user and the VR environment will have the same effect as the modeled setting in the real world. In terms of training purpose for using such simulations, it would provide us extra feedback from the real setting compared with only using pure VR environments.

Apart from the common advantage of using VR in teleoperation, which offers depth information [7] for the remote environment, we also import natural human interaction (e.g. eye gaze and head movements) into the user control part of the simulation. The entire motivation of this research work is to develop a VR simulation that is a sufficiently good 3D representation of reality with an improved user control interface by using natural interaction for the effective training in a particular mining teleoperation setting.

2   Development

The original mining teleoperation setting considered in this research development is a telerobotic control system for conducting remote rock breaking task in mining [2]. A lab-based version of the remote control system has been built mainly for demonstration and testing.

Fig. 1. The real lab-based rock breaker setting

As shown in Figure 1, the real lab-based rock breaker setting consists of a robot arm as the major control device which is very similar to the one used in the real mining setting in terms of its physical structure and possible movements. In addition, a pair of cameras has been integrated into this setting to provide real-time visual feedback from the remote environment back to the user to complete the mining teleoperation task.

2.1   System Architecture

The developed virtual reality simulation for the lab-based setting consists of several components:

1. 3D model of the entire environment
2. User control interface for devices
3. Real-time tracking of rocks
4. Natural interaction based virtual camera control

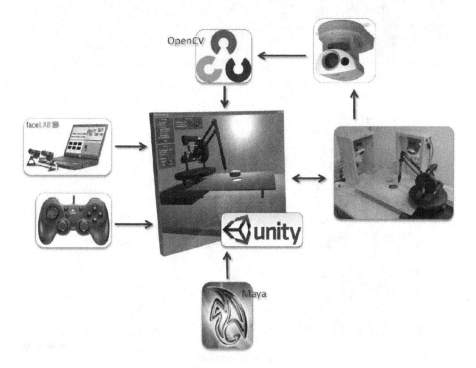

Fig. 2. Overall system architecture for the simulation

The overall VR simulation system architecture is illustrated in Figure 2. A number of software tools as well as hardware interfaces are used to develop the VR simulation. The major difference from building a traditional VR simulation is this system connects the VR environment to the real world setting which is being modeled.

2.2   3D Modeling

The 3D modeling for the entire environment setting is done in Maya [5]. As shown in Figure 3, the modeled virtual objects for being used in the simulation include the robot arm, wooden board and rocks. These models are only static 3D objects therefore they then have been imported into Unity3D [8] to have relative physics in animation (see Figure 4), such as all the possible movements of the robot arm.

Fig. 3. 3D modeling in the simulation

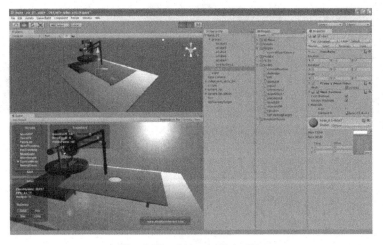

Fig. 4. Simulation in Unity3D

2.3   User Control Interface and Feedback

There are many options for user control interface to connect to the simulation in Unity3D platform. Conventional interfaces for instance mouse and keyboard are not always appropriate for a teleoperation task. Therefore, we chose to integrate a standard Logitech Dual Action Gamepad (see Figure 5) as the major user control interface for our simulation because it is easy to use, simple to implement or integrate into systems and cheap to replace.

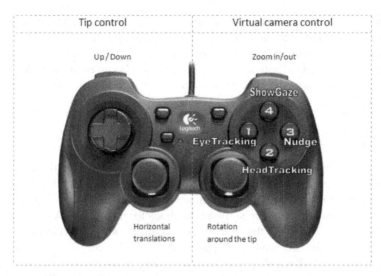

Fig. 5. Gamepad as user control interface

The 3D model of the robot arm is connected to the real robot arm via a UDP network. In practice, it is possible to encounter situations like the real robot arm is moving slower than the virtual one because of network latency or the real one can even be stuck at some point due to unexpected circumstances. Therefore, it would be very helpful for users to have visual feedback regarding the position difference between the virtual robot arm and the real one when such situations occur. In the simulation, we implemented a feature (called "*ghost*") to satisfy this requirement.

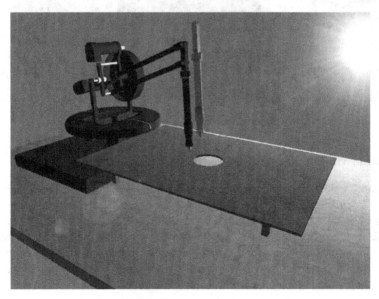

Fig. 6. The *ghost* robot arm

As shown in Figure 6, the *ghost* is actually a second 3D robot arm with a different colour and transparent pattern. It will appear when the position difference/error between the real robot arm and the virtual one exceeds a pre-defined limit. In this way, users have a direct visual feedback of the real robot arm's current position through the *ghost* and the position of the virtual robot arm which represents the intended position to move to.

2.4   Vision Based Rock Tracking

In order to simulate the movements of other objects especially for the rocks in the simulation, we developed a computer vision based rock tracking software approach. This solution is implemented by integrating OpenCV [6] into our simulation with further development of particular software functions for real-time rock tracking.

The basic feature used for the rock tracking is the colour information of the rocks as it is distinguished from other objects in the environment. Figure 7 shows the process of how the rock tracking works by our software solution on top of OpenCV. It takes the real-time video images from the remote cameras (shown in Figure 1) as the source inputs, then feeds them into a filtering function to convert the colour images into black and white where the white bits represent the rocks which need to be tracked. After completion of the filtering process, the position data of the detected rocks will be sent to Unity3D to create corresponding virtual rocks in the simulation. The entire process happens in real-time and it is capable of tracking multiple rocks simultaneously.

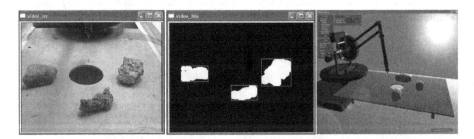

Fig. 7. Rock tracking using OpenCV

2.5   Head Movements and Eye Gaze for Viewpoint Control

The default implementation of virtual camera viewpoint control for the simulation is using the Logitech gamepad. However, recent research has also pointed out the effectiveness of using natural interaction such as human head movements [11] and eye gaze [12] as alternative user inputs for the camera viewpoint control in teleoperation settings. In order to develop such camera viewpoint control modes which are more intuitive than conventional manual interfaces, we integrated another external gaze and head tracking system (*FaceLab* [3]) into our simulation.

The *FaceLab* system (see Figure 8) is a computer vision based tracking device which provides the real-time head and gaze tracking at a 60 Hz frequency without the use of markers. This avoids the need to make the user wear any specialized sensors on their head, offering comfort and flexibility. Head mounted trackers may provide more accuracy and a higher tracking frequency but they are not comfortable to wear for long, therefore they were not considered for our simulation.

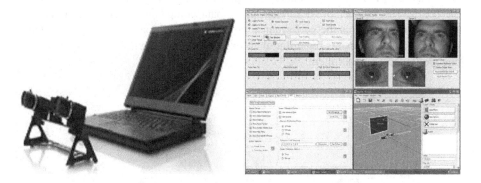

Fig. 8. The *FaceLab* tracking system

The detailed control mapping of using head movements and gaze for the virtual camera in our simulation uses head movements to control the camera position and zoom in/out, and using eye gaze to control the camera pan and tilt functions. This means when a user moves their head either left or right enough (more than a defined threshold limit), the virtual camera in the simulation will start to rotate clockwise/anti-clockwise around the robot arm with a constant speed. Moreover, if the user leans their head towards/backwards to the screen, the virtual camera will carry out corresponding zoom in/out functions. Another essential feature of developing such virtual camera control modes is this will effectively allow users to handle the common multitasking situation in teleoperation [10].

3   Preliminary User Study and Feedback

Compared to the relatively large number of features we intended to test in the simulation, we had a limited number of experimental participants available in the available time frame. Therefore, only a preliminary user study was conducted as the initial evaluation for the VR based simulation at this stage.

The actual experimental setup is shown in Figure 9. A total of 12 volunteers from a local university successfully participated in the study, including 8 male and 5 female, ranging from 21 to 49 years of age ($M_{age} = 27.5$, $SD_{age} = 7.1$). All of them were regular computer users (at least 1 hour a day) either enrolled in a computing/IT related major or working in close areas. They all had prior experience of using a gamepad interface for video games. None of them had any previous experience on any eye tracking or head tracking interfaces as well as the simulation. Several participants had corrected vision but all the participants' eye gaze could be calibrated with the tracker successfully in the user study.

Participants took part in the user study individually. Their experimental task was trying to nudge as many rocks as they could into the hole on the board in a limited task completion time, which was similar to the rock breaking process in the real mining setting. Each participant was given 3 one-minute working time period and in between they were asked to stop as the experimenter would be placing rocks back on the board. The number of rocks each participant completed within the limited time period was recorded as the performance measure. In addition, they were requested to give subjective comments regarding their experience of using this simulation after the completion of the experiment.

Fig. 9. The experimental setup

The overall performance was quite good. Regardless of previous video game experience, every participant was able to complete 4-7 rocks per minute on average. The best ones were able to finish 9-10 rocks per minute on average and the slowest participants did about 3-4 rocks per minute on average.

On the other hand, the subjective feedback from these participants was very encouraging as well. A majority of the participants directly commented that they were able to effectively carry out the rock nudging task in the simulation and they all agreed that this could be a useful training tool for the mining teleoperation task.

They were able to pick up the user control for the devices quickly and they felt the control interface as well as the control mapping was not difficult to get used to. Most participants commented that the entire experimental task was quite competitive and exiting, they felt their performance would be better if they had a bit more time for practice in the simulation.

Almost every participant gave feedback that the head and eye tracking interface for virtual camera control was very interactive and useful for this multi-tasking setting as they had to control the virtual camera and the robot arm simultaneously. Especially for the head leaning to the camera zooming control, they all commented that this was intuitive and exiting.

4   Conclusion and Future Work

In this research, we present the development of a virtual reality simulation for the training of a mining teleoperation task (rock breaking). The entire development includes implementation of the 3D modeling, user control interface, vision based object tracking and natural interaction based virtual camera viewpoint control. A number of features have been implemented in order to enhance user experience of using this simulation. From the results of the preliminary user study reported, initial positive feedback on the effectiveness of using this simulation for the training of the mining teleoperation task has been demonstrated by the experimental participants.

Future work will involve a formal empirical user study for the simulation in terms of different control conditions and testing features. Further improvement on development of the simulation would also be considered in terms of practical deployment of the simulation. Further future enhancements include improving the quality of rock tracking and being able to detect rocks when they are very close to each other.

Acknowledgements. The authors would like to express their appreciation to all the volunteers who participated in the user study. This research was supported by the Information and Human Centred Computing (iHcc) research group in RSCS at ANU, and the Transforming the Future Mine theme under the CSIRO National Mineral Down Under (MDU) Research Flagship and the CSIRO ICT Centre.

References

1. Dai, F., Hopgood, F.R., Lucas, M., Requicha, A.G., Hosaka, M., Guedy, R.A., Bo, K., Foley, J.D., Hagen, P.J.: Virtual Reality for Industrial Applications. Springer, New York (1997)
2. Duff, E., Caris, C., Bochis, A., Taylor, K., Gunn, C., Adcock, M.: The Development of a Telerobotic Rock Breaker. In: Proceedings of FSR 2009, pp. 1–10 (2009)
3. FaceLab: Seeingmachines, Inc. (2012), http://www.seeingmachines.com/product/facelab/
4. Kunkler, K.: The Role of Medical Simulation: an Overview. The International Journal of Medical Robotics and Computer Assisted Surgery 2(3), 203–210 (2006)
5. Maya: Autodesk, Inc. (2012), http://usa.autodesk.com/maya/
6. OpenCV (2012), http://www.opencv.org/
7. Slater, M., Usoh, M., Steed, A.: Depth of Presence in Virtual Environments. Presence 3, 130–144 (1994)

8. Unity3D: Unity Technologies (2012), http://unity3d.com/
9. Zhang, L., Liu, Q.: Application of Simulation and Virtual Reality to Physical Education and Athletic Training. In: Pan, Z., Cheok, A.D., Müller, W., Chang, M., Zhang, M. (eds.) Transactions on Edutainment VII. LNCS, vol. 7145, pp. 24–33. Springer, Heidelberg (2012)
10. Zhu, D., Gedeon, T., Taylor, K.: Exploring Camera Viewpoint Control Models for a Multi-Tasking Setting in Teleoperation. In: Proceedings of CHI 2011, pp. 53–62. ACM Press (2011)
11. Zhu, D., Gedeon, T., Taylor, K.: Keyboard before Head Tracking Depresses User Success in Remote Camera Control. In: Gross, T., Gulliksen, J., Kotzé, P., Oestreicher, L., Palanque, P., Prates, R.O., Winckler, M. (eds.) INTERACT 2009. LNCS, vol. 5727, pp. 319–331. Springer, Heidelberg (2009)
12. Zhu, D., Gedeon, T., Taylor, K.: Moving to the Centre: A Gaze-Driven Remote Camera Control for Teleoperation. Interacting with Computers 23(1), 85–95 (2011)
13. Zyda, M.: From Visual Simulation to Virtual Reality to Games. IEEE Computers 38(9), 25–32 (2005)

Game Mastering in Collaborative Multiplayer Serious Games

Viktor Wendel, Stefan Göbel, and Ralf Steinmetz

Multimedia Communication Labs - KOM, TU Darmstadt,
Rundeturmstr. 10, 64283 Darmstadt, Germany
{viktor.wendel,stefan.goebel,ralf.steinmetz}@kom.tu-darmstadt.de
http://www.kom.tu-darmstadt.de/

The concept of computer-supported collaborative learning (CSCL) emerged more than twenty years ago and has developed various shapes since. Also, the concept of Serious Games has been established during the last years as an alternative and a supplement to traditional learning methods. Serious Games can be used in self-regulated learning scenarios and a variety of successful Serious Games exist today with target groups ranging from preschool to adolescents. Game-based CSCL approaches are emerging during the last years. However, although it is clear that the role of the instructor is of utmost importance in collaborative learning scenarios, only few concepts exist to support the instructor in game-based CSCL environments.

In this paper, we propose a novel concept for the support of instructors in their role as a "Game Master" in collaborative Serious Games. Our concept aims at supporting the instructor by defining necessary information about players, the group and the interactions between group members. It also defines controlling methods and necessary interfaces in order to provide the instructor with the necessary elements to control/steer a game during runtime. We created a framework from our conceptual work and implemented our concept as an extension to an existing Serious Game for training of collaboration skills.

1 Motivation

Today, it has become more and more important to share working activities over computer networks and the Internet and to work collaboratively online or offline. The increasing importance of collaborative working and social skills in today's working environment is one reason why new forms of teaching have found their way into school curricula. Collaborative learning is a concept which is no longer a mere alternative to traditional learning but an established method for teaching self-regulated learning or social skills like communication or teamwork. As today's working life requires both collaboration and teamwork skills as well as knowledge about the use of new media, it seems logical to combine collaborative learning with digital learning. The concept of computer-supported collaborative learning (CSCL) first appeared more than twenty years ago and has developed various shapes until today. One very promising branch is the combination of CSCL concepts with Serious Gaming concepts. It has been shown [1–4] that Serious Games can be used in various learning scenarios and a variety of successful

S. Göbel et al. (Eds.): Edutainment 2012/GameDays 2012, LNCS 7516, pp. 23–34, 2012.
© Springer-Verlag Berlin Heidelberg 2012

Serious Games examples exist today with target groups ranging from preschool to adolescents.

However, to the best of our knowledge, there are only a very limited number of Serious Games adressing collaboration or collaborative learning. Various research [5–7] showed that the role of the teacher in collaborative learning scenarios is vital. They all point out the necessity of an instructor for orchestration and coordination of multiple learning activities as well as interaction between learners. Moreover, until today there rarely exist any concepts for how to integrate teachers in Serious Games for collaborative learning in a way such that they can support the learning process best.

In this paper, we propose a novel concept for the support of teachers/trainers in their role as a "Game Master" in collaborative Serious Games. We focus on the genre of 3D 3rd person multiplayer games as this genre is quite popular and well known among both casual and regular players, thus enabling an easy entry. Our concept aims at supporting instructor by defining necessary information about single players, the group and the interactions between group members. It also defines controlling methods and necessary interfaces in order to provide the instructor with the necessary elements to control/steer a game during runtime. We created a framework from our conceptual work and implemented our concept as an extension to an existing Serious Game for training of collaboration skills which we presented in [8]. Furthermore, we propose an interface for using our framework in similar 3rd person multiplayer games.

The rest of this paper is structured as follows: In Section 2 we discuss related work, in Section 3, we describe our concept in detail and in Section 4 we explain our implementation as an extension to the Serious Game 'Escape From Wilson Island'. We conclude our work with a short summary and a description of next steps.

2   Related Work

2.1   Learning with Multiplayer Games

An overview of games used in educational research is provided by Squire [9]. He describes the various forms and genres of games already being used in education, especially in classroom so far. Those are mainly 'Drill-and-practice' games, simulations, and strategy games. Whereas 'Drill-and-practice' games are mostly utilized for learning by enriching factual recall exercises in a playful way, simulation games can be used to simplify complex systems, i.e. laws of physics, ecosystems (Sim Earth[1]), or politics. On the other hand, high fidelity simulations can be used for realistic training scenarios as often used by military or e.g. flight simulators.

Most educational games developed during the last ten years, especially learning games, were mainly simple simulation games (TechForce[2]) or learning

---

[1] www.maxis.com

[2] www.techforce.de

adventures (Geographicus[3], Winterfest[4]). Those games were created as a playful alternative to learning facts by heart or to provide a playful environment for learning through trial and error (e.g. physics games).

It is however possible to use multiplayer technologies for learning in classroom. Herz [10] argues that "... RPG [5] game persona is the most fully dimensional representation of a persons accumulated knowledge and experience gained in the online environment". Delwiche [11] held online classes using SecondLife[6] and the Massive Multiplayer Onling Game(MMOG) Everquest[7] in order to try out new teaching methods. Mansour and El-Said [12] found that "... playing Serious Games positively influences students' [...] learning performance". In [13], Steinkhler addresses the question of how learning of tomorrow can profit of MMOGs. Wang et al. [14] designed a collaborative learning environment to show how technology can be used to enhance collaboration in learning. However, none of these games provide support for an instructor to be able to assess or control such a game at run-time.

The potential of CSCL is being known and researched for many years [15]. The combination of CSCL technology and gaming technology however, is a rather new field with only few examples. Hämäläinen [1] for example designed an environment for comuter-supported learning for vocational learning. Their findings suggest that game-based learning "may enrich learning and the pedagogical use of technology" but they also point out many remaining challenges like the lack of proof of effectiveness or the role of the teacher in such a scenario. Zea et al. [16] designed a collaborative game for learning vowels adressing children aged 3-4.

2.2   Game Mastering

One of these challenges is the fact that instructors are usually only insufficiently integrated when using game-based approaches for learning in groups or classes and are not able to orchestrate collaborative learning processes properly [7]. It has been argued ([5, 17]) that real-time orchestration is vital for collaborative learning scenarios to be successful. Also, Azevedo et al. [18] argue that externally-facilitated regulated learning (using a human tutor) is more effective than self-regulated learning when using hypermedia. Kreijns et al. [19] state that technological environments can support teachers' abilities to foster productive knowledge construction by helping them to control and assess learning activities.

Tychsen et al. [20] proposed an approach for a virtual Game Master based on the idea of the Game Master role in pen-and-paper roleplay games.

Hämäläinen and Oksanen [7] developed a scripted 3D learning game for vocational learning with real-time teacher orchestration. Their findings indicate that the teacher plays a vital role in knowledge construction processes.

---

[3] www.braingame.de

[4] www.lernspiel-winterfest.de

[5] Role Playing Game, author's note.

[6] secondlife.com

[7] www.everquest.com

3   Concept

As mentioned before, in game-based learning scenarios for self-regulated learning in classroom the role of the teacher is vital. The teacher has various responsibilities in the learning process: observation, orchestration, assistance, correction, or mediation of the learning process and the interactions between learners.

In order to pursue these responsibilities, the teacher needs to be able to observe both the (learning) behavior and the interactions of learners as well as to interfere with the learning process whenever he/she thinks it is necessary. Moreover, the teacher needs to be able to recognize mistakes made by learners and provide them with hints, corrections or advice on what to do better.

In terms of controlling the game, we refer to the teacher as the "Game Master" (GM). We can summarize that the GM's needs mechanisms for

1. Observing the gaming/learning process
2. Controlling/ Influencing / Orchestrating the gaming/learning process.

3.1   Components of the Game

Before we can describe how the GM can observe and control a game, we need to define the components of a game. Again, we focus on 3rd person 3D multiplayer games. For our concept, we can break down such games into the following three parts: *Game World, Players, (Inter)Actions.*

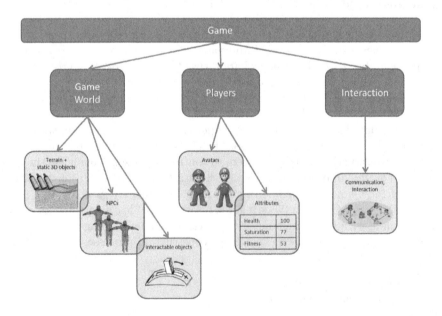

Fig. 1. Game world components

These components can be further subdivided (cf. Figure 1). The *Game World* consists of the level (static 3D objects and terrain), Non-player Characters (NPCs), and interactable objects. The *Players* entity consists of the players' avatars (and their position in the game world) as well as their game relevant attributes (like e.g. health, skills, inventory, etc.). *Interactions* can be categorized as communication (direct or indirect), direct interaction (e.g. trading items, fighting with each other) and derived interaction (spatial proximity to other players).

Group Model. To capture player behavior, learner behavior, and player interactions, we introduce a group model. The group model consists of three elements: a player model, a learner model, and an interaction model. The group model is presented to the GM, in order for him to be able to analyze the learning progress, player preferences and interactions between the players/learning group.

Player Model. The player model describes the preferred style of play. According to Bartle [21], player types in roleplay games can be categorized according to their style of play. They can tend to either act or interact with either the game world or with other players. Along these two dimensions, Bartle defines four player archetypes: the socializer (interacting, players), the killer (acting, players), the explorer (interacting, world), and the achiever (acting, world). Whenever there are parts of the game which can be passed in more than one way, each way stands for a certain style of play. The players choose one of these ways according to their preferences. The player's player model will then be adapted accordingly (see [22]). The GM can use this information to alter other parts of the game which the players will pass next in a way such that it fits their preferred style of play most.

Learner Model. The learner model describes learning behavior as well as learning progress. For the learning progress we use a hierarchical description (cf. [22]) of learning goals. Those are structured in a directed graph where learning objects which have other learning goals as prerequisites are connected with an arrow to those, thus forming a hierarchical graph.

Interaction Model. Whereas the group player model and the group learner model are combinations of the player and learner models of the individual members, the group interaction model is build differently. We differentiate between interactions in terms of

1. communication
2. action

between two or more players.

Communication can take place between two or more players in form of a conversation. Important information for the instructor is: The content of the conversation (topic, offtopic, relation to problems). The number of notions from

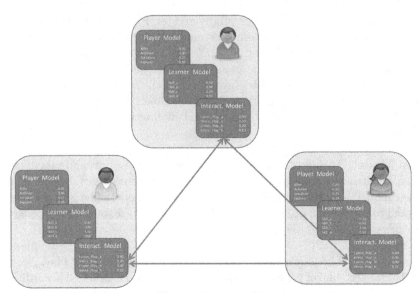

Fig. 2. Group model

each member of the conversation (indicates if only one person is talking or if it is a bidirectional communication). Actions between players can also be unidirectional or bidirectional. Players trading items for example are interacting with each other bidirectionally. Figure 2 summarizes the group model.

3.2   GM Interface

All of the items mentioned in Section 3.1 are game-specific and differ from game to game. We cannot assume that any collaborative 3rd person 3D Serious Game contains NPCs or contains a 'health' avatar attribute. Therefore, in order for the GM to have both a comprehensive overview over the entire game and to be able influence/control it, the game needs to implement an interface describing which information the game provides and which input/control parameter it accepts (Figure 3). Regarding the information, the game needs to specify

- the Game Master's view over the game world,
- relevant (player) attributes and their type,
- game state variables (including the states of game relevant objects),
- NPC variables,
- the player communication (details about which player talks to which other player).

Regarding the input/control parameters, the game needs to enable

- manipulation of parameters for control (e.g. for difficulty)
- altering the game world (difficulty, placing hints, providing second chances)
- talking to players (directly via chat/global messages or indirectly via NPCs)

The above mentioned interface can be implemented by the game itself, thus providing a special GM interface. The GM would then just be a special role inside the game. Another approach would be to implement a stand-alone GM overview and control tool which then can connect to games using the API. Whereas the approach describe in this paper refers to the former, we are currently developing an approach for the latter.

Although visualization of the offered information and the manipulation and control tools is important, it is rather a human-computer interface related problem and thus it is not the focus of this work.

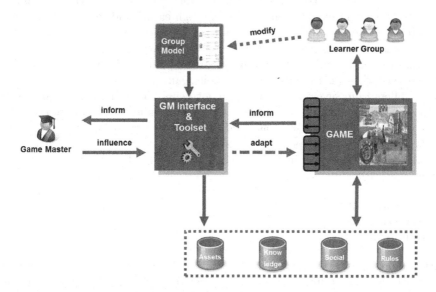

Fig. 3. Game Master interface

4 Prototypical Implementation

4.1 Escape from Wilson Island

We implemented an instance of our Game Master Interface as an extension to the existing Collaborative Serious Game *Escape From Wilson Island* (EFWI). EFWI is a 3D 3rd person multiplayer Serious Game for collaborative learning and teamwork. The collaborative learning features and the game design decisions have been presented in [8]. The narrative context of EFWI is a 'Robinson Crusoe'-like setting. Four players stranded on a lonely island. Their goal is to flee from there. Therefore, they first need to ensure their surviving by gathering food and building a log hut for shelter. After that they need to build a raft to reach a neighboring island where they can lit a signal fire on top of a mountain. The game was designed to foster collaboration. Therefore, several tasks were designed which can only be solved as a team. Additionally, team members have heterogeneous resources, so that they depend on each other.

4.2   Game Elements

The game world consists of the terrain (two islands and surrounding water), static 3D objects like trees and bushes, objects to interact with, and one NPC, an eremite living on the island providing information and help to the players. Objects include palms (can be felled), berry bushes (berries can be gathered), an empty bottle (can be collected), a geyser (to get gas), herons (can be hunted), a fire and a log hut(needed to rest).

Players are represented by their avatars. The relevant attributes are health, saturation, and fitness. Health is decreasing, when a player is drowning or suffering from hunger. Players can increase it through eating and resting. Saturation is decreasing consistently over time and can be restored by eating. If saturation value is too low, health is decreasing. Fitness is decreasing consistently over time and through running or working (like felling palms). If one player's health reaches zero, the game is lost for the whole team. If the value is too low, the player suffers from several penalties, like not being able to run anymore. It can be increased by resting. Furthermore, players have an inventory where they can put game relevant items like tools, food or wood.

Player interactions happen in various ways. Players interact with each other at collaborative tasks. We implemented the following collaborative tasks in the game:

- Carrying palms
- Gathering gas
- Hunting herons

Furthermore, players interact with each other by using the shared inventory, a box which is accessible by every team member. Finally, players interact by chatting with each other. Therefore, we implemented a chat system where players can choose with whom they want to chat. Via checkboxes, they can define who receives their chat messages. Thus, it is possible to talk only to one player, to two other players, or to the whole team.

4.3   Group Model

Our group model at this moment is limited to the player model and the interaction model. As EFWI does currently not contain any direct learning content in form of questions and answers, we have not implemented a learning model so far.

We use a modified version of the player model of Bartle, where we do exclude the player type 'killer' as their are hardly any parts of the game which can be overcome by playing in an aggressive manner. However, we can capture an explorer behavior, an achiever behavior, and a socializer behavior. We introduce three variables, one for each of the player model dimensions we capture. $PM_e(i)$

shows to which extent player i is an explorer, $PM_a(i)$ and $PM_s(i)$ respectively for the achiever and socializer dimension, whereas

$$0 <= PM_e, PM_a, PM_s <= 1 \qquad (1)$$

The variables will be influenced by different player actions, like moving around will increase the explorer value as well as finding special hidden places all over the island. Getting much wood or gathering many berries is an indicator for the achiever. Chatting with fellow players or the NPC will improve the socializer value. Normalizing those values between 0 and 1, improves comparability of the three dimensions.

For the social model, we capture the chat logs and analyze them in terms of which player is talking to which other player(s) how often. Second, we capture which players are solving collaborative tasks together. Third, we capture how long the players' avatars are in spatial proximity to other avatars (exploring the island together, etc.).

4.4   Information

All of the information described above needs to be presented to the Game Master. Therefore, we implemented a Game-Master-View (see 4) which contains different view modes.

1. The GM's camera is freely movable, so that the GM can 'fly' over the island.
2. The GM's camera follows one player.
3. The GM splits his/her camera into four screens, each following one player.

Additionally, the GM can jump to several important locations around the game world and can define such spots himself. The GM has can see all players' attributes like health, saturation, and fitness in form of bars. The GM can see all important game variables. Those are: time, tasks solved (log hut build, raft built, etc.), number of food available, number of palms felled. Additionally, the GM is provided with a list of 'action notifications'. Whenever something notable happens (e.g. a player felled a palm), a notification with timestamp is sent to the GM. The GM can view a minimap of the whole game world displaying players' and the NPC's position. Finally, the GM can can see the chat log and a graphical representation of the player and the interaction model (see 5).

4.5   Control

The GM is provided with various tools for controlling the game. These control mechanisms are divided into

1. character manipulation
2. game world manipulation
3. NPC control

Fig. 4. Screenshot of the Game Master view

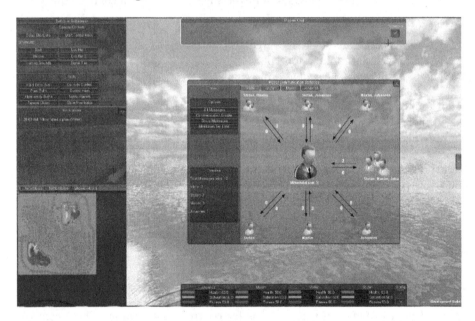

Fig. 5. Screenshot of the detailed communication overview

Regarding character manipulation, the GM is able to influence the way character values change directly. The GM can adapt the rate with which saturation and fitness decrease over time. Furthermore, it is possible to adapt the rate with which health, saturation, and fitness increase or decrease when eating/sleeping/receiving damage through a multiplicative factor.

Regarding game world manipulation, the GM can place and remove interactable objects, like palms, berry bushes, or empty bottles. Furthermore, the GM can give items to players (food, empty or gas-filled bottles, wood). The GM can also influence the degree of difficulty at various collaborative tasks, like setting the strength of currents in the water, or like the size of the movement circle when carrying palms.

Finally, the GM can control the NPC in various ways. He/she can create custom dialogues ad-hoc or chat through the NPC with players. Also, whenever a players triggers the NPC, the GM is asked if he/she wants to control the dialogue.

5 Conclusion

First evaluation studies with students show, that our concept is feasible. It is possible to implement a Game Master component into a 3D 1st/3rd person multiplayer Serious Game providing an instructor with a comprehensive overview and tools to control the game. An instructor can use our GM interface to assess the playing/working progress inside the game having a comprehensive overview over the players, their actions and the game itself. The GM also is able to influence the game in terms of difficulty or give assistance. Due to its generality, our concept is reusable for similar collaborative learning games. However, further studies including professional instructors and educators are necessary in order to evaluate the impact a GM can have on collaborative learning settings using 3D multiplayer Serious Games. Our next step will be to plan and conduct such studies and use the findings to further support instructors at orchestrating digital collaborative games.

References

1. Hämäläinen, R.: Designing and Evaluating Collaboration in a Virtual Game Environment for Vocational Learning. Computers & Education 50(1), 98–109 (2006)
2. Wong, W.L., Shen, C., Nocera, L., Carriazo, E., Tang, F., Bugga, S., Narayanan, H., Wang, H., Ritterfeld, U.: Serious Video Game Effectiveness. In: Proceedings of the International Conference on Advances in Computer Entertainment Technology, pp. 49–55. ACM (2007)
3. McFarlane, A., Sparrowhawk, A., Heald, Y.: Report on the Educational Use of Games: an Exploration by TEEM of the Contribution which Games Can Make to the Education Process. Technical report, TEEM, Cambridgeshire, UK (2002)
4. Sandford, R., Williamson, B.: Games and Learning. In: A Handbook. FutureLab, Bristol (2005)
5. Dillenbourg, P., Järvelä, S., Fischer, F.: The Evolution of Research on Computer-Supported Collaborative Learning. In: Tech.-enhanced Learning, pp. 3–19 (2009)
6. Dillenbourg, P., Jermann, P.: Technology for Classroom Orchestration. New Science of Learning, 525–552 (2010)

7. Hämäläinen, R., Oksanen, K.: Challenge of Supporting Vocational Learning: Empowering Collaboration in a Scripted 3D Game - How Does Teachers' Real-time Orchestration Make a Difference? Comp. and Educ. 59, 281–293 (2012)

8. Wendel, V., Gutjahr, M., Göbel, S., Steinmetz, R.: Designing Collaborative Multiplayer Serious Games for Collaborative Learning. In: Proceedings of the CSEDU 2012 (2012)

9. Squire, K.: Video Games in Education. International Journal of Intelligent Simulations and Gaming 2(1), 49–62 (2003)

10. Herz, J.C.: Gaming the System: What Higher Education Can Learn From Multiplayer Online Worlds. In: The Internet and the University: Forum, pp. 169–291 (2001)

11. Delwiche, A.: Massively Multiplayer Online Games (MMOs) in the New Media Classroom. Educational Technology & Society 9(3), 160–172 (2006)

12. Mansour, S., El-Said, D.M.: Multi-Players Role- Playing Educational Serious Games: A Link between Fun and Learning. The International Journal of Learning 15(11), 229–240 (2008)

13. Steinkuehler, C.A.: Learning in Massively Multiplayer Online Games. In: ICLS 2004: Proceedings of the 6th International Conference on Learning Sciences, pp. 521–528. International Society of the Learning Sciences (2004)

14. Wang, A.I., Øfsdahl, T., Mørch-Storstein, O.K.: Collaborative Learning Through Games–Characteristics, Model, and Taxonomy. Online (2009)

15. De Wever, B., Van Keer, H., Schellens, T., Valcke, M.: Structuring Asynchronous Discussion Groups: the Impact of Role Assignment and Self-assessment on Students' Levels of Knowledge Construction Through Social Negotiation. Journal of Computer Assisted Learning 25(2), 177–188 (2009)

16. Zea, N.P., Sánchez, J.L.G., Gutiérrez, F.L., Cabrera, M.J., Paderewski, P.: Design of Educational Multiplayer Videogames: A Vision From Collaborative Learning. Advances in Engineering Software 40(12), 1251–1260 (2009)

17. Kollar, I.: Turning the Classroom of the Future Into the Classroom of the Present. In: The Classroom of the Future: Orchestrating Collaborative Learning Spaces, Sense, pp. 245–255 (2012)

18. Azevedo, R., Moos, D., Winters, F., Greene, J., Cromley, J., Olson, E., Godbole Chaudhuri, P.: Why Is Externally-Regulated Learning More Effective Than Self-Regulated Learning with Hypermedia? In: Proceeding of the 2005 Conference on Artificial Intelligence in Education: Supporting Learning through Intelligent and Socially Informed Technology, pp. 41–48. IOS Press (2005)

19. Kreijns, K., Kirschner, P.A., Jochems, W., Van Buuren, H.: Measuring Perceived Sociability of Computer-Supported Collaborative Learning Environments. Computers & Education 49(2), 176–192 (2007)

20. Tychsen, A., Hitchens, M., Brolund, T., Kavakli, M.: The Game Master. In: Proceedings of the Second Australasian Conference on Interactive Entertainment, pp. 215–222. Creativity & Cognition Studios Press (2005)

21. Bartle, R.: Hearts, Clubs, Diamonds, Spades: Players Who suit MUDs. Journal of Virtual Environments 1(1), 19 (1996)

22. Göbel, S., Wendel, V., Ritter, C., Steinmetz, R.: Personalized, Adaptive Digital Educational Games Using Narrative Game-Based Learning Objects. In: Zhang, X., Zhong, S., Pan, Z., Wong, K., Yun, R. (eds.) Edutainment 2010. LNCS, vol. 6249, pp. 438–445. Springer, Heidelberg (2010)

Implementing High-Resolution Adaptivity in Game-Based Learning

Florian Berger and Wolfgang Müller

University of Education Weingarten, Kirchplatz 2, 88250 Weingarten, Germany
{berger,mueller}@md-phw.de

Abstract. Adaptivity has long been a key demand for e-learning, but is still far from being an understood feature in game-based learning. Simply transferring paradigms from adaptive e-learning does not suffice, as digital games are highly interactive real-time systems. We are implementing an educational game with real-time adaptivity, based on a generic architecture. The game frequently adapts to over- and under-performers at runtime. After completion, the adaptivity component will be subject to layered evaluation and a controlled trial.

1 Adaptivity in Game-Based Learning

Research on digital educational games has a track record of more than 30 years. [1] In the 1990s, focus shifted to hypertext-based systems, but with the growing acceptance of "serious games" as a learning medium, several academic disciplines invest effort in making educational games more effective and easier to produce.

While personalization has long been a key demand for e-learning tools [2], it is still far from being an understood feature in game-based learning (GBL). This has considerable impact on the effectiveness of educational games. This short paper presents our ongoing work in implementing a serious game with real-time adaptivity, based on a generic architecture.

2 Limits of Legacy Adaptivity Techniques

Conventional e-learning systems follow the paradigm of a learner progressing through a series of mostly textual learning steps, arranged in courses. Consequently, associated adaptivity techniques are concerned with arranging these steps. In 2001, Albert et al. presented EASEL, which allows for WWW-based course creation. [3] Adaptivity is offered as pre-selection during course construction, or by applying document-internal rules. This approach has not changed much over the years, as can be seen in the adaptive hypermedia system (AHS) presented by Vassileva et al. in 2009.[4] The adaptivity of this system consists of content selection and content hiding, as well as link annotation and link hiding, all to be applied when the learner "asks for the next page." Even when real-time concerns are taken into account, as done by Martens in 2006 [5], adaptivity is restricted to displaying information and enabling or disabling user actions.

S. Göbel et al. (Eds.): Edutainment 2012/GameDays 2012, LNCS 7516, pp. 35–40, 2012.

In 2007, Moreno-Ger et al. integrated an adaptable digital game into a learning environment. [6] A pre-test from the environment captured the initial state of knowledge of the learner, which was used to decide which parts of the game could be skipped. Magerko et al. took a similar approach with the game S.C.R.U.B.: a pre-game questionnaire was used to classify the player as of the *explorer, achiever* or *winner* type, after which an adapted game instance would be started. [7] In her 2010 PhD thesis, Hodhod presented the "Adaptive Educational Interactive Narrative System" (AEIS) which aimed at teaching ethics by exposing the player to moral dilemmas. [8] In AEIS, adaptation happened by choosing teaching moments. A student model was updated after each player action, but only used by the pedagogical model after the current dilemma was resolved.

These applications transferred the paradigms of adaptive e-learning to the domain of game-based learning. The result however is a combination of large time windows of player interaction with few points where the system actually adapts to the gathered interaction data. This severely contradicts the fact that digital games are highly interactive real-time systems, with a high frequency of user input and rich possibilities of updating a user model at runtime. This is true even for seemingly slow-paced games like adventures, quizes or puzzles which nonetheless accept user input at fine-grained intervals. It is the authors' belief that adaptation and educational gameplay must not fall apart.

3   Digital Games: High Resolution Real-Time Systems

Digital games are complex systems that involve virtual environments, game mechanics, and entity behaviours, with a layer of graphics, sound, and possibly networking underneath. [9] Input processing and world state update are typically done in a game loop. A rate of 20 loop cycles or more per second is common.

Any adaptation algorithm must be aware that the game state might change at every new cycle of the game loop. The examples presented above did not strive for a fine-granular adaptation and thus took no action based on those changes, apart from collecting interaction data. If the aim is real-time adaptivity instead, there are two implications: 1) the algorithm must take note of and keep up with the changes of the world state, and 2) adaptation calculation must not slow down the game below the desired game loop rate.

There have been practical attempts to put real-time adaptivity into practice outside educational games research. As traditional planning techniques are inapplicable in domains with vast search spaces, Sugandh et al. developed *Darmok*, an adaptive case-based planning system for real-time strategy games. [10] It offers real-time performance while utilizing domain-independent techniques. Another noteworthy implementation is Yannakakis and Hallam's attempt to optimize player satisfaction. [11] In their 2009 paper, they point out the challenges in finding a time window that provides enough input data to the adaptation algorithm while still being short enough to allow for frequent interventions.[1]

---

[1] The final implementation featured a series of overlapping 45 second intervals in a 90 second game, yielding three intervention points.

4   Research Case: A Project Management Game

We are developing *The Project Manager*, an educational game that aims at training project management skills such as parallelising tasks, managing resource constraints, and handling breakages and delays. [12] The game is meant to bring playing and learning together in a meaningful way by utilizing game mechanics for learning purposes. Over the course of several levels, the player is in control of a group of virtual employees that are able to fulfill tasks. In order to pass a level, the player has to make the employees complete a project within given constraints of time and budget.

The adaptive architecture of the Project Manager Game is outlined in figure 1. The game constantly monitors player actions, agent actions and the game world state. The monitoring is integrated into the game loop at 30 steps per second, while adaptive interventions can happen at 1 second intervals.

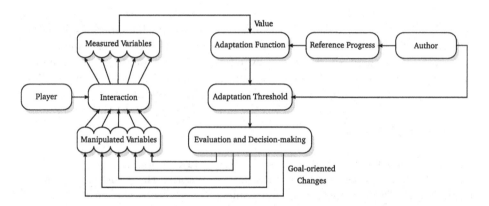

Fig. 1. A flowchart of the framework for adaptive Game-based Learning applications to be implemented

If the player's project progress deviates from a reference progress authored by a domain expert, the adaptation engine triggers appropriate interventions. If a player lags behind the reference progress, the game uses an in-game *tutor* to assist the player. But contrary to other adaptive intelligent tutoring systems (ITS), the game also adapts to *over-peformers*—who exceed the reference progress—by making the game more challenging: breaking machinery, slowing down workers, and other obstacles. Following an *adaptive testing* approach, the game will become more difficult until it matches the player's abilities. Figure 2 shows a screenshot of the game.

At this point, the architecture as shown in figure 1 has been implemented. A vector of percentages of completeness for project milestones over time has been identified as the measured variable to base the adaptation on. The ITS component that adapts to underperforming players is in place. Over-performer adaptivity is currently still work in progress.

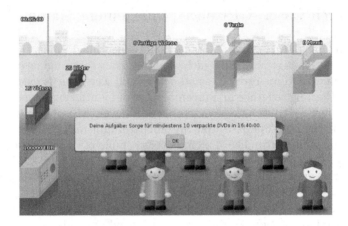

Fig. 2. A screenshot of The Project Manager Game (on-screen text in German)

The game is a unique research case in several respects: while previous projects predominantly skip content as a means of adaptation to over-performers, our game addresses these shortcomings by offering them a deliberately different gameplay experience. Furthermore, we present an architecture which handles adaptivity to over- and under-performing players at the same time.

5   Related Work

Already in 2005, Charles et al. suggested a framework for adaptive games consisting of a loop of monitoring player performance, adapting the game—for example by changing NPCs or the virtual environment—, measuring the effectiveness of the adaptation and re-modeling the player type, all done in real-time. [13] The game presented in this paper is partly an implementation of this architecture, but adapted for educational purposes and extended by an authored performance reference to base the adaptation on.

In 2007, Albert et al. introduced the concept of "microadaptivity" using an example from the ELEKTRA project. [14] Building upon the idea of continuous and implicit assessment, the concept bears great similarity to high-resolution adaptivity. Yet the work presented did not deal with practical intervention frequencies, and the system did not adapt to over-performers. In a follow-up paper, Peirce et al. presented the ALIGN system which separates between game design and educational adaptation and implemented hint-based adaptivity based on Knowledge Space Theory (KST) in real-time. [15] A 2010 paper of Kickmeier-Rust reiterates the concepts of 2007. [16]

Conati and Manske presented a technical report of their implementation of the "Prime Climb Game", which aimed at teaching number factorization. [17] Adaptation was realized using a hinting agent. Their 2009 paper did not give details on the adaptation frequency, but reported averages of 7.6 and 16.3 hints in 10 minute playing sessions. Interestingly there was evidence that the players did not read the hints. The implementation using a less frequent, shorter and simpler hinting sequence was perceived as less intrusive. In the Project Manager Game, the hinting agent will give very short hints, and will refrain from giving hints that it has given before.

A 2011 follow-up paper to [6] by del Blanco et al. introduced a general architecture for the integration of adaptive games in student-centered virtual learning environments. [18] While their architecture features a dedicated channel between adaptation and game engine, the adaptation interventions are expected to be triggered by the learning environment using an abstract representation of the game state. It is questionable whether this architecture is real-time capable for more complex games. Of the three games presented in the paper, none features real-time in-game adaptation.

6   Future Work

The next steps of our work are finishing the Project Manager Game, and then evaluating the adaptivity component. This will be done by using the method of a controlled trial. The trial will be carried out using students of business economics, media and education management and computer science from three universities, split into groups of $n = 50$ to reach statistically meaningful results. The groups will play an adaptive and a non-adaptive version of the game.

Paramythis et al. have suggested a layered evaluation framework for adaptive systems. [19] Their concept involves a decomposition of the adaptive system, and a separate evaluation of interaction monitoring, interpretation, modelling, adaptation decision making, and applying adaptations. The authors will try to follow these recommendations to their best extend, but it is their belief that a layered evaluation approach has to be supplemented with actual user data.

Research of adaptive digital games, especially educational games, suffers from small numbers of test subjects. Our study will add a statistically solid test case to the body of evidence. We will report results in a follow-up paper.

References

1. Malone, T.W.: Toward a theory of intrinsically motivating instruction. Cognitive Science 5(4), 333–369 (1981)
2. Teo, C.B., Gay, R.K.L.: A knowledge-driven model to personalize e-learning. J. Educ. Resour. Comput. 6(1), 3 (2006)
3. Albert, D., Hockemeyer, C., Conlan, O., Wade, V.: Reusing adaptive learning resources. In: Proceedings of the International Conference on Computers in Education, ICCE, vol. 1, pp. 205–210 (2001)
4. Vassileva, D., Bontchev, B., Grigorov, S.: Mastering adaptive hypermedia courseware. Acta Electrotechnica et Informatica 9(1), 57–62 (2009)
5. Martens, A.: Time in the Adaptive Tutoring Process Model. In: Ikeda, M., Ashley, K.D., Chan, T.-W. (eds.) ITS 2006. LNCS, vol. 4053, pp. 134–143. Springer, Heidelberg (2006)

6. Moreno-Ger, P., Burgos, D., Sierra, J.L., Fernández-Manjón, B.: A Game-Based Adaptive Unit of Learning with IMS Learning Design and <e-Adventure>. In: Duval, E., Klamma, R., Wolpers, M. (eds.) EC-TEL 2007. LNCS, vol. 4753, pp. 247–261. Springer, Heidelberg (2007)

7. Magerko, B., Heeter, C., Fitzgerald, J., Medler, B.: Intelligent adaptation of digital game-based learning. In: Proceedings of the 2008 Conference on Future Play: Research, Play, Share, Future Play 2008, pp. 200–203. ACM, New York (2008)

8. Hodhod, R.: Interactive Narrative for Adaptive Educational Games: Architecture and Application to Character Education. PhD thesis, University of York (February 2010)

9. Lewis, M., Jacobson, J.: Game engines in scientific research - introduction. Commun. ACM 45, 27–31 (2002)

10. Sugandh, N., Ontañón, S., Ram, A.: Real-Time Plan Adaptation for Case-Based Planning in Real-Time Strategy Games. In: Althoff, K.-D., Bergmann, R., Minor, M., Hanft, A. (eds.) ECCBR 2008. LNCS (LNAI), vol. 5239, pp. 533–547. Springer, Heidelberg (2008)

11. Yannakakis, G.N., Hallam, J.: Real-time game adaptation for optimizing player satisfaction. IEEE Trans. Comput. Intellig. and AI in Games 1(2), 121–133 (2009)

12. Berger, F.: Evaluating an Implementation of an Adaptive Game-Based Learning Architecture. In: Masthoff, J., Mobasher, B., Desmarais, M.C., Nkambou, R. (eds.) UMAP 2012. LNCS, vol. 7379, pp. 351–355. Springer, Heidelberg (2012)

13. Charles, D., Kerr, A., McAlister, M., McNeill, M., Kücklich, J., Black, M.M., Moore, A., Stringer, K.: Player-centred game design: Player modelling and adaptive digital games. In: Proceedings of the DiGRA 2005 Conference: Changing Views - Worlds in Play (2005)

14. Albert, D., Hockemeyer, C., Kickmeier-Rust, M.D., Peirce, N., Conlon, O.: Microadaptivity within complex learning situations - a personalized approach based on competence structures and problem spaces. In: Proceedings of the 15th International Conference on Computers in Education, ICCE 2007 (2007)

15. Peirce, N., Conlan, O., Wade, V.: Adaptive educational games: Providing non-invasive personalised learning experiences. In: Second IEEE International Conference on Digital Games and Intelligent Toys Based Education, pp. 28–35 (2008)

16. Kickmeier-Rust, M.D.: Micro adaptivity: Protecting immersion in didactically adaptive digital educational games. Journal of Computer Assisted Learning 26, 95–105 (2010)

17. Conati, C., Manske, M.: Evaluating Adaptive Feedback in an Educational Computer Game. In: Ruttkay, Z., Kipp, M., Nijholt, A., Vilhjálmsson, H.H. (eds.) IVA 2009. LNCS, vol. 5773, pp. 146–158. Springer, Heidelberg (2009)

18. del Blanco, Á., Torrente, J., Moreno-Ger, P., Fernández-Manjón, B.: Enhancing Adaptive Learning and Assessment in Virtual Learning Environments with Educational Games. In: Intelligent Learning Systems and Advancements in Computer-Aided Instruction: Emerging Studies, pp. 144–163. IGI Global (2011)

19. Paramythis, A., Weibelzahl, S., Masthoff, J.: Layered evaluation of interactive adaptive systems: framework and formative methods. User Model. User-Adapt. Interact. 20(5), 383–453 (2010)

Turning High-Schools into Laboratories? Lessons Learnt from Studies of Instructional Effectiveness of Digital Games in the Curricular Schooling System

Cyril Brom[1], Vít Šisler[1,2], Michaela Buchtová[1,2], Daniel Klement[3], and David Levčík[3]

[1] Charles University in Prague, Faculty of Mathematics and Physics
Ke Karlovu 3, Prague, Czech Republic
[2] Charles University in Prague, Faculty of Arts,
Nám. Jana Palacha 2, Prague, Czech Republic
[3] Institute of Physiology, Academy of Sciences of the Czech Republic
Vídeňská 1083, 142 00, Prague, Czech Republic

Abstract. Digital games are believed by many to be instructionally effective in the context of the formal schooling system; however, studies investigating this idea empirically are limited and their outcomes are often inconclusive and/or difficult to interpret. Part of the problem is caused by the fact that when conducting a study in an authentic environment, i.e., in a school, as opposed to a laboratory, researchers encounter many common, yet unspoken, technical pitfalls. This paper verbalizes some of these pitfalls and organizes them into 6 Recommendations for "best practice" in field studies on the instructional effectiveness of digital game-based learning (DGBL). These recommendations are based on experience gained during five DGBL studies on more than 700 subjects in the context of secondary education and can be useful to other researchers willing to run similar studies.

Keywords: digital game-based learning, serious games, simulations, secondary schools, instructional effectiveness, empirical studies, learning effects.

1 Introduction

In the past decade, many scholars have argued that serious games present a new instructional technology with many potential advantages in the context of the formal schooling system, e.g. [2, 10, 11]. Nowadays, serious games gradually enter schools [27]. However, at the same time, data supporting the idea of the instructional effectiveness of digital game based learning (DGBL) are still limited, inconclusive and/or difficult to interpret, e.g. [5, 12, 20, see also 24]. Coincidentally, in the neighboring field of educational simulations (including non-computer based simulations), Feinstein and Cannon complained in 2002 that claims about the benefits of simulations have remained inconclusive since the Sixties [9; cf. 29]. Moreover, Moreno also noted that other "technological innovations in the past have been considered promising media to promote learning," [21, p. 2], including motion pictures, radio and television [7; cited from 21, p. 2]; however, the "hopes and expectations were largely unmet" [21, p. 2; see also 19]. Are serious games so

S. Göbel et al. (Eds.): Edutainment 2012/GameDays 2012, LNCS 7516, pp. 41–53, 2012.
© Springer-Verlag Berlin Heidelberg 2012

different from previous instructional innovations or has the serious games community just forgotten its own history? Importantly, in a different neighboring discipline, that of multimedia learning, the research outcomes, as organized by Mayer into the cognitive theory of multimedia learning (CTLM) [19], seem to be generally much clearer and unambiguous. Can DGBL studies be more like those underpinning CTLM than those about which Feinstein and Cannon complained?

One notable difference between these two types of studies is that the former tends to be conducted in a laboratory, while the latter takes place in a real-world setting. Especially digital games for the formal schooling system tend to be studied directly in schools and sometimes with real teachers. The reason for this is because the mere integration of a digital game into the formal schooling environment is difficult and its acceptance by the target audience is not guaranteed: many practical barriers to game integration exist; ranging from the unintelligibility of interfaces and game rules for some teachers and non-players, to a lack of access to equipment, e.g. up-to-date video cards, to barriers posed by fixed lesson times, e.g. [15, 17, 25]. Of course, the authentic context brings more confounding variables. Thus, it seems that two opposing things are needed at the same time: minimizing confounding variables; that is, moving studies to labs, while keeping the studies' external validity, i.e. running them in the real-world context. Can this tension be, at least to some extent, reconciled?

Since 2008 we have conducted five quasi-experimental DGBL studies in the context of secondary education; four of which were comparative and investigated learning effects (as opposed to mere acceptance of a game by students or teachers). These studies involved a total of more than 700 subjects. Based on these studies, and also based on general educational literature, we put together 6 Recommendations that we believe will help remove some of the confounding variables, yet allow for conducting a study in the real-world context or in a laboratory setting that closely approximates the authentic environment.

The goal of this paper is to present these 6 Recommendations. The paper should not be read as a definitive guideline for conducting DGBL studies. First, our advice or counsel refers to the technical aspects of running DGBL studies rather than conceptual issues related to formulating research questions and designing experiments. Second, the list is not exhaustive. Still, in our opinion, the Recommendations could bring us a step closer to the reconciliation of the laboratory/real-world tensions.

The paper proceeds as follows. Section 2 briefly introduces our studies. Section 3 outlines and describes our Recommendations. Section 4 presents a general discussion and our overall conclusions.

Fig. 1. Screenshots from StoryFactory, Orbis Pictus Bestialis, and Europe 2045

2   Assumptions and Design of Our Studies

These Recommendations can be applied to studies with experimental design similar to ours; namely to comparative studies of DGBL learning effects that combine various quantitative and qualitative measures. We now detail our studies' design.

The studies involved Europe 2045 [6], Orbis Pictus Bestialis (OPB) [5], Bird Breeder [22] and StoryFactory [4] (Fig. 1). Our team developed all of them except for Bird Breeder. Europe 2045 is a turn-based, complex, multi-player, strategy game for social science courses. It can be played during a one-day workshop or within a formal schooling framework on a long-term basis (about a month). OPB and Bird Breeder are simulation mini-games for explaining and practicing specific skills: animal training in the case of OPB; and Mendelian genetics in the case of Bird Breeder. Their goals can be achieved within 15 – 30 minutes of playing. Both games can be best used in the formal schooling system for homework assignments or in a practical seminar after a theoretical lecture on a specific topic (for gaining more insight into the topic). StoryFactory is not a game but a 3D toolkit, which helps students learn how to produce short movies in a 3D virtual world and is to be used in ICT/media education classes. The target audience for all the projects is students aged 13 and above.

Our first study (marked as EU1) investigated the acceptance of Europe 2045 as an educational tool by the target audience (N=220), without assessing real learning gains. Students' attitude towards the game was positive and the majority claimed that they learned more than or at least as much as they usually did [6]. Our other studies investigated learning gains, while comparing experimental groups taking part in DGBL activities to control groups receiving comparable "traditional" instruction. Knowledge of subjects was assessed using knowledge tests in (a) pre-test/series of post-tests or (b) immediate post-test/delayed post-test design. A study with OPB (N=100) (OPB1) showed no between-group difference right after the treatment but medium effect size positive learning gains for experimental groups in one month delayed post-tests [5]. However, our preliminary analysis of data from a consecutive study with OPB and Bird Breeder (OPB2) suggests that we failed to replicate these results (unpublished data; N=224). Similarly, our pilot study of the learning effects of Europe 2045 (EU2) showed mixed results [26] (N=153, note: some subjects participated in two studies featuring two different games). Some of our learning gain results, most notably from the OPB2 and EU2 studies, are difficult to interpret due to technical problems encountered while running the studies. Thus, the studies present excellent examples that help explain our Recommendations. The final study employed StoryFactory (SF) and the preliminary analysis suggests a small positive effect size of active exposure to StoryFactory compared to passive exposure (unpublished data). That was the only study conducted on high-school teachers (N=29).

In studies OPB1/2 and SF, after an initial theoretical lecture, each class was randomly divided into experimental and control groups. Both groups received two different treatments that were nevertheless comparable as relates to their educational content and time length. Study EU2 was longitudinal: a whole class of subjects played Europe 2045 about a month as part of their regular education. Therefore, random sampling was not possible. Instead game classes were matched with comparable control classes that also received a set of theoretical lectures on the European Union. In each study a teacher supervised DGBL activities.

3   Recommendations

This section summarizes our research and experimental experiences into Recommendations. In doing so, it verbalizes how to avoid several *technical* pitfalls during DGBL studies conducted in the context of the formal schooling system. Recommendations can be applied most straightforwardly to comparative studies in which classes of high-school students represent a pool of experimental subjects and every class receives a treatment at once or is divided into several groups, each of which receives a different treatment. The Recommendations do not discuss conceptual and methodological issues – how research questions should be formulated, what treatment should be picked for control groups, etc. The descriptions will follow this structure: summary – rationale – an example from one of our studies – take-home message.

Recommendation 1: Reserve a Whole Day for the Experiment

Summary. It is important to design the study so that subjects participate in research activities *only* during the school day on which the study takes place. In particular, (a) the treatment *per se* should start and end at approximately the same time for each class tested, and (b) students should not be involved in other educational activities not controlled by the researchers, nor should they be examined (no matter the subject), during the testing day. If possible, (c) subjects should not be involved in significant extra-curricular activities during the testing day or during the day prior to testing. Also (d) no major exams should take place the day after.

Rationale. Concerning Point (a), in general, subjects' overall mood and attention spans change during the day. Therefore, different performance levels can be expected if one class is examined early in the morning and another before lunch. Concerning Point (b), if students continue with their normal class work the day after the experiment, there is a high risk that some students' attention spans will be disrupted during the experiment (and therefore, performance will be compromised) due to the fact that they either worry they may be examined later that day or think about homework they need to finish for a class during that day. Concerning Point (c), significant extra-curricular activities, such as an official event the previous evening or one scheduled for the evening of that same day, may influence performance. The same applies for major exams the next day (d).

It can be argued that not respecting this Recommendation and conducting the study as part of a regular school day would actually increase external validity and – with a random sampling and a sufficiently large number of participants – would not pose problems for internal validity. While true, this argument is too idealistic. Because the possible influences are numerous and sometimes apply to individual participants, sometimes to part of a class and sometimes to a whole class. The number of classes should be an order of magnitude larger than it usually is in current DGBL studies, e.g. [1, 23, cf. 14], should the experiment be conducted in a "natural" setting. This is too costly. At the same time, our observation, which can be conceived as a working hypothesis, is that the more the experiment looks "laboratory-implemented," the more the high school students concentrate. We suspect that high school students are motivated *less* when undergoing a "natural" experiment (violating this Recommendation) than when undergoing a "laboratory" experiment or when doing the same tasks as part of their regular education. This Recommendation offers general advice on how to keep budgets reasonable at the cost of slightly reducing external validity.

Example. In the OPB1 study, which violated Points (a) and (b), some students tried to work on their homework during the experiment. Others did a sloppy job because they expected to be examined later that day and thus studied the subject in question instead of participating in the experiment (note: they might not have done their homework were this a regular lesson with OPB!). The OPB2 study violated Pt. (c): some students in one class left earlier because they participated in a competition that day.

Take home message. Fear of examination, the need to finish one's homework, fatigue from an important extra-curricular activity that occurred the previous day, or the fact that one is looking forward to an extra-curricular activity on the given day may distract students from experimental activities.

Recommendation 2. Disrupt the Regular School Schedule

Summary: In many countries a formal schooling system implies a fixed schedule and lessons with a fixed duration. It is important to either accept this schedule completely, in particular to accept regular breaks, or disrupt this schedule entirely; ideally by taking students out of the school environment or by conducting a study on days when the regular schedule has been disrupted for the whole school.

Rationale. It may seem that if the experiment takes a whole school day (see Recommendation (1)), the schedule can be changed at the researchers' will. Unfortunately, this is not always the case. First, students often have their regular schedule *internalized*. Second, in some schools, the schedule is made explicit; e.g. by the bell ringing at the beginning and the end of lessons. Third, participants in the experiment have friends in different classes. If the schedule is not disrupted for these friends, they may come to visit the participants during periods that would normally be breaks. All of this means that if the experiment takes place in a real school environment and breaks in the experimental schedule are not matched with regular breaks, participant attention levels may decrease during the would-be regular breaks. It may also be undesirable to allow students from the control and experimental groups to mix together during breaks. Note that usage of a DGBL activity in school implies acceptance of the in-school schedule; however, researchers may want to change the schedule during the research day purely for experimental reasons, e.g. to introduce the experiment or to distribute questionnaires. In such cases, it can help to take students out of school and *model* the real breaks during DGBL activities (but not administer tests, etc.).

Example. In the OPB1 experiment, we wanted to test the effect of students interfacing with the OPB game after a regular expository lecture on the topic of that game. The expository lecture should have lasted the same time as it would have in the real educational setting; i.e. 45 minutes in the Czech Republic. However, before the expository lecture, we had to introduce the whole experiment to the class: that took 10 minutes. Thus, we had 55 minutes after which we wanted to schedule a break. However, as said, the regular lesson lasts 45 minutes. Oddly though, ten minutes before the end of the expository lecture, a high number of participants left to use the restroom and participants' friends started to wander into the class. Ultimately, we had to shorten the introduction to 5 minutes and the supplementary lesson to 40 minutes: a compromise.

Take home message. The regular school schedule should either be accepted or disrupted completely.

Recommendation 3. Work with a "Standardized" Expert Teacher, Who Has Authority Over Students

Summary: Many DGBL activities should be supported by teachers, e.g. [12, 24]. According to our experience, the teacher effect has enormous influence on a study's outcome. Unless the teacher effect is investigated *per se*, all the classes and groups should have the same teacher; one who is, if possible, hypothesis-blind. The teacher should be an expert on the topic and should have authority over the students. Thus, inevitably, the teacher should be part of the research team.

Rationale: According to our experience, expertise levels among regular school teachers differ and teachers occasionally like/dislike particular topics. When supplementary activities are led/taught by different teachers, the outcome can be heavily influenced by the effect of the teacher's *a priori* knowledge, his/her authority, actual mood, attitude towards DGBL, etc.

Example: In the EU2 experiment, we let regular school teachers supervise and teach both the control and experimental groups. Some students (in the experimental group) later complained, in focus groups, that their regular school teacher did not engage less motivated students sufficiently so that they would participate in the game playing. This compromised the game play quality for the whole group (Europe 2045 is a multi-player game). At the same time, there was no similar problem with the control group. Eventually, in terms of learning effects, the data showed no difference between these two particular groups, but we got a positive gain for a different experimental group, compared to its matched control group supervised by a different teacher. It would be an important result, should it be proven that the game works for some teachers but not others. However, to investigate this hypothesis, enough classes must be available (i.e. around at least 30 group pairs) in order to gain statistically interesting results. If it is assumed that the teacher masters DGBL and just the effect of a game, or the presence of some of its features, are investigated, employing the same teacher during the trials would bring less noisy data.

Possible obstacles and solutions. The idea of all groups being led/taught by an expert teacher from the research team is not without drawbacks. However, according to our experience, such drawbacks are relatively minor compared to the teacher effect. First, the experimental design depicted on Fig. 2 (left) is impossible: the teacher cannot be in both groups at the same time. We suggest (and use) the experimental design on Fig. 2 (right). Both groups participate in the "introductory" lecture, but then one group is subject to a given intervention, while another waits. Then the groups are switched.

For some group pairs the experimental group goes first. For others the control group goes first. Our suggestion for the "waiting" group is to use a supplementary activity that is not linked with the educational objective; i.e. one that is relatively easy but not boring, and is motivationally neutral or mildly positive. We used a five-factor personality test and informed the students that they would get the results, which mildly motivated most of them.

The second issue is, as revealed by our focus groups, that with an external teacher, some students may feel that they "do not need to learn as much as they would with their own teacher." As one student put it: "It was a pleasant change from the school routine. We didn't have to learn." (cf. Rec. 1). Generally, because our results showed some learning gains for most students in all our studies (though experimental groups did not always outperform their matched control groups), we do think that this issue is not as troubling as the teacher effect. Arguably, the silent presence of the regular teacher during trials might help, but we do not have enough data to support this claim empirically.

The third point is that the teacher should be hypothesis-blind, which is not always possible if he/she is part of the research team. Two things can help reduce teacher bias to some extent: first, the teaching method should be "standardized". For instance, the teacher should have a set of key points that he/she should mention/focus on in both groups during the interventions. This can be checked by an in-class observer. Second, and more importantly, the research hypothesis should be formulated so that both negative and positive results are meaningful and the teacher's preferences for these outcomes are the same. Obviously, if the teacher is also the main author of the game, and the research question is merely whether this particular game outperforms a different educational activity, the bias is hardly avoidable.

Take home message. The "teacher effect" can corrupt the data. Unless the teacher effect is investigated, it is better to work with one expert teacher from the research team; i.e. one who is hypothesis-blind and has authority over students. If it is not possible for the teacher to be hypothesis-blind, every effort must be made to reduce possible bias.

Recommendation 4. Keep Groups as Small as Possible for Testing Students

Summary: If a DGBL activity is to take place in a real school with a whole class at once (but not e.g. as a homework), it is often desirable to set up the experiment so that the activity in the experiment also employs whole classes. This should be done no matter whether the game used is multi- or single-player. However, when tests are administered after the intervention, the groups should be broken into the smallest subgroups possible. These subgroups should not be allowed to interact with other subgroups when tested.

Rationale: Generally, the class effect tends to be large; similar to the teacher effect. In a field study, researchers are often interested in the class effect generated by the intervention; however, they are not interested in the class effect caused by *testing*. According to our experience, the latter is also large. When all (high school) students are tested at once, it is almost inevitable that some of them start joking during testing, saying right or wrong answers aloud, complaining and cheating (in our research, some students tried to cheat just for fun), or using mobile devices to find the right answers. So far, we have found no instruction that would help to ameliorate these problems. Note that some students always lack motivation to complete tests due to the low-stake problem (see Recommendation 5); however, the risk is high that these students would distract more motivated students and worsen *their* performance. Typically only a few students function as these "motivation reducers", which means that we cannot expect the performance reductions, caused by this effect, to cancel each other out in both paired groups. When students are tested in smaller subgroups, ideally groups of one person, the administrator can better control the subjects. The "motivation reducers" thus influence a smaller number of subjects (of course, an administrator must be present in each subgroup during the entire testing period).

Example: Our studies violated this Recommendation. For instance, in one OPB2 group (in an above-average high school according to the Czech School Inspectorate), one student started contemplating aloud about the administrator's sex life in hopes of attracting the attention of other students (which he eventually did).

Take home-message. It is better to administer tests and distribute questionnaires in subgroups smaller than the original research groups.

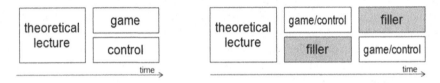

Fig. 2. Two possible designs, the one on the right features a "filling" activity

Recommendation 5. Address the Low-Stake Test Problem

Summary. The low-stake test problem is a general issue [28] and precautions should be taken to rectify it. Notably, (a) questionnaires/tests should not be too long and therefore should ask only the most important questions, (b) the order of questions should be changed in different versions of the tests, (c) the groups taking the tests in the same room should be as small as possible (Recommendation 4), (d) there must be no significant activity taking place after the test (Recommendation 1), (e) steps should be taken to avoid some students completing the test more quickly than others in the same subgroup.

Rationale. Generally, it is well known that in low-stake assessments that have little consequence for students, their motivation to complete the tests is reduced. This problem is discussed even in the context of large scale surveys such as the OECD Program for International Student Assessment (PISA), surveying student aptitude in reading, mathematics and science in more than 60 countries, e.g. [13]. Concerning (a) and (b), performance can decrease over time, for example, due to motivation or fatigue. Because of this, it is often useful, if a test is very long, to divide questions into blocks and present them in a different order in different versions of the test, so that the positions of question blocks are balanced across the test variants and research groups. This helps to separate the effect of fatigue and question difficulty.

Point (c) is actually part of Recommendation 4. Point (d) relates to Recommendation 1: student motivation is generally reduced if they expect a major event such as an exam. Special attention should be paid to delayed post-tests. It is tempting to think that delayed post-tests can be administered in one school class hour during a regular school day. Unfortunately, this is not the case. Ideally, the whole day should be reserved *only* for administering post-tests due to reasons mentioned in Recommendation 1. Because post-tests *per se* would hardly take a whole school day, it is necessary to supplement them with other activities unrelated to the regular school schedule.

Concerning (e), it often happens that some (often less motivated) students complete a test earlier than others. If the "earlier finishers" stay in the test room, they may distract the "late finishers." If the "early finishers" leave, the other students may speed up, thereby filling in tests less carefully. This is because they realize that they can leave as soon as they finish the test. Ideally, each student should have the same amount of time for every question, and each question should be put to all the students in one testing subgroup at the same time. This method is practiced by Mayer in his studies on learning from multimedia [19, p. 44]. However, according to our experience, it also helps when the whole test is divided into several sections, each of which is administered at the same time to every student in the testing group. If a student finishes a section, he/she waits only a few minutes for the next one (in Mayer's approach, every section consists of one question).

Finally, one should note that the official grading of the tests is not always the solution, since it is not possible to grade delayed post-tests (one has to administer them without notifying the students in advance; otherwise, they would study for the test). However, what might help is "gamification" of the testing process, i.e. embedding tests in a game, while making their filling an inherent part of the game-play.

Examples. In the OPB1 study, we measured students' knowledge with eight open-ended questions only. The test took about 15 minutes. For the OPB2 study, we reasoned that it would be advantageous to have twice as many open-ended questions to gain a more extensive sample of students' knowledge. The OPB2 test took about 30 minutes and the lessons learnt are that students left most questions unanswered or wrote just a few words instead of, as expected and required, several sentences. We should have used the shorter version and/or multiple-choice questions. At the same time, some students returned the test after 10 minutes hoping they could go to lunch, while the rest of the class continued working on the test. It was hard to keep the "early finishers" silent for the next 20 minutes. However, this became easier when the test was split into two parts; the second not being administered until 90% of the students had finished the first one (more parts would be even better).

In the SF study with high school teachers at a two-week-long summer school, 29 teachers completed immediate post-tests, but only seven volunteered to complete one week post-tests with eight questions, despite the fact that they could take home a bottle of wine. The test had four closed-ended and four open-ended questions and took 15 minutes. Notably, all teachers had many other things to do since the school year was ending.

Take-home message. The low-stake test problem can be partly addressed by giving questions to students one by one or in small batches and by avoiding administering the test when students are expecting a significant event after the test. It is also useful to change the order of the questions: this helps get balanced answers for all questions despite increasing fatigue/decreasing motivation. Gamification of tests may help too.

Recommendation 6. Avoid Certain Periods of Year

Summary. It is important to avoid conducting the experiment during certain periods of the school year, when low performance can generally be expected, e.g. before the end of the school year or during exam periods. The situation is complicated by the fact that it is often useful to administer delayed post-tests; these tests also should not be administered during the critical periods.

Rationale. The reason is the same as for Recommendations 1 and 5.

Example. We conducted the OPB2 and EU2 experiments in May 2011 and administered the delayed post-tests on roughly 25 June 2011. The school year ends on 30 June in the Czech Republic. While we administered the delayed post-tests, some students in some classes (but not in all classes) openly claimed that they would make no effort to complete the tests because their final marks had already been assigned (on about 20 June). Also, nearly half the students were missing in some classes. Students' average scores on one of the knowledge tests in the Europe 2045 experiment are depicted in Fig. 3. Because the tests were of the same difficulty and we also administered a 3-month delayed post-test (the school year starts on 1 September), attribution of the large decrease in the 1-month post-test scores for the experimental classes to the low-stake test issue seems valid. What's worse, preliminary analysis of the OPB2 study's data suggests that we in fact failed to replicate the OPB1 results (i.e. no difference in delayed post-tests). However, because we do not have a 3-month post-test for the OPB2 study and the scores were really low for the 1-month post-test, we do not know whether to attribute the null results to a lack of difference between the instructional effectiveness of the DGBL activity and the control treatment or to the combination of the low-stake test problem and the floor effect.

Take-home message. It is important to consider the context in which the experiment and the knowledge assessment take place. Was the chosen time of year a distraction for the students?

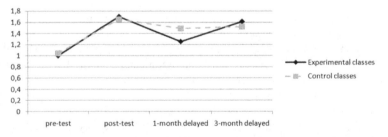

Fig. 3. Normalized averages across the experimental and control classes for the first type of knowledge test administered in the EU2 study (1 equals the average score across the control classes in the pre-test). Note: standard deviations are from 0.43 to 0.52 for all conditions and tests, except for the 1-month post-test, where they are larger: 0.57 (experimental) and 0.6 (control). Note also that the outcome of the second knowledge test is similar.

General Social Science Recommendations. Besides the 6 Recommendations above specific to the DGBL, there are many standard social science recommendations. Newcomers to social sciences, such as computer scientists, should consult introductory text books, e.g. [3]. For instance, sometimes standardized knowledge tests are available. More often though researchers have to compile their own knowledge tests. In such cases, it is vital to identify and replace questions deemed "too easy" and "too difficult" as well as questions that do not distinguish able and less able students, see e.g. [16]. Another useful idea is to consider combining quantitative measures (such as questionnaires with Likert items and knowledge tests) with qualitative measures (such as commentary – e.g. on pictures or specific events) or text writing tasks for subsequent content analysis. While quantitative outcomes often provide a kind of ultimate aggregate description of *what* happened during the treatments, qualitative data can add interesting detail to this picture; they can help to elucidate *how* the gross quantitative outcome was achieved.

Even though these two (and other) general social science recommendations may seem obvious to social scientists, there are many DGBL studies, including our own OPB1 study [5], that do not mention how they (or that they) piloted the knowledge tests and many studies use only quantitative or qualitative methods.

4   Conclusion

When running a DGBL study on learning gains in the context of a formal schooling system, researchers often encounter many technical pitfalls stemming from the authenticity of the environment. In this paper, we have verbalized 6 Recommendations suggesting how to minimize some of these pitfalls:

1. Reserve a whole day for the experiment.
2. Disrupt the regular school schedule.
3. Employ a "standardized" expert teacher, who has authority.
4. Use the smallest groups possible for assessing students' knowledge.
5. Address the low-stake test problem.
6. Avoid certain periods of year.

Generally, Recommendations argue for running a study in a more laboratory-like fashion, while *modeling* the authenticity of the real school setting. This general suggestion can be interpreted as: turn the school into a laboratory, or model a school setting in a laboratory. Both ways help to eliminate some of the confounding variables.

The important boundary condition of the Recommendations is that they were formulated based on our experience with *secondary* education systems. Not all of these recommendations may apply in primary and tertiary education environments, e.g., the low-stake test issue may not be that problematic with younger children. However, some other issues may emerge, e.g., the necessity to keep the study short for primary school students.

We hope that the Recommendations will help to improve the quality of DGBL studies conducted in authentic environments, and that consequently, the empirical research base will become more solid.

Acknowledgments. This work was partially supported by the project *LEES: Learning Effects of Educational Simulations* nr. P407/12/P152 (GAČR) for C.B. and V.Š., and by the IGA MZČR grant NT/13386 for D.K. and D.L. We thank Zdeněk Hlávka, Tereza Nekovářová and Tereza Selmbacherová for their contributions to this research and three anonymous referees for their helpful comments.

References

1. Annetta, L.A., Minogue, J., Holmes, S.Y., Cheng, M.: Investigating the Impact of Video Games on High School Students' Engagement and Learning about Genetics. Computers & Education 53(1), 74–85 (2009)
2. Barab, S., Thomas, M., Dodge, T., Carteaux, R., Tuzun, H.: Making Learning Fun: Quest Atlantis, A Game Without Guns. Educational Technology Research & Development 53(1), 86–107 (2005)
3. Babbie, E.R.: The Practice of Social Research, 13th edn. Wadsworth Publishing (2012)
4. Bída, M., Brom, C., Popelová, M., Kadlec, R.: StoryFactory – A Tool for Scripting Machinimas in Unreal Engine 2 and UDK. In: Si, M., Thue, D., André, E., Lester, J.C., Tanenbaum, J., Zammitto, V. (eds.) ICIDS 2011. LNCS, vol. 7069, pp. 334–337. Springer, Heidelberg (2011)
5. Brom, C., Preuss, M., Klement, D.: Are Educational Computer Micro-Games Engaging and Effective for Knowledge Acquisition at High-Schools? A Quasi-Experimental Study. Computers & Education 57, 1971–1988 (2011)
6. Brom, C., Šisler, V., Slavík, R.: Implementing Digital Game-Based Learning in Schools: the Augmented Learning Environment of Europe 2045. Multimedia Systems 16(1), 23–41 (2010)
7. Cuban, L.: Teachers and Machines: The Classroom Use of Technology Since 1920. Teachers College Press, New York (1986)
8. Egenfeldt-Nielsen, S.: Beyond Edutainment: Exploring the Educational Potential of Computer Games. PhD thesis. University of Copenhagen (2005)
9. Feinstein, A.H., Cannon, H.M.: Construct of Simulation Evaluation. Simulation & Gaming 33(4), 425–440 (2002)
10. de Freitas, S.: Learning in Immersive Worlds. Joint Information Systems Committee (2006), http://www.jisc.ac.uk/eli_outcomes.html (accessed March 16, 2012)
11. Gee, J.P.: What Video Games Have to Teach Us About Learning and Literacy. Palgrave/St. Martin's, New York (2003)
12. Hays, R.T.: The Effectiveness of Instructional Games: A Literature Review and Discussion, Technical Report 2005-004, Naval Air Warfare Center Training Systems Division, Orlando (2005)
13. Hopfenberg, T.N.: Students' Test Motivation in PISA. In: Proc. EARLI, pp. 498–499 (2011)
14. Huizenga, J., Admiraal, W., Akkerman, S., ten Dam, G.: Mobile Game-based Learning in Secondary Education: Engagement, Motivation and Learning in a Mobile-city Game. Journal of Computer Assisted Learning 25(4), 332–344 (2009)

15. Klopfer, E.: Augmented Learning: Research and Design of Mobile Educational Games. MIT Press, Cambridge (2008)
16. Izard, J.: Trial Testing and Item Analysis in Test Construction. Module 7. In: Quantitative Research Methods in Educational Planning. UNESCO International Institute for Educational Planning (2009)
17. Ketelhut, D.J., Schifter, C.C.: Teachers and Game-based Learning: Improving Understanding of How to Increase Efficacy of Adoption. Computers & Education 56, 539–546 (2011)
18. Malone, T.W.: Toward a Theory of Intrinsically Motivating Instruction. Cognitive Science 5(4), 333–369 (1981)
19. Mayer, R.E.: Multimedia Learning. Cambridge University Press, New York (2001)
20. Mayer, R.E., Clark, R.C.: Simulations and Games in e-Learning. In: E-Learning and the Science of Instruction, 3rd edn., ch. 16, pp. 369–400. John Wiley & Sons (2011)
21. Moreno, R.: Instructional technology: Promise and pitfalls. In: Technology-based Education: Bringing Researchers and Practitioners Together, pp. 1–19. Information Age Publishing, Greenwich (2005)
22. Novak, M., Wilensky, U.: NetLogo Bird Breeder Model. Center for Connected Learning and Computer-Based Modeling, Northwestern University, Evanston, IL (2007), http://ccl.northwestern.edu/netlogo/models/BirdBreeder
23. Papastergiou, M.: Digital Game-Based Learning in High School Computer Science Education: Impact on Educational Effectiveness and Student Motivation. Computers & Education 52, 1–12 (2009)
24. Sitzmann, T.: A Meta-analytic Examination of the Instructional Effectiveness of Computer-based Simulation Games. Personnel Psychology 64, 489–528 (2011)
25. Šisler, V., Brom, C.: Designing an Educational Game: Case Study of 'Europe 2045'. In: Pan, Z., Cheok, D.A.D., Müller, W., El Rhalibi, A. (eds.) Transactions on Edutainment I. LNCS, vol. 5080, pp. 1–16. Springer, Heidelberg (2008)
26. Šisler, V., Buchtová, M., Brom, C., Hlávka, Z.: Towards an Empirical–Theoretical Framework for Investigating the Learning Effects of Serious Games: A Pilot Study of Europe 2045. In: Applied Playfulness. Proceedings of the Vienna Games Conference 2011: Future and Reality of Gaming, pp. 16–36. Braumüller Verlag, Vienna (2012)
27. Wastiau, P., et al.: How are digital games used in schools? Complete Results of the Study. European Schoolnet (2009), http://games.eun.org/upload/gis-synthesis_report_en.pdf (accessed: March 16, 2012)
28. Wise, S.L.: Strategies for Managing the Problem of Unmotivated Examinees in Low-Stakes Testing Programs. The Journal of General Education 58(3), 152–166 (2009)
29. Wolfe, J., Crookall, D.: Developing a Scientific Knowledge of Simulation/Gaming. Simulation & Gaming 29(1), 7–19 (1998)

Application of NXT Based Robots
for Teaching Java-Based Concurrency

Łukasz Szweda, Daniel Wilusz, and Jakub Flotyński

Department of Information Technology, The Poznań University of Economics
Mansfelda 4, 60-854, Poznań, Poland
{szweda,wilusz,flotynski}@kti.ue.poznan.pl

Abstract. Education in the field of computer programming is a challenging task, in particular when some complex issues are introduced for non-computer science students. A number of simplified programming languages, environments and simulation software have been developed in recent years to support both teaching as well as self-learning of different programming techniques. However, there are no solutions for teaching in the domain of concurrent programming in the Java language. In this paper we present our original concept of studies using NXT robots to teach Java-based concurrency. An NXT robot equipped with Java virtual machine seems to be a good solution to improve teaching concurrent programming. Actions performed in real-time by robots allow students to observe the performance of their applications and quickly identify mistakes in their code.

Keywords: teaching programming, edutainment, Lego NXT, concurrency.

1 Introduction

In recent years introductory courses in computer science have become complex in terms of both the volume of knowledge to be acquired and the sophistication of widely used programming tools. This situation resulted from continuous advances in computer science. Contemporary students would be bored if they had to study in the manner practiced by the previous generation [10]. Once it was an exciting challenge to find the mean of a set of numbers, however, in the era of the Internet, PlayStation and Tablet PCs it is considered to be boring and purely theoretical – and as such, currently, not very attractive to students. The fact that computer devices can be met everywhere makes new expectations emerge; for instance, GUIs, database or distributed systems are often introduced quite early in computer science studies. Introduction of new and more advanced concepts in courses requires more time which makes it very difficult to pass on relevant knowledge within merely several semesters. The Computing Curricula 2001 Report indicates a proportional increment of the number and complexity of subjects to be dealt with by students to the level of sophistication of problems they need to face [11].

Computer science needs to tackle two major problems that have a negative impact on the quality of education:

S. Göbel et al. (Eds.): Edutainment 2012/GameDays 2012, LNCS 7516, pp. 54–64, 2012.

— complexity – the volume of detailed aspects in programming has risen rapidly over recent years;
— lack of stability – present programming languages, libraries and tools for teaching programming are evolving very quickly [16].

The problems mentioned above lead to a paradox. On one hand, growing complexity lengthens establishment of effective teaching strategies (including educational and teaching materials). On the other hand, increasingly rapid progress of computer science is observed.. As a result, teaching materials and strategies quickly become obsolete and outdated. Finding solutions that reduce the level of sophistication and mitigate effects of rapid changes in computer science is a crucial issue for contemporary education.. The most obvious reason for the complexity and instability of computer science is its lifetime. Since the climax of the Pascal language 25 years ago the size of the society working on software development has significantly increased. Nowadays, there are lots of people and companies engaged in development of technology. When a new promising technology such as Java emerges, those people and businesses invest their time and energy in promoting it. From this point of view rapid changes to Java and its API may be perceived as a measure of success. The fact that Java developed faster than its predecessors stems from people's excitement towards the language which has propelled its further evolution.

Despite all the problems, the aptness of Java as a basic programming language seems to be unquestionable. Its rivals are either obsolete or — as in the case of C# — they have numerous similarities. Accordingly there are no reasons to replace this popular and well-proven tool with any other brand name. However, the issue of complexity and instability remains to be solved to enable effective teaching of Java programming.

Concurrency programming is an example of one of the complex issues that students need to face quite early. Topics related to threads, resource sharing, locks and semaphores cause potential misunderstanding and a lot of unidentified errors across the code. The problems mentioned above require a new approach for teaching concurrency which would simply identify and exclude anomalies caused by improperly implemented threads.

In this paper we propose a use of NXT robots for teaching Java concurrency. The remaining of the paper is organized as follows. In Section 2 the educational environments are presented. Next, areas of using physical, programmable robots are described. Section 3 describes and evaluates a study prepared by the authors of this paper, which aims at improving education of Java-based concurrency. Finally, Section 4 concludes the paper and indicates future works.

2   The Platforms Supporting Education in the Domain of Computer Programming

Instead of forcing the students to learn advanced aspects of programming with the industrial aspects of implementing Java programs, one should rather make them acquainted with programming using an environment which is strongly bounded with Java, and simultaneously user friendly [17]. Unfortunately, Java has been developed for experts, not for aspiring programmers. Therefore, there are plenty of inconveniences and technicalities which make understanding Java more difficult with no previous programming knowledge. That is why it seems practically impossible to successfully teach students with little programming experience advanced aspects of Java programming, in particular such complex features as concurrency.

2.1   Karel – The Robot

In the 70s Rich Pattis, graduate student of Stanford University, came to the conclusion that it will be easier to teach fundamentals programming issues if students have a possibility to learn this concepts in a new and simple environment, instead of using enterprise-driven approach. Inspired by success of LOGO, Seymour Papert's project in MIT, Rich Pattis created a pilot programming environment in which students teach a robot to solve simple problems. The robot was named Karel as a tribute to the Czech drama writer, Karel Capek [12].

Karel is a basic robot embedded in a very simple world. By giving a series of commands we can make it perform certain tasks. The process of defining those commands is called programming. At the first, Karel knows only few predefined commands, however, a crucial part of programming is teaching Karel new commands which expand its capabilities.

While programming Karel to perform a task one should accurately write out the relevant commands so that the robot can properly interpret what it is intended to do. In particular the source code has to comply with a series of syntactic rules which specify which commands and linguistic forms are allowed. Predefined commands and syntactic rules define the Karel programming language. This language bears some resemblance to Java. Owing to this fact it is easy to switch between those two dialects. Karel and Java programs have a very similar structure and include the same basic elements. The most important difference between the two languages is that the scope of Karel programming language is narrow, i.e. it does not have many commands and rules. It is easy, for example, to learn the entire language within several hours. Then the student knows Karel's capabilities and knows how to define its activities in the program. Details when compared to Java are easier to master. Despite this fact, one can easily find out that the solution to a problem may turn out to be a big challenge. Solving problems constitutes the essence of programming and the rules are only a minor obstacle.

Undoubtedly, Karel is a step in the right direction. However, this technology has been simplified excessively. Although we can discuss basic aspects of programming methodology, such as: object-orientation, decomposition, encapsulation and hiding information, there is little time left for more advanced issues including the concurrency. As a result, Karel is a good choice to facilitate education of Java basics; however, when it comes to more sophisticated Java issues, new stimulating environment is required.

2.2   Scratch – MIT Solution

The Scratch environment, developed by the MIT research team in collaboration with Lego company was inspired by the fact how children put blocks together into certain structures. These two teams decided to implement in their tool the idea of Lego blocks to facilitate programming education. In other words scratch grammar is a collection of graphic blocks used for programming. As in case of Lego blocks, the graphic blocks are characterized by proper projections and joints implying how the blocks fit to each other [18]. Similar to Karel, there is no irritating syntax and implementation details which make the concept difficult to understand. The advantage of programming in Scratch is that it provides a lot of enjoyment and enables the programmer to mix graphics, animations, photos and sounds. One can also learn elements which are not present in Karel, e.g. using listeners and interactions. Scratch users can also face multiple threads. Several behavior elements can be used at once what enables the multiple threads to work simultaneously on a Scratch's graphical layer. Is it then a perfect tool for learning programming and advanced aspects related to that? Unfortunately not; it has been already said that, unlike Karel, Scratch has no irritating syntax. However, the problem is that there is practically no programming syntax, and little correlation is provided with Java programming. As a result, advanced Scratch users not necessary become advanced in Java programming. All aspects of programming are purely conceptual. Simplification of the tool also eliminates crucial elements of multiple threads which we are unable to present, e.g., race condition[1].

2.3   Using Robots in Education

Numerous works present psychological and educational aspects of teaching by means of robots. Recently, Lego Mindstorms NXT robot has been utilized in education very intensively because it is a flexible tool, appropriate for various applications [1], that may meet individual educational needs of students [2,3] and improves their social behavior [4].

In the project of A. K. Lui et al. [5], robots have been used to improve enriched learning in groups with individual supervisors. The work of G. D. Chen et al. [6] presents a robot with emotions, interacting with students in a mixed reality learning environment. The experiment of R. B. Osborne et al. [7] uses NXT Mindstorms robots in service-oriented training based on scientific, mathematical and computing fundamentals.

In the area of technical applications, robots are convenient tools for teaching both low- [8], as well as high-level programming [9], introducing students to the automata theory [19] and developing interactive educational platforms hiding implementation details [20].

However, even if a lot of training solutions have been proposed, all these proposals do not address teaching multithreading and concurrent programming.

---

[1] Race condition is a phenomena in the system or process causing that the output of the system is dependent on the timing of other events [21].

3   Using Lego NXT to Teach Java-Based Concurrency

In order to stimulate the education of complex Java issues, we have prepared a case study. The aim of the study was to teach non-computer science students the concept of concurrency in Java. We decided to use NXT based robot operating under the LeJOS environment [13], in order to facilitate education. The idea behind the study was to allow the student to observe the execution of many parallel, independent threads on the example of NXT robot activities. Although the students had a basic Java knowledge, we measured the progress of their knowledge concerning concurrency, by conducting entrance and exit tests.

3.1   The Environment of the Study

The main component of the study environment was a robot constructed from the Lego Mindstorms NXT 2.0 8547 bricks set [15]. The robot had a form of a tank utilizing three motors, an ultrasonic sensor, a touch sensor and a color (RGB, light) sensor. An NXT firmware was replaced by LeJOS, which enabled the robot to be programmed in Java. In addition, the study required the 32 bit Java development kit and the 32 bit Eclipse IDE. Moreover, Eclipse was extended by the LeJOs plugin, which allowed for automatic integration with LeJOS library and convenient compilation, transmission and execution of the program in the NXT brick [14]. Compiled code was uploaded to the NXT brick via USB and after that could be executed standalone, without direct real-time control from a PC.

3.2   The Study

The study was performed by students working in pairs with the Lego NXT robot and the Eclipse environment (Figure 1). Their task was to program, during a 75-minutes-long class, the robot in Java and to observe the robot's behavior.

The properly programmed robot should switch its operation modes (guard, attack and retreat) depending on data received from sensors. When operating in the guard mode the robot was supposed to rotate clockwise, make a beep noise, display the current mode, make a beep sound and check, using a proximity sensor to check whether there is an object in the range of 20 cm. After the robot located an object, it switched into the attack mode. The robot shot a ball twice, swung and played a high tone. Next, it switched into the retreat mode and rotated by approximately 180 degrees and ran at full speed for three seconds. In any time the robot could be switched off by pressing the touch sensor.

The students were supposed to implement a thread to examine the touch sensor all the time the robot was operating. The study required use of threads in the guard mode, in which the rotation, the proximity check, and the beep noise should be performed in parallel. Moreover, the threads implementing shooting the ball, moving the robot one side another, playing scary tones and switching different colors on LEDs had to be properly implemented, executed and managed during attack.

Fig. 1. Students and NXT based robots during the exercise

Because students were not familiar with the LeJOS API, we prepared a Robot class, which allowed student to focus only on aspects of concurrency. The Robot class implementation is presented in Figure 2. Its methods are listed and shortly described below:

— beepUp() – allowing the robot to play increasing tones;
— display(String text) – printing any text on an NXT screen;
— forward(int speed) – making the robot to run at defined speed;
— getProximity() – returning the distance to the closest object;
— isTouched() – informing if the touch sensor has been pressed;
— playTone(int frequency, int duration) – playing a tone of given frequency by a specified period of time;
— rotateClockwise(int speed) – turning the robot with given speed;
— rotateCounterClockwise(int speed) – turning the robot with given speed;
— shoot(int shots) – shooting a ball given number of times;
— stop() – stopping the motors;
— switchLights() – switching on the lights;
— turnOffLight() – turning off the lights.

The exercise enabled presenting the students different aspects of concurrency. A race condition was experienced by students observing different messages on the NXT screen or the unexpected motor stops until the threads were properly controlled. In addition, the students could observe improper robot's behavior if some threads (i.e., the one responsible for playing the tones, or rotating the robot) were forgotten to be interrupted. Moreover, the effects of not-handled exception thrown by the java.lang.Thread.interrupt method were visible as well and thus had to be properly handled. In Figure 3 code responsible for the attack and retreat modes, that was especially difficult to implement for students, is presented. In the method implementing the attack mode, the students often forgot to interrupt the threads at the end of the mode. This resulted in continuation of the noise, swing and colors threads and was visible as improper robot's behavior. In the retreat mode, the students have to use NXT library carefully, as the LeJOS environment does not allow setting the time of robot's engine operation. In result, it was necessary for students to sleep the thread, otherwise robot would not perform any moving action.

```java
import lejos.nxt.*;
import lejos.nxt.ColorSensor.*;

public class Robot {
    // Sensors initialization
    private UltrasonicSensor usonic = new UltrasonicSensor(SensorPort.S4);
    private TouchSensor touchsens = new TouchSensor(SensorPort.S1);
    private ColorSensor color = new ColorSensor(SensorPort.S2);

    /**
     * Rotates the robot clockwise
     * @param speed of engines (100-1000)
     */
    public void rotateClockwise(int speed) {
        Motor.A.setSpeed(speed);
        Motor.B.setSpeed(speed);
        Motor.A.backward();
        Motor.B.forward();
    }

    /**
     * Displays text on LCD
     * @param text to display
     */
    public void display(String text) {
        LCD.clear();
        LCD.drawString(text, 0, 0);
    }

    /**
     * Gets the distance to the nearest object (red from ultrasonic sensor)
     * @return distance in cm
     */
    public int getProximity() {
        return usonic.getDistance();
    }
```

Fig. 2. The snippet of the Robot.class

The study required from participants careful software implementation by revealing their mistakes during software tests performed on the robot. Such construction of the study aimed at stimulating students to rethink their code in order to overcome multithreading traps. Note that, due to the complexity and mutual dependence of the robot tasks, it was not possible to program the robot behavior without using threads and concurrent programming. Thus, to complete the exercise, the students were forced to learn more deeply about Java threads, their synchronization and mutual communication. Note also, that it was not yet-another annoying theoretical exercise of producer-consumer problem, typical for a course on concurrent programming.

```java
public void attack() throws InterruptedException {
    mode=ATTACK;
    robot.display("Attack mode");
    Thread noise = new NoiseRobo();
    noise.start();
    Thread swing = new SwingRobo();
    swing.start();
    Thread colors = new ColorsRobo();
    colors.start();
    robot.shoot(2);
    noise.interrupt();
    swing.interrupt();
    colors.interrupt();
    Thread.sleep(100);
    retreat();
}

public void retreat() throws InterruptedException {
    mode=RETREAT;
    robot.display("Retreat mode");
    robot.rotateCounterClockwise(800);
    Thread.sleep(1500);
    robot.forward(800);
    Thread.sleep(3000);
    robot.stop();
    guard();
}
```

Fig. 3. The attack and retreat modes implementation

3.3   Educational Results of the Study

The study described above was our first approach to use robots in order to facilitate Java education. Moreover, the relatively small group of participants caused that the exercise results had to be perceived demonstratively only.

Eleven non-computer science students participated in the study. They attended the Internet of Things classes at the interdisciplinary Master course concerning economics, computer science, telecommunication and some aspects of physics. Before and after the exercise, the students were required to attend a quiz consisted of theoretical as well as practical (requiring Java code snippets analysis) questions. The questions verified their knowledge and understanding in the area of the following aspects:

— Java classes and methods concerning concurrency,
— sequence of instructions performed by concurrent threads,
— interrupting threads,
— sharing variables by many threads,
— executing threads.

The test results are summarized in Table 1 and discussed below.

Table 1. The rates of results of entrance and exit tests, grouped by question type

Question type	The entrance test: correct answers	The exit test: correct answers	Change
Java concurrency classes	36%	82%	46%
Sequence of instructions performed by concurrent threads	36%	64%	28%
Interrupting threads	55%	82%	27%
Sharing variables by many threads	91%	100%	9%
Executing threads	82%	82%	0%
Average	**60%**	**82%**	**22%**
Std. dev.	**22% points**	**22% points**	-
Max	**100%**	**100%**	-
Min	**20%**	**40%**	-

The research revealed that the highest progress achieved concerned the familiarity of Java thread classes and methods (the increase by 46 %). The observation of the students behavior showed that in comparison standard IDE based only classes, they were more engaged to fulfill the task when using the robot. This engagement should cause better Java knowledge acquisition. The second identified progress was achieved by the students in the area of understanding how instructions of parallel threads are executed by Java virtual machine. At the beginning of the exercise only 36% of the students answered correctly the questions concerning race condition. However, after performing the study and analysis of the robot's behavior, the understanding of race condition increased by 28% points. We may expect that the visualization of the way the threads accomplish their tasks, had positive educational effects. Another positive educational effect was achieved in the area of thread interruption and exception handling. During the entrance test about 55% of students gave correct answer and after the exercise this ratio increased to 82%.

On the other hand the issue of sharing variables among different threads appeared to be quite intuitive and, in this particular case the exercise had no possibility to influent the students' knowledge, as correct answer ratio rose from 91% to 100%. Similarly the issues concerned creation and running of threads was quite intuitive and could not reveal the potential of the robot.

The use of NXT robot increased the curiosity of students and caused their high engagement in the task, as they strongly wanted to see the robot in action. The utilization of educational robot allowed achieving good results in teaching quite complex issues such as race condition or exception caused by interrupting threads.

4 Conclusions and Future Works

Although simplified programing languages, simulation environments and robots supporting computer education have been used for decades, the effective education in the domain of concurrent programming is still a challenging task. The existing teaching environments lack the possibility to depict Java concurrency issues and cannot support teaching in this field.

The proposed study, which utilized the NXT robot, revealed the positive impact on students' education. Robots illustrating a multi-thread application are a milestone in teaching concurrency. The students observing anomalies in robots behavior in real-time, are stimulated to identify bugs in the code and thus became more careful when implementing concurrency.

Concurrency and multithreading are not the only challenging issues. Such concept as Service Oriented Architecture (SOA) or Event Driven Architecture (EDA) can also be depicted by some exercises utilizing NXT robots. Moreover, robots allow for getting student involvement in learning process by making classes more interesting. However, use of robots is only a supporting part of classes, useful in effective introduction to programming concepts. Facilitated issues should be also presented (in the complementary manner) in the standard way, to allow students to gain necessary programming skills.

As for the future work, we plan to propose more studies with NXT robots to teach programming in such domains as SOA and EDA services as well as service orchestration, swarm intelligence and pattern recognition.

References

1. Eubanks, A.M., Strader, R.G., Dunn, D.L.: A comparison of compact robotics platforms for model teaching. Journal of Computing Sciences in Colleges, Consortium for Computing Sciences in Colleges 26(4), 35–40 (2011) ISSN 1937-4771
2. Virnes, M., Sutinen, E., Kärnä-Lin, E.: How children's individual needs challenge the design of educational robotics. In: Proceedings of the 7th International Conference on Interaction Design and Children, Chicago, USA, June 11-13, pp. 274–281 (2008) ISBN 978-1-59593-994-4
3. Virnes, M.: Robotics in special needs education. In: Proceedings of the 7th International Conference on Interaction Design and Children, Chicago, USA, June 11-13, pp. 29–32 (2008) ISBN 978-1-59593-994-4
4. Kanda, T., Shimada, M., Koizumi, S.: Children learning with a social robot. In: Proceedings of the Seventh Annual ACM/IEEE International Conference on Human-Robot Interaction, Boston, USA, March 05-08, pp. 351–358 (2012) ISBN 978-1-4503-1063-5

5. Lui, A.K., Ng, S.C., Cheung, Y.H.Y., Gurung, P.: Facilitating independent learning with Lego Mindstorms robots. ACM Inroads 1(4), 49–53 (2010) ISSN 2153-2184
6. Chen, G.-D., Chi, Y.-L., Huang, C.-W., Fan, C.-Y., Wu, C.-J.: Design a Partner Robot with Emotions in the Mixed Reality Learning Environment. In: Chang, M., Hwang, W.-Y., Chen, M.-P., Müller, W. (eds.) Edutainment 2011. LNCS, vol. 6872, pp. 457–463. Springer, Heidelberg (2011)
7. Osborne, R.B., Thomas, A.J., Forbes, J.R.N.: Teaching with robots: a service-learning approach to mentor training. In: Proceedings of the 41st ACM Technical Symposium on Computer Science Education, Milwaukee, USA, March 10-13, pp. 172–176 (2010) ISBN 978-1-4503-0006-3
8. Jipping, M.J., Calka, C., O'Neill, B., Padilla, C.R.: Teaching students java bytecode using Lego mindstorms robots. ACM SIGCSE Bulletin 39(1), 170–174 (2007) ISSN 0097-8418
9. Pedersen, R.U., Nørbjerg, J., Scholz, M.P.: Embedded programming education with Lego Mindstorms NXT using Java (leJOS), Eclipse (XPairtise), and Python (PyMite). In: Proceedings of the 2009 Workshop on Embedded Systems Education, Grenoble, France, October 11-16, pp. 50–55 (2009) ISBN: 978-1-4503-0021-6
10. Miller, D., Nourbakhsh, I., Siegwart, R.: Springer Handbook of Roboics. Springer, Heidleberg (2008)
11. Computing Curricula 2001 Computer Science, ACM, IEEE, http://www.acm.org/education/curric_vols/cc2001.pdf
12. Pattis, R., Roberts, J.: Karel The Robot: A Gentle Introduction to the Art of Programming, 2nd edn. Wiley (1995)
13. LeJOS, Java for Lego Mindstorms, http://lejos.sourceforge.net/
14. The LeJOS NXJ Tutorial: Using Eclipse, http://lejos.sourceforge.net/nxt/nxj/tutorial/Preliminaries/UsingEclipse.html
15. Lego.com midstorms products, http://mindstorms.lego.com/en-us/products/default.aspx
16. Roberts, E.: The Dream of a Common Language: The Search for Simplicity and Stability in Computer Science Education. ACM SIGCSE Bulletin Homepage 36(1) (March 2004) ISBN:1-58113-798-2
17. Roberts, E.: An Overview of MiniJava. ACM SIGCSE Bulletin Homepage 33(1) (March 2001) ISBN:1-58113-329-4
18. Resnick, M., Maloney, J., Monroy-Hernández, A., Rusk, N., Eastmond, E., Brennan, K., Millner, A., Rosenbaum, E., Silver, J., Silverman, B., Kafai, Y.: Scratch Programming for All. Magazine Communications of the ACM - Scratch Programming for All CACM Homepage Archive 52(11) (November 2009)
19. Hamada, M., Sato, S.: Simulator and Robot-Based Game for Learning Automata Theory. In: Zhang, X., Zhong, S., Pan, Z., Wong, K., Yun, R. (eds.) Edutainment 2010. LNCS, vol. 6249, pp. 429–437. Springer, Heidelberg (2010)
20. Kazerouni, A., Shrewsbury, B., Padgett, C.: Using the NXT as an educational tool in computer science classes. In: Proceedings of the 49th Annual Southeast Regional Conference, Kennesaw, USA, March 24-26, pp. 67–69 (2011) ISBN 978-1-4503-0686-7
21. Race condition, http://en.wikipedia.org/wiki/Race_condition

The Effect of Learning Mechanics Design on Learning Outcomes in a Computer-Based Geometry Game

Jan L. Plass, Bruce D. Homer, Elizabeth O. Hayward, Jonathan Frye,
Tsu-Ting Huang, Melissa Biles, Murphy Stein, and Ken Perlin

Games for Learning Institute,
New York University,
The Graduate Center of the City University of New York

Abstract. A computer-based geometry game was adapted to allow for play using a conceptual rule or an arithmetic problem-solving mechanic. Participants (n = 91) from an urban middle school were randomly assigned to experimental conditions. Results suggest that play in the number condition was more situationally interesting than play in the rule condition. Participants in the rule condition were found to perform better in the game than those in the number condition. Learning outcome results suggest that in the number condition, but not the rule condition, playing more levels in the game diminishes the gain from pretest to posttest. For the design of games for learning, results highlight the importance of choosing a game mechanic that reflects the intended learning outcomes.

1 Introduction

Over the past decade, interest in developing computer-based games and simulations for learning has been ever growing (Gee, 2007; Squire, 2003). A number of influential books and articles have argued that well-designed games embody a broad variety of learning theories and are in line with some of the "best practices" of learning (e.g., Collins & Halverson, 2009; Gee, 2003; Mayo, 2007; Plass, Homer & Hayward, 2009). However, in order to realize the potential of games to foster the acquisition of specific knowledge and skills in players, designers have to address a series of challenges. For example, how should essential elements in the game be represented through iconic information to be more easily comprehended (Plass et al., 2009)? What design patterns can be formulated that help designers apply evidence from empirical research to make games effective for learning (Plass, Perlin, & Isbister, 2010)? How does visual design affect emotion, and how do these emotions affect learning (Um, Plass, Hayward & Homer, 2011)? The question addressed in the present paper extends our previous research by asking: How does the design of the learning mechanics affect learning outcomes in a geometry game.

We define learning mechanics as "patterns of behavior or building blocks of learner interactivity, which may be a single action or a set of interrelated actions that form the essential learning activity that is repeated throughout a game" (Plass et al., in press, p. 13). We argue that one of the key factors in designing effective games for

---

S. Göbel et al. (Eds.): Edutainment 2012/GameDays 2012, LNCS 7516, pp. 65–71, 2012.

learning is that the learning mechanics reflect the specific content to be learned, and that they reflect the specific user actions that will foster the acquisition of the related knowledge or skills.

In our work, we employ Evidence Centered Design as the framework that allows us to design these learning mechanics and assess their impact on learning. Evidence Centered Design (ECD; Mislevy, Almond & Steinberg, 2003) provides a useful framework for developing games for learning purposes. ECD requires designers to be specific about what skills, knowledge or other traits are being assessed, and what learners need to do, say, or create in order to provide evidence of the variables being assessed. A well-developed game for learning should include specialized learning mechanics (i.e., specialized activities grounded in learning sciences) that are mapped onto corresponding game mechanics (Plass et al., in press).

The current study employed a single player puzzle game that focused on geometry concepts of angles. This game was designed to allow for manipulation of the learning mechanic, which was implemented in two variants. Middle-school students were randomly assigned to play one of two versions of a math game, Noobs vs. Leets. In the first version, which we call the Rule version, players were asked to apply a geometry rule to an angle to solve an angle problem. In other words, in order to solve an angles problem, the players were asked to identify which rule they would apply but did not specify the numeric answer. Rules included the supplementary angles rule, complementary angles rule, opposite angles rule, etc. In the second version, which we call the Number version, players were given the same angles problems but were asked to calculate the angle and click on the correct number value to solve for the angle. In other words, instead of identifying the rule they used to solve the problem, learners were asked to specify the numeric answer. Learning outcomes, situational interest, and game performance were dependent variables.

2   Method

Participants and Design

Participants were 91 students from an urban school in a major Northeastern city. There were 33 sixth graders and 58 eighth graders. 43 participants were females (47%). Each participant was randomly assigned to one of two versions of the game: rule and number. In the rule condition, participants played the version that required them to solve problems with geometry rules, whereas in the number condition, they played the version that required them to do arithmetic calculation. Two participants were excluded as they had outlying scores on the arithmetic fluency pretest or on the pretest of geometry skills. The resulting total of 89 participants was included in the analyses.

Procedure

Participants were randomly assigned to conditions. First, they were administered a measure of math fluency and a pre-test of geometry knowledge that was timed for a period of 10 minutes. Once these were completed, participants engaged independently in a 25-minute game-play session of the game, Noobs vs. Leets. Participants were given the instruction: "When playing the game, do the best you can." Participants played the game on desktop computers using a mouse. Game-play instructions were provided through cut-scenes and in-game tutorials. An experimenter was also available during this time for questions about game play. At the end of the game-play session, participants were instructed to stop all play activity. Participants then completed geometry post-test for a period of 10 minutes. After the post-test was administered, participants completed a situational interest survey and a play-testing protocol.

Materials

Noobs vs. Leets is a single player puzzle game that focuses on geometry concepts of angles. The game was designed to investigate the learning mechanic of rule application. The game runs in a web browser on desktop computers. The object of the game was to unlock angles, allowing the 'noob' character to free a fellow 'noob' from a cage. By unlocking angles, players open paths that the character can traverse. In the rule version of the game, angles are solved by clicking on the angle or angles to be solved and then selecting the appropriate rule. For example, a player could click on a known angle and an unknown angle that together make a right angle and then select the 'complementary rule' button to unlock an angle. In the number version of the game, angles are solved by clicking on an angle and selecting the correct degree of the angle. For example, a player could click on a locked right angle and then click the '90°' button (Figure 1). For complex angles, players would have to calculate the correct number of degrees of the angle.

The game is divided into six chapters, each consisting of 8-10 levels and focusing on a specific angle concept. These concepts include simple, complementary, supplementary, vertical, triangle, and quadrilateral. Both versions of the game contain an identical first chapter, which mixes response types, and focuses on simple angle types such as acute, obtuse, right, and straight. Each chapter begins with a cut-scene introducing and explaining the concept for that chapter. Each level within a chapter progressively increased in difficulty. Levels are complete when a player has unlocked a pathway for the noob to reach the caged noob. On some levels, immobile or mobile 'leet' characters block some pathways that a player could solve, requiring the player to unlock a pathway around the 'leet'. See Figure 1 for a screen shot of each game version.

Fig. 1. Two Game Mechanics in *Noobs v. Angles* Game: *Number* version (left) and *Rule* version (right)

Measures

Participants were first given measure of math fluency. The measure consisted of 160 simple addition and subtraction arithmetic problems. Participants were provided 3 minutes to complete as many problems as possible. The measure of math fluency was adapted from the *Woodcock Johnson – III Math Fluency* subtest (McGrew & Woodcock, 2001), which was modified by randomizing the presentation of problems, excluding multiplication problems, and added additional two and three digit problems, so as to make the type of calculation comparable to the arithmetic employed in solving for angles.

Participants also completed a pre-test and post-test of geometry knowledge. A teacher with experience teaching middle school math designed these measures. Items were adapted from questions from yearly exams based on New York state standards. The two measures consisted of nearly identical problems, with slight variations to the specific degrees used or angle being questioned.

Participants were also administered the *Situational Interest Survey* (Linnenbrink-Garcia et al., in press). The language in the situational interest measure was simplified to ensure comprehension in our middle school sample. In addition, the measure was modified to be relevant for game play. The Situational Interest Survey asked participants to use a 7-point Likert scale to indicate their level of agreement with twelve statements, such as "The game was exciting," "The things I learned from the game are important to me," and "I thought the game was interesting."

3   Results

Situational Interest

In order to investigate the situational interest in the game, we conducted a between-subjects ANCOVA, controlling for number of levels completed and grade level. This analysis yielded a marginal main effect for condition, $F(1, 82) = 3.64$, $p = .06$, $\eta^2 = .05$, such that the number condition ($M_{adjusted} = 5.45$, $SE = .20$) demonstrated greater situational interest than those in the rules condition, ($M_{adjusted} = 4.90$, $SE = .20$).

Game Performance

In order to examine the effect of condition on game performance, an ANCOVA was performed on the total number of levels completed in the game, with grade level added to the model as a covariate. The analysis yielded a effects for grade, $F(1, 89) = 9.014$, $p = .004$, $\eta^2 = .10$, as well as condition $F(1, 89) = 7.16$, $p = .009$, $\eta^2 = .08$. Participants who were in the 6th grade ($M = 23.84$, $SD = 7.40$) completed significantly fewer levels than those in the 8th grade ($M = 28.52$, $SD = 7.32$). Individuals in the rule group completed more levels ($M_{adjusted} = 28.88$, $SE = 1.06$) than individuals in the number group ($M_{adjusted} = 24.85$, $SE = 1.07$). This suggests that those in the rule group performed better in the game than those in the number group (Figure 2).

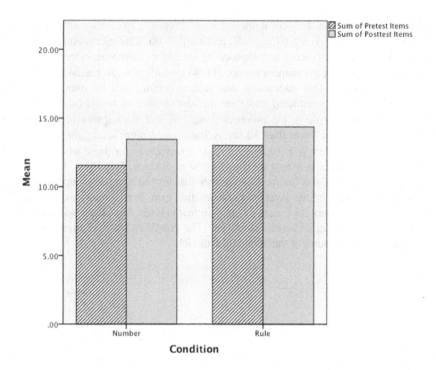

Fig. 2. Pre- v. Post Test Results for Number vs. Rule groups

Geometry Learning Outcomes

A two-way repeated-measures 2 (Time: Pretest vs. Posttest) x 2 (Question Type: Arithmetic vs. Concept) ANCOVA was conducted using average of correct responses as the dependent variable. Condition was a between-groups factor, and arithmetic fluency pretest and number of levels completed were covariates. A custom RM-ANCOVA model was run with time, question type, arithmetic fluency pretest, and levels completed entered as main effects, and time by condition, time by level, condition by level, and time by condition by level as interaction terms. Main effects were found for time, $F(1, 84) = 12.61$, $p = .001$, partial $\eta^2 = .13$ and question type, $F(1, 84) = 45.16$, $p < .001$, partial $\eta^2 = .35$. Therefore, there existed overall differences in the responses due to time, such that scores on the outcome measure increased from the pretest ($M_{adjusted} = .50$, $SE = .01$) to the posttest ($M_{adjusted} = .57$, $SE = .01$). There was also a main effect of question type, such that participants in both groups were more successful on the conceptual rule-based questions ($M_{adjusted} = .74$, $SE = .01$) than on the arithmetic questions $M_{adjusted} = .35$, $SE = .01$), across the pretest and posttest measures. There were also main effects for both covariates on the outcome measures: arithmetic fluency pretest, $F(1, 84) = 23.51$, $p < .001$, partial $\eta^2 = .22$, and levels completed, $F(1, 84) = 16.09$, $p < .001$, partial $\eta^2 = .16$.

These main effects were qualified by significant interactions. There was a two-way interaction between time by condition, $F(1, 84) = 6.05$, $p = .02$, partial $\eta^2 = .07$, represented in Figure 1, as well as a time by level interaction, $F(1, 84) = 4.67$, $p = .03$, partial $\eta^2 = .05$. Of greater theoretical interest is the three-way interaction among time by condition by level, $F(1, 84) = 5.67$, $p = .02$, partial $\eta^2 = .06$. This interaction is shown in Figure 3. When the results were decomposed by condition, there was simple interaction effect of time by level for the number group, $F(1, 41) = 4.49$, $p = .04$, partial $\eta^2 = .10$, but not for the rule group. This interaction was further decomposed by running separate analyses for those who completed less than median number of levels (< 30) or more levels (≥30) for individuals in the numbers condition. For participants in the number condition who completed fewer than 30 levels, there was a significant gain from pretest to posttest, $F(1, 24) = 5.55$, $p = .03$, partial $\eta^2 = .19$, whereas for those who completed more than 30 levels, there was no gain from pretest to posttest, $F(1, 16) = .174$, *n.s.* The graphic representation of this interaction suggests that for the number group, but not for the rule group, playing more levels diminishes the gain from pretest to posttest. In contrast, for the rule group, the extent of the gain from pretest to posttest was consistent, irrespective of the number of levels completed. The condition by level interaction term did not significantly account for variance in the model.

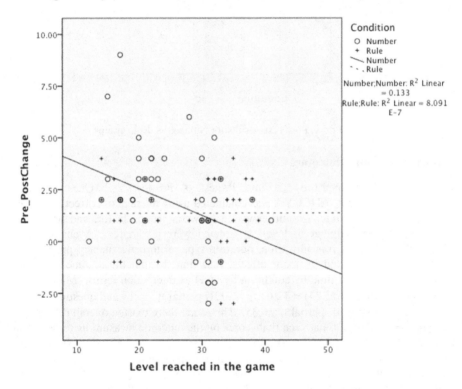

Fig. 3. Three-way interaction among time by condition by level

4   Discussion

The present study investigated how variation of the learning mechanic in a geometry puzzle game affected situational interest, game performance, and learning outcomes.

The number condition resulted in greater situational interest than the rule condition, suggesting that calculating the arithmetic solution for angles yields greater intrinsic interest. However, individuals in the rule condition performed better in the game. Finally, with regard to learning outcomes, results suggest that in the number condition, but not the rule condition, playing more levels in the game diminishes the gain from pretest to posttest. In contrast, for the rule group, the extent of the gain from pretest to posttest was consistent, irrespective of the number of levels completed. Overall, the results suggest that while calculating the arithmetic solution to geometry problems may be more situationally interesting, over time, this approach yields diminishing returns. These findings indicate that having an arithmetic understanding of how to solve geometry problems may promote learning outcomes in the short term, but in order to sustain gains in learning, having a conceptual rule-based understanding is necessary. Results also indicate that the choice of the game mechanic in a learning game can have significant impact on the learning outcome. Future work should examine the effects of other design factors, and also if the effects found in the current study are different for different types of games and academic areas.

References

Collins, A., Halverson, R.: Rethinking education in the age of technology: The digital revolution and schooling in America. Teachers College, NY (2009)

Gee, J.P.: What video games have to teach us about learning and literacy. Palgrave Macmillan, New York (2003)

Gee, J.P.: Good video games + Good learning. Peter Lang, New York (2007)

Linnenbrink-Garcia, L., Durik, A.M., Conley, A.M., Barron, K.E., Tauer, J.M., Karabenick, S.A., et al.: Situational interest survey (SIS): An instrument to assess the role of situational factors in interest development (in press)

Mayo, M.J.: Games for science and engineering education. Communications of the ACM 50(7), 30–35 (2007)

McGrew, K.S., Woodcock, R.W.: Technical Manual: Woodcock-Johnson III (2001)

Mislevy, R.J., Almond, R.G., Steinberg, L.S.: On the structure of educational assessments. Measurement: Interdisciplinary Research and Perspectives 1, 3–67 (2003)

Plass, J.L., Homer, B.D., Chang, Y.K., Frye, J., Kaczetow, W., Isbister, K., Perlin, K.: Metrics to Assess Learning and Measure Learner Variables in Simulations and Games. In: El-Nasr, et al. (eds.) Game Telemetry and Metrics. Morgan Kaufman (in press)

Plass, J.L., Homer, B.D., Milne, C., Jordan, T., Kalyuga, S., Kim, M., Lee, H.J.: Design Factors for Effective Science Simulations: Representation of Information. International Journal of Gaming and Computer-Mediated Simulations 1(1), 16–35 (2009)

Plass, J.L., Homer, B.D., Hayward, E.O.: Design Factors for Educationally Effective Animations and Simulations. Journal of Computing in Higher Education 21(1), 31–61 (2009)

Plass, J.L., Perlin, K., Isbister, K.: The Games for Learning Institute: Research on Design Patterns for Effective Educational Games. Paper presented at the Game Developers Conference, San Francisco, March 9-13 (2010)

Squire, K.: Video Games in Education. International Journal of Intelligent Simulations and Gaming 2(1) (2003)

Um, E., Plass, J.L., Hayward, E.O., Homer, B.D.: Emotional Design in Multimedia Learning. Journal of Educational Psychology (December 19, 2011) Advance online publication, doi:10.1037/a0026609

A Serious Game for Architectural Knowledge in the Classroom

Philip Mildner, Christopher Campbell, Mark Himmelsbach,
Christoph Malassa, Marco Miczka, and Wolfgang Effelsberg

University of Mannheim, Mannheim, Germany,
Department of Computer Science IV,
{mildner,effelsberg}@informatik.uni-mannheim.de,
{ccampbel,mhimmels,chmalass,mmiczka}@mail.uni-mannheim.de

Abstract. In this paper we present a serious game on the topic of architecture. The game was developed in association with an architect and is intended to be used in classrooms to deliver architectural knowledge to young students. It focuses on a modular story pattern to allow an easy integration of further game and learning content. With its modern 3D graphical interface it is well suited for illustrating various aspects of architecture.

Keywords: serious games, education, architectural knowledge.

1 Introduction

Serious Games nowadays are used in a variety of application fields. One of their main purposes is the transfer of knowledge, so it is quite a natural application scope to use them in classrooms as an alternative way of knowledge transfer [7]. We propose a serious game that delivers architectural knowledge to young students. Architecture itself can be found in many different disciplines, from statics and geometry, different building materials, stylistic eras, to the effect of light and shadow or sound. Through its strong visual aspects architecture is well suited for the presentation in a graphical computer game. The goal of our game is to provide an understanding of the different aspects of architecture to young students and to increase their interest in this topic. While the game can be played without any further explanation its primary purpose is to be played as part of a guided course in schools. Instead of only delivering explicit learning material the game focuses on giving an overview of the wide field of disciplines that are included in architecture. E. g., students can play the game and afterwards discuss with their teacher what they have learned about architecture in general, or a specific architecture topic that was covered in a part of the game.

The game was developed within the scope of a so-called team project at the University of Mannheim. In this kind of project a group of four to eight master students of business informatics work together for a year. Similar projects like [1] have shown the effectiveness of such projects. The project participants are able to learn about game development, serious games and team work while

S. Göbel et al. (Eds.): Edutainment 2012/GameDays 2012, LNCS 7516, pp. 72–77, 2012.

young students in schools can gather knowledge on architecture by playing the game. This particular team project was created in association with an architect who delivers knowledge about the topic of architecture to students. She already conducted projects in schools with students in primary and middle schools with traditional learning material[1]. The idea of this team project was to transfer her approach to a digital game in order to demonstrate the variety of application fields that are connected to architecture.

2 Game Overview

A main goal of the project was to create a modular game design that allows for an easy integration of further modules into the game. In the project the term *module* was used for a level/scene of the game that can be played on its own so that the game consists of a set of modules. With such a design students who participate in the project are able to create their own complete modules while students who join the project later can easily contribute additional content. At the same time this concept gives players a high level of freedom how they want to experience the game. Ideally, players should have the possibility to freely change between available modules by moving on the axis of different dimensions such as location, time, or actor. Consequently, instead of using a pure linear story a *Hero's Journey* approach was chosen. In such a story line the game starts with a short linear introduction scene and then moves on to a bigger section where the player can freely choose from a set of scenes or levels. After the player solved a certain set of tasks he is allowed to move on with the story, leading to a unique linear finishing scene of the game [3].

The game itself was implemented as a 3D adventure. In adventures in general, a player has to complete tasks or solve riddles in order to proceed. While the majority of the existing adventure games are set up in a 2D environment, a 3D environment can greatly promote the illustration of architectural topics. Unity3D[2] has been chosen as the game development platform. With its ability to run on different platforms it is well suited for use in schools. Integrated authoring tools for the creation of serious games, such as [4], were not considered as it was desired to have the biggest possible freedom in the game creation process.

During the design phase of the game efforts have been made to create a proper *flow* for the gaming experience [2]. The knowledge transfer of the game is of an implicit character. This is in contrast to other educational games where learning and fun phases are strictly separated [5]. In our game there is no such distinction. Although the game is set up so that the player is aware of the fact that architectural knowledge is to be delivered, the knowledge itself is implicitly embedded into the game's story line. As the game is designed to be played as part of a school lesson this should be an adequate compromise between awareness of the learning intent and fun of the gameplay.

---

[1] http://www.kunst-raum-bildung.de/Architekturvermittlung/
StadtteilDetektive.html
[2] http://unity3d.com/

A second aspect to ensure game flow is to dynamically adapt the difficulty of the game to the player's skill level. To integrate such a mechanism into our game a tutoring system was chosen. While changing the whole structure of the riddles can be quite complex, an adaptable level of hints is easy to implement. In this way the player can actively ask for help if he or she is stuck at a certain point, or the game can automatically detect if a player needs help by, e. g., measuring the time the player needs for solving a task. With this design the game is not intended to be used as primary learning material as the learning success cannot be assured through a game only [6]. Instead, with its implicit character, the game can be used as an accompanying tool for a course on architecture.

3   Implementation

The player starts the game in the role of a young student who has the task of writing an essay on stylistic eras of architecture for school. As the young student does not know where to start with his writing he seeks advice from a professor in the neighborhood. Being an expert in time travel the professor agrees to help the young student. Before the professor can explain anything relevant a lab accident happens in which the student gets trapped in a time machine the professor possesses. The student then travels through different time epochs where the time machine loses its energy modules. In order to travel back to the present time the player has to collect the lost energy modules to fully repair the time machine.

We argue that the story concept is well suited for this kind of game. First, the time travel scenario gives broad possibilities on the delivered learning content. Within the scenario it is easily possible to bring new architectural content into the game by creating a new module on the desired epoch or by adding new content to an existing module. Because of the non-linear composition of the modules the game can be extended without changing key aspects of the story. Second, the players have the opportunity to discover various aspects of architecture along with the character of the game. As the game proceeds the game adds content to a virtual notebook that the character uses to write his essay. These notes are generated dynamically by the player's actions and can be used in a subsequent discussion of the game. In this way, each player can tell his own story by solving tasks in other ways or in a different order, or leaving out some tasks or modules completely.

In the following sections two out of the four implemented game modules (see Figure 1) are presented in further detail.

3.1   Ancient Egypt Module

This level takes the player to the ancient Egypt. As an introduction to the scenery, the time machine falls from the sky, crashing into one of the Egyptian pyramids. In front of the pyramid the player recognizes the energy device he will be looking for throughout the story of the module. The player finds himself trapped within the room of the pharaohs sarcophagus. Since the roof has been crushed, rocks are spread in the whole scene, blocking the way out. By pushing them into the correct positions, the path can be unblocked. Unfortunately, the way out is blocked again so the player needs to examine the next room and find an irregularity. One of the walls in the room is not really robust, and finding and pushing a hidden button causes a huge pendulum to crush it. Behind it, there is a hidden way, which the player has to follow. He needs to keep his eyes open for irregularities, since there are traps on the floor, causing a huge rock to follow the player. At the end of the secret way, the player can finally leave the pyramid.

Arriving outside, the player finds himself standing in front of the huge pyramid, in a desert with little vegetation and burning heat (see Figure 1(a)). As mentioned before, the player should remember about the energy device; he needs to find the place where he has seen it before. After arriving there, he recognizes that it has disappeared. Footprints lead him from the pyramid to the Sphinx, where a camel herder stands who is in possession of the energy device. After a short explanation, he offers to give back the energy device if the player takes his camels to a well for watering. On the way to the well the player is confronted with a statics riddle in which he has to pass a canyon by using a bridge. The player has to choose from different kinds of bridges from which only one can carry both the player and the camels.

The architectural learning aspects in this module are colors and their combination, sound and acoustics, proportions, properties of materials, structures and construction, as much as statics. The player needs to use some of the aspects specifically in order to fulfill a task, others are just influencing the situation and the player's subconsciousness. The hieroglyphs and the yellow white sandstone within the pyramid create an harmonic and warm atmosphere. The hard and structured surface of the stones make the inside of the pyramid uncomfortable and dull, which is completely appropriate for its use as a grave. When moving the character through the inside of the pyramid, the footsteps on the hard stone can be heard, while moving over the sand in the desert causes a calm sound. Additionally, the echo of every sound is very intensive within the pyramid; outside, there is none. In the first room, where stones must be moved, a scraping sound is heard, causing the player to realize that there are two hard objects scratching against each other. Within the pyramid, there is complete silence since the walls are extremely thick. Only near the hole in the roof, some cries of birds and calm blowing of the wind can be heard. Outside, those effects are much louder. Since the pyramids and the sphinx are implemented in a similar size to the originals as well as with respect of the distance to each other, the player gets to know the proportions and gets to think about the difficulty to build such landmarks without modern tools.

3.2 Futuristic Module

In this module the player is stranded in the future. On its chaotic odyssey through time, the time machine has lost a battery in the year 2245. The battery

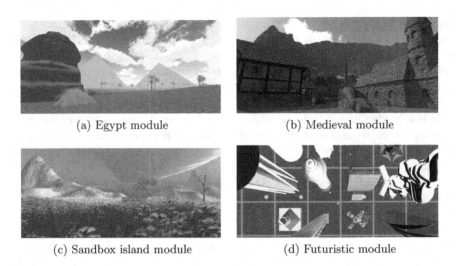

(a) Egypt module   (b) Medieval module

(c) Sandbox island module   (d) Futuristic module

Fig. 1. Screenshots of the implemented game modules

has been picked up by a future historian who is only willing to return it if the player helps him with the following problem: The historian owns a museum for ancient architecture, and a thief has stolen five museum objects. Each museum object is tagged with a tracking device, so the historian has a list of buildings next to which the thief has hidden the stolen objects. The historian asks the player to jump onto a flying platform and look for the objects. In order to provide a better overview of the map of the futuristic city, the perspective will be from above as long as the player is located on the platform (see Figure 1(d)). When the player has found the five missing objects, the historian will be very pleased; he asks the player to return each one to its correct socket in his museum. Each socket has a name tag, and the player has to decide where he or she puts down which object. Finally, the historian is so delighted that he returns the time machine battery to the player. The player returns to the time machine and continues the game.

The architectural learning outcomes of this scenario are manifold. First of all, the player will get a certain impression of futuristic architecture. Building shapes and materials are not randomly selected but based on the most modern buildings of today. They provide an impression of how future buildings will perhaps look. Additionally, the player will have to deal with switches of perspective when he or she is flying around on the platform to find the missing objects. The player will receive a picture of a building he or she has to identify according to its shape and appearance. The building might be recognizable from a certain distance, but in order to get there, the player will have to think about a path between the other buildings and, having decided on a path, map it to the view from above. Finally, the player will learn something about architectural epochs when he or she has to put each object on the socket with the corresponding nameplate.

4 Conclusion

In this paper we have presented the design and implementation of a serious game that is intended to be used in schools to teach students architecture. We have focused on a modular game design to allow an easy extension of the existing game content in another iteration of the project. The implemented modules cover different aspects of architecture, including statics, landmarks and the effects of light and shadow which have been developed in association with an architect. All modules are integrated into an adventure game setting which allows for an implicit transfer of the learning content while the player enjoys the game.

As a next step it is planned to bring the game to classrooms so that it can be played by grad school students. The results of the game sessions then can be evaluated in terms of the gaming experience and the actual learning outcome. Another focus of the evaluation will be on how the combination of game and lessons influences the learning experience. Furthermore, more architectural content will be added to the game to increase the amount of learning material.

Acknowledgements. We would like to thank the architect Bettina Gebhardt who is dedicated to the transfer and propagation of architectural knowledge for her valuable input on the architecture that was integrated into the game. We also would like to thank Prof. Dr. Heinz Jürgen Müller for his assistance in the project planning and execution.

References

1. Chaffin, A., Barnes, T.: Lessons from a course on serious games research and prototyping. In: Proceedings of the Fifth International Conference on the Foundations of Digital Games - FDG 2010, pp. 32–39. ACM Press, New York (2010)
2. Cowley, B., Charles, D., Black, M., Hickey, R.: Toward an understanding of flow in video games. Computers in Entertainment 6(2), 20:1–20:27 (2008)
3. Göbel, S., Mehm, F., Radke, S., Steinmetz, R.: 80Days: Adaptive Digital Storytelling for Digital Educational Games. In: Proceedings of the 2nd International Workshop on Story-Telling and Educational Games (STEG 2009), CEUR Workshop Proceedings, vol. 498 (August 2009)
4. Göbel, S., Salvatore, L., Konrad, R.: StoryTec: A Digital Storytelling Platform for the Authoring and Experiencing of Interactive and Non-Linear Stories. In: 2008 International Conference on Automated Solutions for Cross Media Content and Multi-Channel Distribution, pp. 103–110. IEEE (November 2008)
5. Prensky, M.: Digital Game-Based Learning. Paragon House (2007)
6. Squire, K.: Changing the Game: What Happens When Video Games Enter the Classroom? Innovate 1(6) (2005)
7. Wong, W.L., Shen, C., Nocera, L., Carriazo, E., Tang, F., Bugga, S., Narayanan, H., Wang, H., Ritterfeld, U.: Serious video game effectiveness. In: Proceedings of the International Conference on Advances in Computer Entertainment Technology - ACE 2007, pp. 49–55. ACM Press, New York (2007)

Evaluation of Competence Development in WoW

Steven Rausch, Uwe Faßhauer, and Alke Martens

PH Schwaebisch Gmuend, University of Education,
Dep. of Vocational Pedagogics and Dep. of Computer Science,
Oberbettringer Str. 200,
73525 Schwaebisch Gmuend, Germany
alke.martens@ph-gmuend.de

Abstract. This paper summarizes an evaluation in World of Warcraft (WoW), which took place in 2011 and 2012. The Massively Multiplayer Online Role Playing Game, which is currently played by thousands of players worldwide, lends itself for an investigation of several things, e.g. of competencies required for management and leadership positions. In the evaluation shown in this paper it has been possible to show that basic competencies can be trained in WoW playing, but also, that the investigated target group is inherently complex. The latter insight can be a good basis for future research.

1 Introduction

In the last years, the public and also the scientific discussion about Online-Roleplaying games has increased. Scientists have investigated Online-Roleplaying games from several different perspectives, e.g. how to use these games for teaching and training [15], [19], development of addiction, social aspects like communication, development of social networks, up to more technical aspects from the perspective of computer sciences [14]. The evaluation presented in this paper has a strong background in pedagogical and psychological research, combined with structural insights from computer science. From pedagogical and psychological sciences, the development and training of different (well defined) types of competencies is a well-known field of research. We have taken basic concepts from Vocational Pedagogies, e.g. the definition of competencies, and we investigated the development of competencies in a Massively Multiplayer Online Role Playing Games (MMORPGs) at the example of World of Warcraft (WoW). From the perspective of the development of a company, the development of competencies is for example related to the ability to work in a team, abilities for leadership, and the ability to organize things. Such competencies can only be developed, if a training environment provides certain structures, which are comparable to structures in organizations and companies. Such structures can be easily located in WoW. For example, we have *guilds* as one structural unit. Aspects stemming from analysis of companies, but which can be re-located in WoW, are hierarchical structures, responsibilities for certain tasks, exchange of tasks between

S. Göbel et al. (Eds.): Edutainment 2012/GameDays 2012, LNCS 7516, pp. 78–88, 2012.

members of a structure (e.g. a Guild), planning of dates and activities for central organized ventures, resource management, training of enrollees, and quality management.

The evaluation was planned in a three step manner: first, the notion of competencies in the field of business and company development has been investigated and clearly defined for our purpose. Afterward, the obvious game structures have been investigated and mapped to the central terms of development of competencies, and last but not least, the questions for the online evaluation and for structured interviews have been developed, based on both prior steps. The questionnaire has been developed with the system EvaSys. The size of the sample has been $n = 647$. After establishing certain filter questions, e.g. age, a remainder of $n = 608$ persons answered the questionnaire in a correct and usable way. The semi structured interviews have been executed with ten players, which can look back on a very long playing tradition. At the end, the results of the interviews have been compared with the results of the online investigation.

The remainder of the paper is structured as follows: in the next section, we will provide a short introduction into the field of development of competencies and roles in business. The central terms for our investigation will be defined. Afterward, these central terms will be mapped to WoW, which is explained in the third section. The fourth section shows methods, structure and execution of the empirical investigation. The most interesting results will be explicated. A critical discussion and outlook will finish the paper.

2   Development of Competencies and Roles

The term *competence* has its roots in old Latin (*competens* means something is suitable, fair, fitting). The current usage of the term can be traced back to Noam Chomsky and the research field of linguistics. Today, a plethora of potential definitions can be found, depending on the perspective of research, e.g. psychology, school education, vocational training, and the like. Erpenbeck and Rosenstiel [5] noted a comparably precise definition, which we can translate to English and map to our field of application. They defined that competencies are dispositions for self-organization of complex adaptive systems (meant in this context are for example human beings), which have been developed based on generalized development processes, and which allow reflective, creative problem solving, especially in the context of general classes of complex (but meaningful) situations. At the core of competencies are abilities, qualifications and knowledge, expanded by rules, norms, and values, which steer the self-organized actions [1]. A special focus in the context of industrial organizations is on being competent in decision-making and in taking over of responsibility for actions. Parts of the decision-making competence are social competencies, self-competencies, professional competencies, and methodological competencies (see also [10]). The following list shows a mapping of aspects of these competencies in relation to certain terms and competencies in the WoW world. As can be seen in the following list, almost all the areas overlap – with the exception of professional competencies. Sometimes, even the usage of terms is equivalent:

1. Professional competence
   - Special knowledge
     In virtual worlds, this is for example: knowledge about player character, talents, abilities, values,...
     In the business world (real life), we find: rules, norms, technical terms,...
   - Comprehensive knowledge
     Virtual world: mechanics of the game, game content, game principles, game rules, theories about the game,...
     Real (business) world: technical knowledge, language knowledge, private knowledge (general education),...
   - Economic knowledge
     Virtual world: management of resources, money, material,...
     Real (business) world: investment, growth, finance,...
2. Methodological competence
   - Critical thinking and ability to judge
     Virtual world and real world: control, optimization, revision, verification,...
   - Application of strategic and creative abilities
     Virtual world and real world: ability to solve problems, tactic acting, improvisation, application of methods ...
   - Acting in a team
     Virtual world and real world: feedback, acceptance, help, support,...
   - Planning and organizing abilities
     Virtual world and real world: collecting information, usage of resources and utilities, time management,...
   - Ability to interact
     Virtual world: steering and interacting with the own avatar
     Real world: application of technical or scientific methods
3. Social competence
   - Communication
     Virtual world and real world: eloquence, usage of dialects, faculty of speech,...
   - Conflict
     Virtual world and real world: conflict management, conflict solution, give-and-take,...
   - Negotiating skills
     Virtual world: cooperation, representation of interests, ...
     Real world: cooperation, efficiency, argumentation,...
   - Leadership abilities
     Virtual world and real world: leading, motivation, control,...
4. Personal competence (soft skills)
   - Autonomy
     Virtual world and real world: having an own opinion, decision making,
     ...

– Ability and techniques to act
  Virtual world and real world: concentration, power management,
– Flexibility
  Virtual world and real world: multitasking, reaction on new situations,
  openness,...

Gebel, Gurt, and Wagner [9] have been able to show in a study, that the development of competencies in computer games cannot be neglected. They found out,
that there are very likely multiple levels of competencies, which can be acquired
and developed in computer games, and which can potentially be transferred to
non-game situations. This research is also supported by others, as [6], [7] [12],
[13], [16]. Aspects of different competencies, which can (potentially) be trained
in computer games, are according to [11]: knowledge about complex systemic
dependencies, e.g. in business industry, knowledge and insight into physical-
mechanic procedures, or even knowledge about historic and cultural aspects.
Informal exercises can be used to train analytic and strategic competencies,
organization and coordination activities, and also techniques of meta-cognitive
self-steering (e.g. problem-centered attention). Naturally, all these competencies
can only be developed and trained in certain special games – not all the aspects
can be transferred to all the computer games. Moreover, in the context of these
investigations, it is important to differentiate between two major standpoints: is
the focus of interest on competencies, which the players can develop via playing
the game, and which then can be transferred to real-life settings – or is the focus
of interest on being a competent player (e.g. knowing how to act and interact
in the "in-game world", and only there). The study presented in this paper has
a focus on the question, if (and to which extent) the game-related requirements
and potentials related to competencies correspond to the players' self-evaluation.

Lampert, Schwing, and Teredesai [13] investigated five very famous games
(WoW, Counterstrike, FIFA09, the German version of The Sims 3, and Far-
mVille). In their study, they restricted their research on five fields of competencies, which they assumed can be trained and developed in computer games. They
focused on cognitive competencies, like perception, attention, and concentration,
on social competencies, like interaction, communication, and cooperation. Additionally, they investigated personality related competencies, like self-reflection
and self-control, and senso-motoric aspects, like hand-eye-coordination and time
of reaction. Last but not least, media competence / media literacy has been
investigated with respect to knowledge about media, knowledge about media
design aspects, and purposeful usage of media. These five competences have
been called game-immanent competencies. The authors have been able to show
the existence of these competencies in the investigated games.

Next to the notion of competences, the concept of roles plays an important
part – same in business development, as in computer games. A role summarizes the rights and duties of an individual in a certain position, his function,
position and the tasks he has to fulfill. Other members of a group (or team)
make their assumptions about behavior and responsibilities based on the role in
the group of an individual. Belbin [21] described nine roles of team members.

Fruitful team work is according to his assumption based on the fact that certain personal competencies are required for taking over a certain role in a team. The constellation of roles and related competencies results in efficient (or inefficient) team structures (independent of the number of roles represented in the team). Belbin's nine roles are: co-ordinator (leads the team), shaper (develops systematics and strategies), plant (person for innovations and creative ideas), monitor evaluator (works towards quality and control), implementer (best in shaping and designing things), team worker (helps the other team members and supports the team structure), resource investigator (takes over tasks like communication and moderation), completer (responsible for organization and planning), and the specialist (offers special knowledge and information). When comparing the roles and structures in teams in WoW, we found out (as will be shown in the subsequent section), that these roles can be mapped to the roles in WoW teams. Thus, an assumption can be that the roles a person plays in a game might support the development of certain competencies, which might then be transferred to the real world outside the game. Vice versa, it might also be that persons with certain roles in real life tend towards taking over a similar role in the game world. Also this aspect will be explicated in the following.

3   MMORPGs at the Example of WoW

The MMORPG WoW has been brought to public by the game developers Blizzard Entertainment end of 2004. WoW is a role playing game which is located in a fantasy or science fiction world. The game can be played via the Internet and is based on a persistent virtual 3D animated game world (virtual world). Several thousands of players can play and "populate" in this game world at the same time. To take part in this game, a player must buy a certain software part and an account. Additionally, the player has to decide about a game server. Currently, in Europe there are more than 265 servers available, at least 87 of these are available with German language. A server where the game world can be played is called realm in the WoW language. Usually, the game server contains a client program containing mainly the data, which is used to represent a piece of the virtual world on the player's local computer. Steering of program execution and processes, same as the non-player characters and the core game engine are located on the server (and remain there). The virtual game world is called persistent, which means that no roll back is possible. Actions and activities in the virtual world have permanent effects and cannot be canceled after execution. Moreover, the virtual world is permanently developing, independent of the absence or presence of a player. A player has no possibility to save a certain state of the game (or the world) to return to this point in time. Thus, all game activities are real-time activities, e.g. speaking or chatting, acting, fighting, same as cooperation with other players or with non-player characters (see also [3]). In the game, players are represented by their virtual characters, called avatars. Each character is an individual, which is developed by the player based on a set of two fractions (alliance or horde), certain races (six per fraction, e.g. elves, dwarfs, human, gnome) and ten classes (like warrior, paladin, druid), and the player's own vision of optical appearance (regarding clothing, outside appearance, pattern of behavior, weapons, and the like). During their game life, avatars can develop special skills, and they can learn a certain profession, collect experience points and collect or buy things. Thus, the virtual character is not fixed but developing all the time. Generally, there are two modes of playing WoW, which can be summed up as PvP (Player versus Player) or PvE (Player versus Environment). The PvE version contains also interactions with non-player characters.

Regarding the inherent team structures in WoW, we find *groups* as the smallest entity. Here, two to six players come together, most of the time with regards to a certain (short time) goal. The next bigger entity is the *raid*, containing two to eight groups or up to 40 players. In contrast to these more temporal communities, another bigger entity is the *guild* a community which usually has a longer time of existence (some guilds can be called permanent). From a certain level in the game, each player is allowed to form a guild. The structure of a guild can be compared to that of a business organization: usually, there exists a leader, there are sometimes certain teams, and there exists in most cases an implicit role model for members of the group. Guilds can exists over very long periods of time; some guilds have their own internet presence, and some guilds can be seen as virtual social communities in the sense of [4] and [18]. In WoW, guilds can be separated into at least four categories: fun guilds, family guilds, raid guilds, and pro guilds. The fun guilds are communities, which come together with a focus on having fun. Most of the time they come together by chance. Fun guilds usually have only few rules and responsibilities. Family guilds focus on the social interaction, communication and contact between their members. Sometimes, this social network is transferred to the world outside WoW (e.g. the Internet but also the real life). Main goal of this community is also having fun. In contrast to that, the raid guilds focus on fight and offered (organized) raids. Goal of these communities is to be most successful in raids, thus they focus on strategy development and organization. Members have to follow comparably strict rules and have a set of responsibilities. Last but not least, the pro-guilds are communities which take this a step further: they focus on international contests and competitions. Their goal is to be the best in direct comparison to other pro guilds. Rules and responsibilities are stricter than in raid guilds. Members of these guilds must have a certain level of game knowledge and must fulfill certain requirements. To become member of a pro guild, the player has to apply for a position in the team. In all the guilds, decisions are usually taken by the leader of the guild. Democratic structures are seldom found.

4   Empirical Research: Methods and Results

In our investigation, we compared the characteristics of players in their real life (professional life) and in their virtual life in WoW. The focus has been on certain potential influences between these two fields. The method we used has been online questionnaire, as all the players are usually found online. The online questionnaire consisted of closed questions. A number of interviews (open questions) has been used after the evaluation of the online questionnaire to put more focus on certain aspects. The participants have been anonymized (same in real life and in WoW, i.e. also their avatar's names and the names of their guilds or other comparable data). The questionnaire, as well as the interview, is used as an instrument for self-reflection (or self-estimation). Basic assumption for such a kind of evaluation is that the players are aware of their motives and their behavior, and are willing and able to give away this information (see also [2]). Scientifically, all results of this investigation have to be evaluation from this perspective. Thus, we have not focused on finding out what the reality might be, but on what the perception of players is.

The questionnaire is structured in three major parts, which covered a set of seven different subsections:

1. Comparison of the required competencies in WoW and in the professional life
2. Comparison of the role in WoW and in the professional life
3. Transfer between the competencies in WoW and the professional life

Answering the questionnaire took about 30 minutes. The questions have been made as simple as possible. The population is given by all German speaking persons, which are active as players in WoW at the time where the evaluation took place (estimated numbers of users see [22]). An automatic filter excludes the following groups of persons: all persons under the age of 15, persons who don't lay WoW and persons which are only single-players (non PvP players). A pretest has been executed with 11 players. Afterward, the online questionnaire has been revised. The evaluation started with contacting 14 editors of WoW websites, asking them to publish the questionnaire on their news part. However, this has not led to many participants. Thus, as a next step, 18 MMORPG and WoW forums have been used to establish special topic oriented threads, and more website editors have been contacted. The ten players, which have been selected for participation in the interviews, have been selected by direct contacting the players in the forums. Finally, a sum of $n = 647$ WoW players have participated in the evaluation. After answering the filter questions, 39 persons have been deleted from the investigation. The investigated sample finally contained $n = 608$, all of which completed the questionnaire.

In the following, the seven sub-parts of the investigation will be shortly sketched, together with the results.

Part 1: General information: (containing demographic information, professional activities, education, current employment)
Most of the participants are male (86%). Female players, which took part in the online questionnaire, are usually older than their male co-players. Around 69% of the persons are between 20 and 29 years old (29% were between 14 and 19, 9% between 30 and 39). 62% of the participants work in a certain profession, 32% still go to school or to Universities. Only 5% are unemployed. Regarding the professional activities and related questions, the number of participants has thus been reduced accordingly. Most of the participants ($n = 608$) have a

baccalaureate (high school diploma) or an equivalent. 16% have a Bachelor or Master from a University.

Part 2: General information in WoW: (containing information about playing activities: how long, since when, why)
64% of the $n = 608$ play since more than 4 years, 92% play since more than 2 years. This leads to the impression that playing WoW is a long-term activity. Most of the participants 61% stated that they play between 10 and 29 hours per week (called "normal players" in our investigation). 49% play WoW as a daily activity – most of them are working in a profession. Only 1% of the participants stated that they play only at the weekends. Most of the participants stated that "having power" (related to knowing how to play, having influence, and owning game-related items) is their major motive for playing WoW. Only a small amount of players seem to look for friends (20%). Playing together with other real life persons is what 86% of the participants confirmed. In contrast to that, escapism or the wish to change their role has not been confirmed by the participants.

Part 3: Virtual Community: (related to server, game mode, guild, details regarding the guild, and role of the participant in the guild)
75% of the participants stated that they are member of a guild. 12% are part of a fixed entity, and 13% are becoming part of a group only by chance. Regarding all participants ($n = 647$) a number of 90% are members of a guild, 9% are members in several different guilds. 32% of the participants stated that they have a leadership role in the guild or in the team. A relation to demographic data seems not to exist.

Part 4: Organized Activities: (how often does the participant take part in organized activities, details about activities, role in the activities)
98% of the participants ($n = 608$) stated that they take part in organized activities, 82% on a regular basis. The activity which is most frequently occurring is the raid (98%). Other group activities (33%) have only been found in fun & family guilds. Additionally, a comparison of the resulting data revealed that raid and pro-guilds have a set of abilities, which are required for becoming a member of such a group. A focus has been found in required competencies related to team work, flexibility, steering, and interaction. Surprisingly, most of the raid guild members stated that social competencies are not that important. Very important, however, are method competencies, team orientation, and strategic thinking. This is shown in figure 1, where the ratios for critical thinking and judgment and decision making are depicted in % in relation to the different guilds.

Part 5: General Information About Professional Activities: (kind of profession, role in the business, circa income)
The results of this part show that 43% of the participants are working in business industries in the private sector. Every tenth participant is working at a University. 53% are working as employees, only 23% are trainees or apprentices. Circa a third of all the participants are working in a kind of leadership position. A comparison of the data revealed that these persons usually take over a

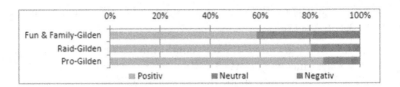

Fig. 1. Diagram for critical thinking and judgment and decision making (fun & family guild: $n = 70$, raid guild $n = 287$, pro guild $n = 225$) [17]

leadership role in their guild. Only a third of the participants without a leadership role in real life took over a leadership role in WoW. However, they supported the idea of "trying out leadership" in the virtual (and thus assumed as save) environment.

Part 6: Professional Communities: (here, the participants are asked about their professional communities and their roles in the professional communities, e.g. existence and structure of teams, and the roles in the team)
55% of the participants have to work in teams or have to interact with teams on a daily basis. 75% of the participants stated that their role is best comparable to "helps the other team members and supports the team structure". Surprisingly, competencies in organized WoW activities are rated higher than competencies required in professional activities. An assumption might be in this context that the WoW system gives more information about concrete competencies, and thus makes an estimation of competency levels easier, than the blurred usage of the term in real life.

Part 7: Transfer of Competencies: (self-estimation of participants related to interactions and relations between their competencies and roles in WoW in comparison to real life)
48% of the working and employed participants ($n = 397$) stated that there is a positive influence: the virtual activities and roles positively influence their professional activities, especially regarding competencies, abilities, and skills. Less than 1% feel a negative influence. 61% of the participants, which took over a leadership position in the virtual community ($n = 131$), stated that they feel a positive influence in their professional activities. All the participants, which stated to see a positive influence relating their virtual activities to their professional activities noted that they see the strongest influence in team oriented competencies (85%), in conflict management (75%), and in leadership qualities (65%). Less important is specialist expertise.

The comparison revealed that in fun & family guilds members in most cases rated the positive influence of the game higher, than members of the raid and pro guilds. Approximately half of the participants stated that they tried to act in certain roles in the virtual world with the goal to become better in a similar role in real life. The semi structured interviews gave no new insights but supported all the assumptions sketched above.

5 Discussion and Outlook

Regarding the chosen method (self reflection) and the chosen instruments (online evaluation and semi structured interviews), the empirical investigation sketched in this paper has to be seen rather critically regarding the new insights and the new information it can provide. As in all online evaluations, also in our investigation, we have been confronted with the usual problems of the relation of the sample to the whole group and the cooperation of the participants. As the participation has been voluntary, a relation between the actual participants and all the persons, who have not participated, cannot be made. This investigation allows only insight about the participants, but no generalization on all the players of WoW. Moreover, the WoW community seems currently to be swamped with online evaluations, so that most players are annoyed and not willing to answer just another questionnaire. A bias can be seen in the facts sketched in part 3 of the questionnaire: from $n = 608$ participants, 48% are members of raid guilds, 38% are members of pro guilds, and only 13% are members in fun & family guilds. This might be a result form the spreading of the questionnaires on the community pages: fun & family guild members seem to be less active in these web pages, than the others. This is important for our research, as fun & family guilds (which are two different types of guilds but have a comparable structure, and thus are taken together in this investigation), have a complete other intern structure and different roles than raid and pro guilds. Especially with focus to our target group, i.e. professionals with certain competencies, which are required for certain roles, this leads again to a bias. Raid and pro guilds provide leadership and team structures, which are better comparable to classical structures in professional environments. Thus, a future work might be to focus on these groups or to investigate the development of competencies in a group adapted manner.

Generally, regarding our initial question: "which competencies can be developed by playing WoW and how can these be re-used in real life?", it can be stated that we have not found any definite statements, but clear tendency. A large amount of participants stated that they think that a transfer of competencies from WoW to professional activities takes place, especially in the field of team competence and social competence.

References

1. Bader, R., Mueller, M.: Unterrichtsgestaltung nach dem Lernfeldkonzept: Dokumentation zum BLK-Modellversuchsverbund SELUBA "Steigerung der Effizienz neuer Lernkonzepte und Unterrichtsmethoden in der dualen Berufsausbildung" der aender Nordrhein-Westfalen und Sachsen-Anhalt. Bertelsmann, Bielefeld (2002)
2. Bortz, J., Doering, N.: Forschungsmethoden und Evaluation fuer Human- und Sozialwissenschaftler. 4. Aufl. Springer, Heidelberg (2006)
3. Choi, B., Lee, I., Choi, D., Kim, J.: Collaborate and Share: An Experimental Study of the Effects of Task and Reward Interdependencies in Online Games. CyberPsychology & Behavior 10, 591–595 (2007)

4. Doering, N.: Virtuelle Gemeinschaften als Lerngemeinschaft!? Zwischen Utopie und Dystopie. In: DIE Zeitschrift fuer Erwachsenenbildung, pp. 30–32 (2001); Deutsches Institut fuer Erwachsenenbildung (DIE) e.V. Bonn (1999)
5. Erpenbeck, J., von Rosenstiel, L. (Hrsg.): Handbuch Kompetenzmessung. Erkennen, verstehen und bewerten von Kompetenzen in der betrieblichen, paedagogischen und psychologischen Praxis. Schaefer-Poeschel Verlag, Stuttgart (2003)
6. Fritz, J., Lampert, C., Schmidt, J., Witting, T. (Hrsg.): Kompetenzen und exzessive Nutzung bei Computerspielern: Gefordert, gefoerdert, gefaehrdet. Zusammenfassung einer Studie. 3 Baende. Vistas (66), Berlin (2011)
7. Gebel, C.: Schnell reagieren, cool bleiben, planen und probieren. Kompetenzpotenziale populaerer Computerspiele. In: Dittler, U., Hoyer, M. (Hg.) Machen Computer Kinder dumm?, pp. 147–162. Kopaed, Muenchen (2006)
8. Gebel, C.: Kompetenz erspielen - kompetent spielen? Merz 54(4), 45–50 (2010)
9. Gebel, C., Gurt, M., Wagner, U.: Kompetenzfoerderliche Potenziale populaerer Computerspiele. Studie des Muenchner Inst. f. Medienpaedagogik, JFF (2005)
10. Kauffeld, S.: Kompetenzen messen, bewerten, entwickeln: ein prozessanalytischer Ansatz fuer Gruppen. Schaeffer-Poeschel, Stuttgart (2006)
11. Klimmt, C.: Der Nutzen von Computerspielen. Ein optimistischer Blick auf interaktive Unterhaltung. Merz 48(3), 7–11 (2004)
12. Klimmt, C.: Die Nutzung von Computerspielen. Interdisziplinaere Perspektiven. In: Quandt, T., Wimmer, J., Wolling, J. (Hrsg.) Die Computerspieler. Studien zur Nutzung von Computergames, pp. 57–72. VS Verlag fuer Sozialwissenschaften, Wiesbaden (2008)
13. Lampert, C., Schwing, C., Teredesai, S.: Kompetenzfoerderung in und durch Computerspiele(n). In: Fritz, et al. (Hrsg.) Kompetenzen und exzessive Nutzung bei Computerspielern: Gefordert, gefoerdert, gefaehrdet (3 Bd.). Vistas (66), Berlin (2011)
14. Maciuszek, D., Ladoff, S., Martens, A.: Content Design Patterns for Game-based Learning. International Journal of Game-Based Learning 1(3), 65–82 (2011)
15. Martens, A., Maciuszek, D. (Gast Hrsg.): Zeitschrift fuer eLearning. Themenheft Lehren und Lernen in virtuellen Welten 1(12), 7 (2012)
16. Mattes, T.: Organisationale Kompetenz. Eine experimentelle Untersuchung der Wechselwirkung von organisationalen Rahmenbedingungen auf erfolgreiche organisatorische Handlungen im Rahmen eines Online Rollenspiels. Frankfurt School of Finance & Management, Dissertation (2010)
17. Rausch, S.: Kompetenzentwicklung in MMORPGs am Beispiel von World of Warcraft, Masterareit (M.Sc.) im Fach Ingenieurpaedagogik an der PH Schwa3bisch Gmuend (2011)
18. Sander, F.: Virtuelle Gemeinschaften. Entwurfsfassung, Diplomarbeit. Staufen (July 30, 2005), http://www.kreativrauschen.de/artikel/virtuelle-gemeinschaften-einfuehrung/ (download: August 25, 2011)
19. Steinkuehler, C.: Cognition and learning in Massively Multiplayer Online Games: A critical Approach, PhD. Thesis, University of Wisconsin, Madison (2005)
20. Offizielle World of Warcraft Homepage Online, http://eu.battle.net/wow/de/ (last checked March 2012)
21. Belbin, M.: http://www.belbin.com/ (last visited: March 29, 2012)
22. WoW in Zahlen: mmodata.net, Analyse Ibe Van Geel (last visited: March 29, 2012)

"This Game Is Girly!" Perceived Enjoyment and Student Acceptance of Edutainment

Michail N. Giannakos[1,*], Konstantinos Chorianopoulos[2], Letizia Jaccheri[1], and Nikos Chrisochoides[3]

[1] Norwegian University of Science and Technology, Trondheim, Norway
{mgiannak,letizia}@idi.ntnu.no
[2] Ionian University, Corfu, Greece
choko@ionio.gr
[3] Old Dominion University, VA, USA
nikos@cs.odu.edu

Abstract. Serious video games that enable students to engage into topics as mathematics through an enjoyment process are becoming increasingly popular. However, there is lack of empirical evidence on the relationship between students' enjoyment and their intention to use serious video games. This study is about a storytelling serious video game, which has the goal to improve the mathematical skills of players. The game has a plot, featuring a story in which a mission is assigned to the player. The story and the mission are used to stimulate the students' interest and motivate them to play the game. The empirical study is a controlled experiment to which 46 Gymnasium (middle school) students participated. Results confirmed the positive effects of the enjoyment on students' intention to use storytelling serious games. Notably, we found that gender has a moderating effect on the relationships between enjoyment and intention to use the game. The results of this study suggest that games with a storytelling component might be attractive to girls.

Keywords: Storytelling, Serious, Video Game, Enjoyment, Mathematics, Experiment.

1 Introduction

Many authors argue that the growth of serious games has a large impact on learning procedures. Studies indicated that playing video games gives learners a "mental workout" and the structure of activities embedded in video games develops a number of cognitive skills [12]. The emergence of serious games has further facilitated the wide adoption of learner-centered education and other changes in educational practices. Video games have drawn significant attention from educational institutions and business organizations due to the potential educational and cost benefits;

---

* This work was carried out during the tenure of an ERCIM "Alain Bensoussan" Fellowship programme. The research leading to these results has received funding from the European Union Seventh Framework Programme (FP7/2007-2013) under grant agreement no 246016.

S. Göbel et al. (Eds.): Edutainment 2012/GameDays 2012, LNCS 7516, pp. 89–98, 2012.

however, the introduction of video games in teaching is often complex, and learners do not always use them as expected [19]. For instance, difficulties in technology are some of the most widespread barriers for effective serious game adoption.

The purpose of the empirical experiment is to examine whether and how enjoyment affect learners' intention to use the storytelling serious video games. First we designed and developed a serious storytelling math game. The video game named "Gem-Game" and is targeted to children that attend first and second class of Gymnasium (middle school). Afterwards, we elaborated on an experimental procedure that includes surveys with constructs regarding students' enjoyment and intention to use the storytelling serious game. They played the game during a school hour, after which they completed the respective survey.

Despite that serious gaming is one of the main categories of entertainment computing, limited research exists concerning effect of entertainment characteristics of serious games on learners' intention to use these games. Our work is grounded in existing theoretical frameworks [7, 13], which propose the factor of enjoyment for understanding games.

This study is centered on two research hypotheses: about the relation between enjoyment (H1) and Intention to use serious games and how this relation is influenced (moderated) from student gender (H2) (Fig. 1).

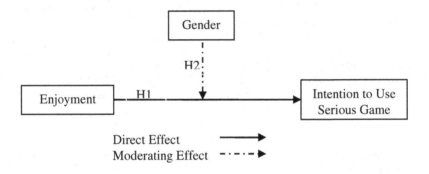

Fig. 1. Path Diagram of the research hypotheses

Strong empirical evidence indicates that the motivation basis of human decisions relies on the so-called approach system. The activation of this system results positive mental and cognitive states [3]. For the perspective of video games, player enjoyment is the most important goal. Enjoyment is deemed as a most appropriate measure of motivation because enjoyment measures how the game helps achieve the task related objectives. Venkatesh et al. [17] report that enjoyment (instruct motivation) has no direct effect on intention to use a system. However, the sense of enjoyment while the students learn through a serious game reduces anxiety and help students feel confident about their success. Therefore we hypothesize that:

H1. *Students' enjoyment has a positive effect on their intention to use serious storytelling game*

One of the most consistent results in studies of video games is the difference among boys and girls [13]. Some researchers (i.e. [1]) indicate that the difference rise from the fact that boys are more familiar and experienced with video games. Bruner et al., [5] mention that competition and violence may deter girls from playing video games. Another study [4] reveals that females prefer puzzle, adventure and managerial games and males prefer sport, strategy and role playing games. These differences can be explained by the fact that girls and boys are differ systematically on neurocognitive tests relevant to the use of digital games [4]. In addition, males consider games as more useful learning tools because they accommodate to their neurocognitive propensities [6]. In view of the above, it can be assumed that the effect of enjoyment on students' intention to use serious games is differentiated among boys and girls. Therefore, the following hypothesis is formulated:

H2. Students' gender has a significant moderating effect on the relationship between enjoyment and intention to use serious game.

2   Methodology

2.1   The Game: Gem-Game

The main purpose of Gem-Game[1] is to improve the mathematical skills of players [10]. The main character (Peter) moves up or down dependent on the operation executed by the player. So the students also get a visual idea of increasing quantity when adding and decreasing quantity when subtracting.

Most notably, the game has a plot, featuring a story in which a mission is assigned to the player. The story and the mission are used to stimulate the students' interest and motivate them to play the game (fig. 2). The dialogues and the plot are funny, so that it does not resemble rigid book or common computer-based exercises.

According to Vogler [18] each storytelling game consists of some common stages; our game's design (Fig. 2) follows Vogler's storytelling structure. In the first stage, the hero is situated in the ordinary world; in our game the hero named Peter is in his bedroom and looking for his dog. Then the hero is presented with a problem or event that necessitates leaving the comfort of the ordinary world, Peter's dog, Lucky has been kidnapped. Next, the hero meets a mentor or someone who may offer advice or guidance, the fairy guides Peter to collect 30 diamonds. Once the hero commits to the adventure, he begins the problem-solving process. During this process, the hero encounters various challenges that must be overcome in order to progress. In this stage Peter has to play and win the game in order to collect the necessary diamonds (Fig. 3). When Peter collected the diamonds, the fairy is appeared, fairy called the witch, witch is appeared and gets the diamonds, release the dog and the moral aspect of the game is presented.

---

[1] Gem-Game: http://scratch.mit.edu/projects/geostam/1292162

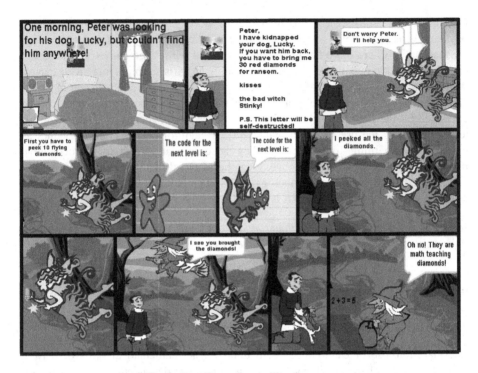

Fig. 2. Gem-Game Storytelling Structure

The ultimate goal of the player is to retrieve his dog by collecting diamonds. To achieve the ultimate goal, Peter must win the 3 stages (fig. 3). In particular, Peter must correctly add/subtract in order to earn diamonds. For example, if Peter is positioned on line 6, and the diamond is on line 1, the player must write -5 in order to gain the diamond. The player completes each stage by collecting 10 diamonds.

The first stage has only positive integers, the second stage has only negative integers, and the last stage has both positive and negative integers. Moreover, at each stage Peter wears a different uniform: a flyer uniform in the first stage; a diver uniform in second stage; and a helicopter uniform in the third stage.

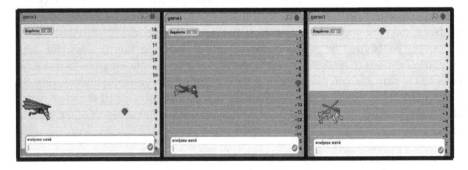

Fig. 3. Video game stages air (left), sea bed (center) and helicopter (right)

2.2 Sampling and Procedures

The sample of participants in this study was comprised of 46 students. Of the 46 participants, 29 were boys and 17 girls. All of the students who participated in the experiment were volunteers and around 13-14 years old, attended the second grade of gymnasium (middle school), and they were taught the same syllabus on mathematics and informatics. The experiment took place in a Greek state gymnasium. They played the game during a didactical hour, after which they completed the respective survey. The study was conducted over a weekly period from November 14–18, 2011. In addition, students played video games at school once a week for 4 weeks before the experiment in order to minimize the effect of students' enthusiasm. The game play was conducted on Windows desktops with a 17-inch screen using headsets.

2.3 Measures

After the game play, students completed a paper-based survey. The surveys gathered feedback of students' enrolment with the storytelling serious math game. The survey consisted of two factors adopted from prior studies (Table 1). The factors are enjoyment (ENJ) and Intention to Use Storytelling Serious Game (IUSSG). ENJ refers to the extent to which the activity of using a storytelling serious game is perceived to be personally enjoyable [15, 17], and IUSSG refers to the degree of students' willingness to play a storytelling serious game [9]. In both cases, 5-point Likert scales (1 = strongly disagree, 2 = disagree, 3 = neither agree nor disagree, 4 = agree and 5 = strongly agree) were used to measure the variables.

Table 1. The Research Factors and their Respective Items

Factors	Operational Definition	Items	Source
Enjoyment (ENJ)	The degree to which the activity of using a storytelling serious game is perceived to be personally enjoyable.	Studying is more interesting using Gem-Game (ENJ1).	[17]
		Using Gem-Game is fun (ENJ2).	
		I like using Gem-Game (ENJ3).	
		I enjoy those aspects of my studying that require me to use Gem-Game (ENJ4)	
Intention to Use Storytelling Serious Game (IUSSG)	The degree of students' willingness to play a storytelling serious game.	I plan to use Gem-Game for studying in the future (BI1).	[9]
		I intent to continue using Gem-Game for studying in the future (BI2).	
		I expect my use of Gem-Game to continue in the future (BI4).	

Except for the data provided by surveys, this study gathered information from conversation/interview with teachers and researchers' observations. These data provide a vehicle in order to interpret and validate the results in the Discussion and Conclusions section.

2.4   Data Analysis

The data were separated into two groups by performing median split on ENJ. Afterwards, an independent samples t-test was conducted in order to examine the effect of ENJ on students' IUSSG. In the next step, it was examined if students' gender influences the relationship between ENJ and students' IUSSG (H2). To test the moderating effect of students' gender, the correlation coefficient between ENJ and IUSSG of the males and females was tested by simple regression. Then, the coefficient R from the result of regression analysis and the sampling N was used to conduct Fisher's Z-transformation analysis.

3   Research Findings

Fornell and Larcker [8] proposed three procedures to assess the convergent validity of any measure in a study: (1) composite reliability of each construct, (2) item reliability of the measure, and (3) the average variance extracted (AVE).

First, we carried out an analysis of composite reliability and dimensionality to check the validity of the scale used in the survey. Regarding the reliability of the scales, Cronbach`s α indicators was applied and the results of the Cronbach's test show acceptable indices of internal consistency in the three scales considered: ENJ (*0.91*), and IUSSG (*0.97*).

In the next stage, we evaluated the reliability of the measures. The reliability of an item was assessed by measuring its factor loading onto the underlying construct. Hair et al. [11] recommended a factor loading of 0.6 to be good indicator of validity at the item level. As Table 2 presents, all items exhibited factor loadings that were higher than 0.6, with no cross construct loadings, indicating good discriminant validity [11]. Consequently, it is possible to use a sole factor for representing each theoretical construct.

The third step for assessing the convergent validity is the average variance extracted (AVE); AVE measures the overall amount of variance that is attributed to the construct in relation to the amount of variance attributable to measurement error. Convergent validity is found to be adequate when the average variance extracted is equal or exceeds 0.50 [11].

Table 2. Summary of Measurement Scales

Factors	Items	Mean	S.D.	CR	Loadings	AVE
Enjoyment	ENJ1	4.05	2.39	0.91	0.87	0.66
	ENJ2	3.55	2.28		0.62	
	ENJ3	3.40	2.54		0.90	
	ENJ4	3.90	2.20		0.83	
Intention to Use	IUSG1	3.30	2.34	0.97	0.84	0.72
Storytelling Serious	IUSG2	3.00	2.29		0.87	
Game	IUSG3	2.70	2.00		0.84	

To examine the H1 hypothesis, the empirical data were divided into two groups based on the students' responses. We perform a median split on ENJ (*3.25*) and we used a t-test having the ENJ as an independent variable and the IUSSG as a dependent. As it can be seen from the outcome data in Table 3, ENJ exhibits a highly significant impact on IUSSG.

Table 3. Hypotheses testing using t-tests

Dependent Variable	Mean (S.D.)		T	Results
	Low	**High**		
IUSSG	Enjoyment (ENJ)			
	1.88 (1.36)	3.70 (2.33)	3.02*	H1 (Accepted)

* p< 0.01.

The objective of this stage is to examine if students' gender influences the relationship between ENJ and IUSSG. To examine that moderating effect (H2), the correlation coefficient between ENJ and IUSSG of males and females students was used. The simple regression of males and females was conducted among ENJ and students IUSSG. Table 4 shows the R for the males and for the females at ENJ. Then, the coefficient R from the regression analyses and the sampling N was used to conduct a Fisher's Z-transformation analyses. The Fisher's Z-value of ENJ is *2.04 > 1.96*; the one-tailed test shows that the correlation coefficients are not significant at the 95% significant level [2]. The results mean that these data provide strong evidence that learners' gender has a significant moderating effect on the relationship between ENJ and IUSSG (supporting H2).

Table 4. Testing the moderating effect of gender using Fisher's Z-transformation analysis

	Male (N=29)	**Female (N=17)**	**Significance test (<1.96)**	**Results**
ENJ→IUSSG				
Correlation coefficient R	.665*	.125*	2.04[a]	H2 (Accepted)

*Represents that coefficients are significant at 0.01 or above.
[a]The critical value for Z is 1.96 for *p* < 0.05.
ENJ, Enjoyment; STF, Satisfaction; HAP, Happiness; IUSSG, Intention to Use Storytelling Serious Game.

In fig. 4 we can clearly observe the moderating effect of gender on the relationship among ENJ and IUSSG, in addition boys with high ENJ have the same IUSSG with girls with low enjoyment, as such, enjoyment affects mostly boys.

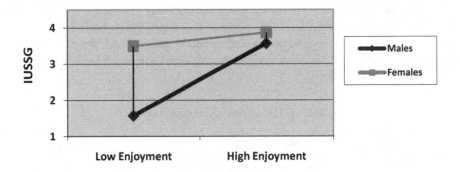

Fig. 4. The moderating effect of gender

4   Discussion and Conclusions

The main objective of the presented study is to explore the dependency between ENJ and IUSSG. In particular, the findings indicate that ENJ has a positive effect on students' IUSSG. Another conclusion of this study is the moderating effect of students' gender on the relationships between ENJ and IUSSG. An interesting discovery is observed; girls who are low enjoyed with the game have the same IUSSG with boys who are high enjoyed. This result can be possibly explained by the fact that boys are more familiar and experienced with video games [1], as such is more difficult to change their attitude (ENJ). But if you will change their attitude then they will reward it with their behavior.

The study has also produced a number of interesting qualitative findings that illustrate the impact of the entertainment nature of games on students' behavior. At the end of the study students suggested that they should even play on their own laptop in classroom, and they could even use it at home in order to study in this way. Another crucial issue was students' sense during the experiment. Based on the researcher observation in the lab it can be presumed that most of the students felt "exited". Researchers' opinions regarding the "excitement" of the students arise from the comments of the students, such as "awesome," during and after the experiment. Teachers present were asked to observe students playing the game, but they were not actively involved. In particular, teachers thought that students who played the game seemed so immersed that their behavior changed, and they appeared to be very interested in the game. In general, the results counter positive emotions and beliefs for the use of serious game.

The survey findings revealed that girls affected less from enjoyment (Fig. 4). On the other hand boys are greatly affected as boys with low enjoyment are not likely to use the game. Serious game developers should strive to increase students' intrinsic motivations, and make them feel enjoyment. Especially for the case of boys, serious games must updated (e.g., characters, story-line), in order to meet the needs of today's students, as they are used to play state of the art games.

Although our study provides evidence for the serious games adoption and gender issues, there are also some limitations. Firstly, the subjects were secondary education students from Greece, but beliefs and perceptions may differ among countries. Secondly, self–report method (surveys) was used to measure research variables, so some of the results might have a common method biased. However, we eliminate that bias by interpreting the results with some qualitative methods (observations, light interviews). Third, other demographic variables (i.e., age, educational level) may have contingent effect on serious gaming, which limits the extent of the generalization to other populations.

Further studies should investigate the effect of entertainment attributes on students' actual performance, under different context and over longer periods. In addition, research is also needed to examine students' attitude and performance with latest technologies (Augmented-Mixed Reality, 3D games).

Acknowledgements. The authors would like to thank all of the students and the schools' staff for their participation in the experiment. This work is also supported by the Marie Curie project (MC-ERG-2008-230894) CULT (http://cult.di.ionio.gr) under the 7th Framework Program (FP7) and NSF grants: CCF-1139864, CCF-1136538, and CSI-1136536 and by the Richard T. Cheng Endowment.

References

1. Baenninger, M., Newcombe, N.: Environmental input to the development of sex-related differences in spatial and mathematical ability. Learning and Individual Differences 7, 363–379 (1995)
2. Baron, R.M., Kenny, D.A.: The moderator-mediator variable distinction in social psychological research: conceptual, strategic, and statistical considerations. Journal of Personality and Social Psychology 51(6), 1173–1182 (1986)
3. Berridge, K.C.: Pleasures of the brain. Brain Cogn. 52, 106–128 (2003)
4. Bonanno, P., Kommers, P.A.: Gender differences and styles in the use of digital games. Educational Psychology 25(1), 13–41 (2005)
5. Brunner, C., Bennett, D., Honey, M.: Girl games and technological desire. In: Cassell, Jenkins (eds.) From Barbie to Mortal Kombat: Gender and Computer Games, pp. 72–89 (1998)
6. Casey, M.B.: Gender, Sex, and Cognition: Considering the Interrelationship between Biological and Environmental Factors. Learning and Individual Differences 8(1), 39–53 (1996)
7. Cowley, B., Charles, D., Black, M., Hickey, R.: Toward an understanding of flow in video games. Comput. Entertain. 6(2), Article 20 (2008)
8. Fornell, C., Larcker, D.F.: Evaluating structural equation models with unobservable variables and measurement error. Journal of Marketing Research 48, 39–50 (1981)
9. Giannakos, M.N., Vlamos, P.: Educational webcasts' acceptance: Empirical examination and the role of experience. British Journal of Educational Technology (2012), doi:10.1111/j.1467-8535.2011.01279.x
10. Giannakos, M.N., Chorianopoulos, K., Jaccheri, L.: Math is not only for Science Geeks: Design and Assessment of a Storytelling Serious Video Game. In: Proc. of ICALT (2012)

11. Hair Jr., J.F., Black, W.C., Babin, B.J., Anderson, R.E., Tatham, R.L.: Multivariate data analysis, 6th edn. Prentice-Hall International, Upper saddle River (2006)
12. Johnson, S.: Everything bad is good for you: How today's popular culture is actually making us smarter. Allen Lane, London (2005)
13. Nakatsu, R., Rauterberg, M., Vorderer, P.: A New Framework for Entertainment Computing: From Passive to Active Experience. In: Kishino, F., Kitamura, Y., Kato, H., Nagata, N. (eds.) ICEC 2005. LNCS, vol. 3711, pp. 1–12. Springer, Heidelberg (2005)
14. Phillips, C.A., Rolls, S., Rouse, A., Griffiths, M.: Home video game playing in schoolchildren: a study of incidence and patterns of play. Jour. of Adolescence 18, 687–691 (1995)
15. Salem, B., Rauterberg, M., Nakatsu, R.: Kansei Mediated Entertainment. In: Harper, R., Rauterberg, M., Combetto, M. (eds.) ICEC 2006. LNCS, vol. 4161, pp. 103–116. Springer, Heidelberg (2006)
16. Sweetser, P., Wyeth, P.: GameFlow: a model for evaluating player enjoyment in games. Comput. Entertain. 3(3), 3 (2005), doi:10.1145/1077246.1077253
17. Venkatesh, V., Speier, C., Morris, M.G.: User acceptance enablers in individual decision making about technology: toward an integrated model. Decis. Sciences 33, 297–316 (2002)
18. Vogler, C.: The writer's journey: Mythic structures for writers. Michael Wiese Productions, Studio City (1998)
19. Yi, M.Y., Hwang, Y.: Predicting the use of web-based information systems: self-efficacy, enjoyment, learning goal orientation, and the technology acceptance model. International Journal of Human-Computer Studies 59(4), 431–449 (2003)

Towards a Social Game Interaction Taxonomy

A Social Gaming Approach towards Peer Knowledge Sharing and Participation in Serious Games

Johannes Konert, Stefan Göbel, and Ralf Steinmetz

Technische Universität Darmstadt, Multimedia Communications Lab - KOM
Rundeturmstraße 10, 64283 Darmstadt, Germany
{johannes.konert,stefan.goebel,
ralf.steinmetz}@kom.tu-darmstadt.de

Abstract. *Serious Games for Learning* are often designed as singleplayer, storytelling-based games. Even though immersion into the story and adaption to the player's abilities are pedagogically well designed, players can have misconceptions or get stuck with game quests. Then they seek for assistance from friends or online. Accessing hints, solutions and help of others directly in the gaming context can improve the game play and learning experience. Additionally the users from *Online Social Networks* can be connected to the game as a valuable resource of know-how if they are provided with participation possibilities. The concept of *Peer Education* is valuable for teaching and assessment among peers with similar learning targets. Thus in this paper an approach towards *Social Serious Games* is presented. Existing *Social Media* interaction patterns and singleplayer, story-based game situations are brought together respecting the *Interaction Mapping Patterns 1:1* and *1:n*. The resulting three dimensional *Social Game Influence Taxonomy* is presented as well as the technical implementation as a middleware to connect existing *Serious Games* with *Online Social Networks* for *Peer Knowledge Sharing* and participation.

Keywords: Serious Games, Social Games, Social Learning, Peer Knowledge Exchange, Social Interaction Patterns, Social Serious Games.

1 Motivation

Since ancient times games have been used for learning and training ("History of Games Timeline," n.d.). Social Games played by more than one player are used for knowledge transfer between individuals by means of competition or cooperation. In the last years *Online Social Games* became popular as they utilize the *Social Media* components of *Online Social Networks* (OSN) as interaction patterns between players during game play. If these interaction patterns are categorized and structured to specifically support assistance, guidance and help among users on one side (concept of *Peer Tutoring*) and the rating, assessment and quality control of creative, user-generated game content on the other side (concept of *Peer Assessment*) such a connection between computer games and *Online Social Networks* can be used to enhance the knowledge transfer, adaption and learning experience in *Serious Games*.

S. Göbel et al. (Eds.): Edutainment 2012/GameDays 2012, LNCS 7516, pp. 99–110, 2012.
© Springer-Verlag Berlin Heidelberg 2012

Currently most *Serious Games for Learning* (SGL) are for single players only and based on digital storytelling concepts in order to allow an adaption and personalization to the single player in the targeted knowledge domain. Speed of game play, flow of challenges and guidance as well as selection of events happens according to the player's needs. A maximum of immersion and minimum of frustration and hindrance is favored for the player's experience of gaming and learning (Chen, 2007). Still, such adaptation and flow control cannot perfectly match the player's needs because the computational model representation of player's learning, playing and assumed skills is a simplified abstraction. This results in situations during game play where additional information is needed by the player, a riddle is misunderstood and thus not solvable or the player has memorized misconceptions about the targeted learning topic and needs individual instructional support.

In such situations a player can benefit from human resources connected to his game play experience. It is the aim of currently ongoing research to connect the mentioned *Serious Games for Learning* to *Online Social Networks* and use the available *Social Media* for interaction between players and non-players.

The interaction types and kind of participation that can be used to connect OSN users to the player(s) of *Serious Game(s)* and vice versa is the focus of this paper. It presents the first version of a taxonomy about game situations in singleplayer, story-telling *Serious Games for Learning* and the identified interaction patterns for a connection to *Online Social Networks*.

2   Related Work

The underlying work of this paper is inspired by the interaction patterns that are used by players of *Social Casual Games;* games that are casually played or with easy to use interfaces which are connected to OSNs (Loreto & Gouaïch, 2004). *Ines de Loreto* and *Abdelkader Gouaïch* identify *Asynchronous Play* as one important characteristic of such games. Players interact by e.g. exchanging items or favors, but do not have to be online or in the game at the same time. As *Nick O'Neill* states in his criteria list about Social Games, these games are mostly *turn-based* and *casual games* connected to OSNs, but still *Multiplayer* in a sense that there is an *awareness of others' actions in games* (O'Neill, 2008). We summarize these four criteria as *Casual Multiplayer*, which means a singleplayer game play, but multiplayer atmosphere due to asynchronous play and awareness – and thus interplay - of the activities of others. *Asynchronous Play* and *Casual Multiplayer* are a basis for the targeted *Social Game Interaction Taxonomy*.

A broader view to *Social Media* interaction patterns in general is given in (Crumlish & Malone, 2009). A somewhat simplified list focusing the interaction patterns between users of *Social Media* applications can be found at (Julien, 2011) and will be used in this paper later on.

Sociological analysis of interactions of individuals in their organizational and private social networks have shown the benefit of information exchange among peers; especially if they are not closely but weakly tied . Based on *Social Network Analysis* (SNA) this strength of weak ties is explained by Marc Granovetter in (Granovetter, 1973). That indeed weakly tied 'strangers' are willing to contribute information, assistance and help depends on them consciously belonging to the same social group or having the same, non-competitive goals (Constant, Sproull, & Kiesler, 1996).

From a pedagogical point of view fostering the knowledge transfer between peers of a social group (e.g. classroom peers) is valued beneficial for personality and social competency development, learning by teaching, additional supplement to instructors teaching and provides individualized learning experiences (Damon, 1984). The potential of Peer Education (Tutoring and Assessment) has been investigated in the field of web-based collaboration and online tutoring (Mohammad, Guetl, & Kappe, 2009; Stepanyan, Mather, Jones, & Lusuardi, 2009; Westera & Wagemans, 2007). Results show the motivational benefits and improved social and knowledge skills. Currently ongoing research investigates the effect of Peer Education in a structured classroom-setup to learning and motivation based on the concepts of *Asynchronous Play* and *Casual Multiplayer* (Konert, Richter, Göbel, & Bruder, 2011).

3   Approach

To enhance the game play of one player in a singleplayer, story-based *Serious Game for Learning* by added content or influence from outside, we identified 3 dimensions to address for creating a taxonomy:

1. *Game Situations* (distinct contexts in the game a player can be confronted with)
2. *Mapping Patterns* (one to one, one to many, many to one, many to many)
3. *Social Media interaction patterns* (Julien, 2011)

Each of these dimensions needs to be elaborated as a discrete list of items. The cells of the resulting three-dimensional grid then can be filled with specific implementations of interactions in the context of SGLs connected to OSNs taking into account the concept of *Peer Education*.

Such a taxonomy is expected to help developers of *Serious Games* to enhance the learning by implementing functionality to support the interactions listed in the taxonomy. Examples of such beneficial functionality can be: players who can get assistance from outside the game without pausing (their game), non-players and related persons who can contribute to game play and influence it or other players who can contribute hints, solutions and complement guidelines.

Social Serious Game Definition

In this paper a taxonomy and approach is presented how to enhance *Serious Games* by *Social Game* components. The enhances variant of Serious Games will be defined as Social Serious Games:

> A *Social Serious Game* is a *Serious Game* with all components mandatory for a *Social Game*.
> This includes the use of Social Media interaction patterns for *Peer Education* as listed in the *Social Game Interaction Taxonomy*.

4   Dimensions

4.1   Game Situations

The list of *Game Situations* has been developed in cooperation with CEOs of two game development studios in the area of Frankfurt, Germany. It focusses on the genre of adventure *Serious Games* which are singleplayer and story-based. The list is currently neither considered to be completed nor evaluated to be accurate, but is expected to be of value to relate the *Social Media* interaction patterns to it. *Game Situations* identified so far are listed in Table 1.

Table 1. Game Situations identified in story-based Serious Games for Learning

#	*Game Situation*	*Description*
1	Game Start	Introduction Scene, normally without interaction possibilities for the player except a skipping possibility
2	Game Scene	A general game scene without any specific situation as listed next
2.a	NPC Dialog Scene	A non-person character is in conversation with the player and waits for the player to answer (e.g. from a given list of dialog options)
2.b	New Quest Scene	The user reads and receives a new quest to solve. Quests can be of type Information Seek, Inventory Quest or Riddle
2.c	Branching Scene	The player can decide between several choices (not dialog) for the further development of the game story. Usually these branches in the scene graph of the game are irrevocable
2.d	Minigame Scene	A game in the game that is in itself enclosed like a memory, puzzle or equation to solve.
2.e	Conflict Scene	A fight or situation demanding a time-critical reaction from the player.
2.f	Quest Solving	The player solves a quest
3	Situation Loops	The player reaches no further progress and repeats actions several times or comes along same place without any contextual change (inventory, quests, environment)
4	Savegame	The current game status is saved for later re-loading
5	Game End	The player closes the game application

4.2   Mapping Patterns

It is the intention of the authors of this paper to extend the currently mostly one-way connections between (social) games and OSNs by focusing mainly the other way around: Information flow from social networks into games and participation possibilities from social network users. Considering both ways between games and OSNs, the mapping patterns listed in Table 2 can be identified. The patterns *n:n* and *n:1* are listed for consistency reasons (shown *italic*) and will later on not be considered, as this paper focusses on singleplayer games.

Table 2. Mapping Types identified for the connection of game players and users of OSNs

Mapping Type	Description
1:1	One player in game interacts with one specific user in the OSN
1:n	One player in game interacts with many users in the OSN
n:n	*Many players of the game interact with (the same) many other players in the OSN*
n:1	*Many player of the game interact with (the same) one specific user in the OSN*

4.3   Social Media Interaction Patterns

The *Social Media* interaction patterns listed in Table 3 are structured and described in (Julien, 2011). As they are originally described for interactions between two users of the (same) *Social Media* application, the descriptions here focus on the interaction between game players and users of OSNs which are per definition Social Media applications (Boyd, 2009). As posting, sharing and updating are similar they are grouped and later on referred to as *Post* only. *Buy* and *Play* are shown *italic* as they will later on not be taken into consideration anymore, because they do not fulfill the criteria of a direct influence to or response by another user or many users as defined in ("interaction - definition of interaction by the Free Online Dictionary, Thesaurus and Encyclopedia.," n.d.). Finally eight interaction patterns are left for the taxonomy.

Table 3. Social Media interaction patterns (Julien, 2011)

#	Social Media interaction pattern	Description
1	Post	A user can store new content
	Share	A user can share content
	Update	A user can quickly share a short piece of information
2	Vote	A user can favor or disfavor a content element
3	Comment	A user can respond to specific content element
4	Chat	A user can communicate directly with another user
5	Tag	A user can enrich content with metadata
6	Invite	A user can ask another user to perform an action
7	Connection	A user can establish a link to another user
8	Join	A user can associate himself with an interest group
	Buy	*A user can directly purchase a product or make a donation*
	Play	*A user can engage with a game*

4.4   Taxonomy Model

The *Mapping Pattern* as the second dimension has only two characteristics which we will take into account. Thus the three dimensional taxonomy can be listed as two

Tables; one for each *Mapping Pattern*. The Tables consist of the eleven *Game Situations* as rows and the eight *Social Media* interaction patterns as columns. Most of our identified interaction types to be listed in these Tables are valid for *1:1* and *1:n* simultaneously. Interactions incoming to the game player are in several cases only suiTable for the *1:1 Mapping Pattern* only. Still, Table 4 contains the data for both *Mapping Patterns* and the ones only valid for *1:1* are printed *italic*. There are no interaction types only valid for *1:n*. Explanations for the interaction type examples used in the cells are listed below as Table 5.

First Conclusions

The Tables 4 and 5 are currently work in progress and not yet evaluated or proven and do not claim to be totally complete. Still it is valuable to interpret them and draw some intermediate conclusions and discuss them for the game development of *Social Serious Games*. As seen in Table 4 especially *Vote* tends to be a *Social Interaction* that suits well both *Mapping Patterns 1:1* and *1:n*. The most differences between *1:1* and *1:n* exists for *Post*, as content contributions are made individually and not collective. Thus the differences are mainly the incoming content (I:) for *Game Situations*. Additionally, cooperation modes are not applicable in a *1:n Matching Pattern* of a singleplayer SGL, but for the embedded minigames a (massive, cooperative) multiplayer mode is imaginable as well as a (massive) sidekick concept for *Conflict Scenes* in such games (e.g. a scene with a boss opponent).

For a technical implementation it seems to be reasonable (based on the number of interactions in the Table) to focus on the support of *Post* and *Vote* first, then on *Comment*. Concerning the examples in the Table 4 individuals (*1:1*) might be a most valuable source for creative content, hints or solutions for game situations as for *1:n* most content-related (*Post*) incoming (*I:*) entries are not valid. However, many (*1:*n) connected users, e.g. the friends connected to the player in an *Online Social Network* tend to be a valuable source for *Vote* results and recommendations. As seen in Table 4 this is the only column where all items are available for both *Mapping Patterns*. Because more people can possible contribute in *1:n*, the *Vote* might be even of more value here compared to *1:1*. A combination of both (*Post, Vote*) could be a content contribution of individuals, voted by many others for recommendation.

In both Mapping Patterns it seems to be suitable to *Post* the status (achievements), *Vote* with likes and send invitations from the ongoing game to the connected other users in order to raise awareness and call for participation. It can be assumed that such interactions become more valuable if the recipients are invited to take action, e.g. combining it with a call for a *Vote* or content *Post* to involve them into ongoing game play.

For minigames and *Conflict Scenes* (all scenes with time-critical reactions demanded) *Chat* and *Connection* can be considered to be implemented as they allow a collaborative or competitive scenario in the otherwise singleplayer game play.

Table 4. Social Game Influence Taxonomy (Incoming interactions to the game marked as *I:*, outgoing as *O:*, items only for *1:1* are *italic*)

#	Game Sit.	Post	Vote	Comment	Chat	Tag	Invite	Connection	Join
1.	Game Start	*I: inventory equipment* / O: status	I: inventory equipment, scene selection				O: rec., streaming	*I/O: cooperation*	*I: cooperation,* streaming
2.	Game Scene	*I: solution, question, pers. content* / O: status, screen, solution, question	I: scene selection, assessment / O: content rating	I: solution / O: solution	I/O: consultation	*I: content location* / O: content location	O: rec.	*I/O: cooperation*	*I: cooperation*
2.a	NPC Dialog Scene	*I: dialog option,* names / O: dialog decision	I: dialog option, traits	*I: dialog answer*	*I: dialog takeover*			*I: dialog takeover*	O: join decision (indirect)
2.b	New Quest Scene	*I: tasks, rewards,* item donation, item repairing, params / O: quest decision, question	I: available quests, tasks, rewards, quest parameters / O: quest likes	I: banter / O: notes, restrictions		I/O: categorization	O: rec.	*I/O: cooperation*	*I: cooperation*
2.c	Branching Scene	*I: false decision items* / O: branch decision	I: branch options / O: branch likes	I: banter					
2.d	Minigame Scene	I: game content	I: minigame options / O: minigame likes				I: content rec. / O: rec.	I/O: cooperation, competition	*I: cooperation,* competition
2.e	Conflict Sc.		I: traits, difficulty, tactics, inventory		I: barter, acclamation		O: sidekick	I: sidekick	I: sidekick
2.f	Quest Solving	*I: rewards* / O: rewards	I: assessment / O: quest likes	*I: shouts of victory,* questions, remarks / O: remarks		I/O: categorization	O: rec.		
3.	Situation Loops	*I: assistance* / O: assistance request			I/O: consultation	*I: content location*	O: assistance request	*I/O: cooperation*	
4.	Savegame	O: savegame, status	I: likes, usages	I: likes / O: remarks		I/O: categorization	O: rec.	I/O: affiliation	I: usage
5.	Game End	*I: questions* / O: status, solutions, question	I: assessment / O: likes	I: barter, acclamation (at stream)					I: rec.

Description of Influences

Table 5. Description of influence type examples used in Table 4

acclamation (at stream)	sympathy or antipathy concerning the consumed (live) screencast video stream of the game played
affiliation	dynamic membership in an ad-hoc group of interest of all users connected or liking the same content, e.g. savegame
available quests	influencing the availability of quests a player can choose
branch options	influence to the available game branches a player can choose
branch likes	players and/or users can express their (dis)favor
categorization	players and/or users can edit or add metadata
content location	placing items in the game context, map or area
dialog takeover	the dialog is not any more answered by a NPC, but by humans
false decision items	contribution of (creative) but wrong answers to a question or decision to make
item donation/repair	other players/users owning items can help by donation or repair
join decision (indirect)	NPC dialogs can ask players for favorites or memberships resulting in joins e.g. of affiliated interest groups in OSNs.
params	abbreviation for parameters, e.g. difficulty, time restrictions
rec	abbreviation for recommendations, e.g. recommending a quest
restrictions	players/users can express (by text) self-imposed restrictions making the game e.g. more fun or harder
sidekick	Assistance player restricted to competition support, not capable of interacting with story pacing (e.g. co-fighters)
usages	who/how many other used this item

Other influences are not explained explicitly as they are assumed to be self-explaining.

Research Questions

From the above discussed conceptual ideas the following research questions have been identified to be focused on in future research.

- RQ1: Do game developers value the taxonomy as reasonable covering the main influence kinds for their *Serious Games for Learning*?
- RQ2: Do players value such features in games for *Peer Education* and knowledge transfer?
- RQ3: Are players more engaged and reach further in the game if games are enhanced by the *Social Game Influence Taxonomy* system?
- RQ4: Can the awareness of *Serious Games* be increased for non-players by the participatory effects and interactivity caused by the use of the *Social Game Interaction Taxonomy* compared to (passive) wall posts?

4.5   Middleware Design

Technically the taxonomy is used in a framework that works as a component-based service middleware between existing *Serious Games* that use the offered services and different *Online Social Networks*. As identified in the conclusions of section 4.4 (Model) *Post* and *Vote* are the main *Social Influence Patterns* to be supported first. Consequently the architectural diagram drafts the *Social Game Content Integration* component for *Posts* and the *Social Game Influence System* for *Votes* (see figure 1).

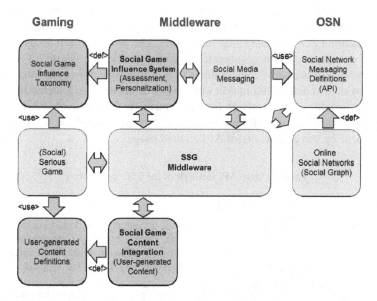

Fig. 1. Middleware design for *Social Serious Game* (SSG) middleware legend: <def> for definition, <use> for usage (access)

Content Integration for Posts

Game developers use the defined content definitions (to be described in a future paper focusing content integration) to fetch or store user-generated content from the middleware repository. This can be hints, screenshots, screencast streams and other formats existing in the game or social network on one side or provided hints, solutions, questions from users of OSNs or from other players on the other side.

Influence System for Votes

Game developers use the defined interaction patterns of the *Social Game Interaction Taxonomy* and invoke concrete influences by selecting a pattern and setting parameters like number of answers, timeout and so on. The middleware component *Social Game Influence System* then instantiates the influence, sends messages to the OSNs, collects feedback and provides the result to the game. Aspects of the service implementation cover content filtering, abuse protection, data privacy policies and the dynamic rendering of the influence system's web interface for users who respond to messages and follow the invitations (links) embedded in the wall posts (e.g. on facebook). Technically supported are right now: single choice, multiple choice, *n out of m* choices, ordering, text gap, image upload and combination of these, e.g. singechoice with the option to add new options with a text field.

Technical Components

The middleware has been developed as a *Java Servlet* application supporting multiple games and multiple-user access. It is designed to connect to multiple OSNs that support the *OAuth* authentication system and provide access to the profiles and graphs via an *Application Programming Interface* (API). The provided web-access for users to vote and contribute content is generated by a *Google Web Toolkit* (GWT) servlet of the middleware. All access to content items is as well possible for game instances via the API provided from the SSG middleware. A list of the main API methods is shown in Table 6. Beside a few methods for authentication that set and check a HTTP access-cookie (not listed) all methods are designed stateless to reduce the interdependencies and complexity of API method usage.

Table 6. Main API methods of the SSG middleware

API method	Functionality
allocateContent	Prepares the receiving of a content item. Usual parameters are metadata about the game, game scene, player, description or type of content. The types are a predefined list that can be extended by game developers with proprietary keys. The method returns a unique *contentId*.
uploadContent	Uploads the content for the given *contentId* to the middleware. This can be textual or binary and does not need to be readable by the middleware
getContentInfo	Based on filter information gives as parameters a result list of all stored and visible content is returned from the middleware. The list contains all metadata, but no content itself.
downloadContent	For specific *contentIds* the content can be downloaded and be parsed according to the content type.
prepareInfluence	Prepares one influence pattern as defined in the taxonomy. These are available as enum values. Usually the minimum parameters are a question (to state) and multiple- or single-choice answer options depending on the selected pattern. Returns a unique *influenceId*.
startInfluence	The defined influence (using the *influenceId*) can be made visible. Parameters are only the timeout. This triggers publication to social networks. If no one participated a default result is returned. If uncommented by users, the posts are deleted after timeout from OSN walls.
fetchResult	Using the *influenceId* the preliminary or final result can be fetched.

5   Outlook

The described taxonomy and the middleware will be further shaped during ongoing implementation and tests. We plan to evaluate the usability and find answers for research questions RQ2-RQ4 with a user study at the end of 2012. Therefore a 3D *Serious Game for Learning* will be connected to the middleware using the *Social Game Influence System* and the *Social Game Content Integration*. A qualitative study has been conducted in April and May 2012 as interviews with six CEOs or senior software developers of German game studios that develop *Serious Games*. The transcription of interview data and results of the analysis will help to answer RQ1.

The ongoing research aims to find technological solutions, approaches and patterns to prove the improvements for knowledge exchange and learning in *Social Serious Games*.

Acknowledgements. Parts of this work are funded by the HA Hessen Agentur (HA 258/11-04).

References

Boyd, D.: Social Media is Here to Stay... Now What? Microsoft Research Tech Fest, Redmond (2009), http://www.danah.org/papers/talks/MSRTechFest2009.html (retrieved)

Chen, J.: Flow in Games (and Everything Else). Communications of the ACM 50(4), 31–34 (2007), doi:10.1145/1232743.1232769

Constant, D., Sproull, L., Kiesler, S.: The Kindness of Strangers: The Usefulness of Electronic Weak Ties for Technical Advice. Organization Science 7(2), 119–135 (1996), http://www-2.cs.cmu.edu/~kiesler/publications/PDFs/ Constantkindness.pdf (retrieved)

Crumlish, C., Malone, E.: Designing Social Interfaces: Principles, Patterns, and Practices for Improving the User Experience (Animal Guide), p. 520. Yahoo Press (2009), http://www.amazon.com/Designing-Social-Interfaces-Principles-Experience/dp/0596154925 (retrieved)

Damon, W.: Peer education: The untapped potential. Journal of Applied Developmental Psychology 5(4), 331–343 (1984), doi:10.1016/0193-3973(84)90006-6

Granovetter, M.S.: The strength-of-weak-ties perspective on creativity: a comprehensive examination and extension. The American Journal of Sociology 78(6), 1360–1380 (1973), doi:10.1037/a0018761

History of Games Timeline (n.d.), http://www.historicgames.com/ gamestimeline.html (retrieved April 28, 2012)

Julien, J.: Social Media Interaction Pattern Library. The Jordan Rules (2011), http://thejordanrules.posterous.com/social-media-interaction-pattern-library (retrieved May 8, 2012)

Konert, J., Richter, K., Göbel, S., Bruder, R.: Knowledge Sharing in the classroom - A social network approach for diagnostic assessment and learning together. In: Proceedings of the 11th IEEE International Conference on Advanced Learning Technologies (ICALT). IEEE, Athens (2011), http://ieeexplore.ieee.org/xpls/ abs_all.jsp?arnumber=5992341&tag=1 (retrieved)

Loreto, I.D., Gouaïch, A.: Social Casual Games Success is not so Casual. Word Journal of the International Linguistic Association (2004)

AL-Smadi, M., Guetl, C., Kappe, F.: PASS: Peer-ASSessment Approach for Modern Learning Settings. In: Spaniol, M., Li, Q., Klamma, R., Lau, R.W.H. (eds.) ICWL 2009. LNCS, vol. 5686, pp. 44–47. Springer, Heidelberg (2009)

O'Neill, N.: What exactly are social games? Social Times (2008), http://www.socialtimes.com/2008/07/social-games/ (retrieved January 18, 2011)

Stepanyan, K., Mather, R., Jones, H., Lusuardi, C.: Student Engagement with Peer Assessment: A Review of Pedagogical Design and Technologies. In: Spaniol, M., Li, Q., Klamma, R., Lau, R.W.H. (eds.) ICWL 2009. LNCS, vol. 5686, pp. 367–375. Springer, Heidelberg (2009)

Westera, W., Wagemans, L.: Help me! Online Learner Support through the Self- Organised Allocation of Peer Tutors. In: Abstracts of the 13th International Conference on Technology Supported Learning & Training, pp. 105–107. ICEW GmbH, Berlin (2007), http://hdl.handle.net/1820/2075

Interaction - definition of interaction by the Free Online Dictionary, Thesaurus and Encyclopedia (n.d.), http://www.thefreedictionary.com/interaction (retrieved May 14, 2012)

Mobile Worlds: Mobile Gaming and Learning?

Sonja Ganguin[1] and Anna Hoblitz[2]

[1] University of Paderborn, Institute for Media Studies, Department of Media Education
and Empirical Media Research, Germany
sonja.ganguin@uni-paderborn.de
[2] University of Paderborn, Institute for Media Studies, Department of Media Economics,
Germany
anho@mail.uni-paderborn.de

Abstract. A mobility shift in the usage of media is characterizing today's society and influences the way people communicate, amuse and learn. In this paper a basic correlation between mobile gaming and mobile learning is explored. Therefore a quantitative study among 597 students, as the most intense user of mobile media, was conducted. The results of the study show that mobile gamers are capable of a broader and more sophisticated range of activities regarding their mobile phone usage. Significant differences can be stated for the search of information, the organization of everyday life, the creative and entertaining usage, as well as the educational applications.

Keywords: Mobile Media, Mobile Communication, Mobile Gaming, Mobile Game-based Learning.

1 Introduction

Nowadays, mobile phones are common: research studies prove a 'full supply' and people tend to own a second phone. Especially with the launch of Apple's iPhone in 2007, smartphones gained popularity and acceptance. The integration of mobile- and smartphones in our everyday life influences media practices as well as the ways people communicate amongst each other. Due to the enhancement of the range of functions of mobile phones, different communication possibilities emerge and a series of "m"-neologism arise, such as m-gaming, m-learning, m-commerce or m-entertainment [1]. Especially the trends of mobile gaming and mobile learning will be studied in detail, in order to elucidate how a possible combination of both activities can emerge in the sense of mobile game-based learning.

Today, mobile gaming is often associated with mobile- or smartphones. However, the starting point of m-gaming can be traced back to the first handheld consoles, in particular the Gameboy, in the mid-1980s. The first game on a mobile phone was 'Snake' in 1997 installed on Nokia phones. Due to the technical development of smartphones and tablets m-gaming becomes more and more important [2]. According to Soh and Tan [3] there are three main lines of progress for the growing of the mobile gaming market: high (and still rising) penetration rate, technology features which become increasingly suitable for gaming (e.g. audio and video quality) and

S. Göbel et al. (Eds.): Edutainment 2012/GameDays 2012, LNCS 7516, pp. 111–120, 2012.
© Springer-Verlag Berlin Heidelberg 2012

enhanced network connectivity – the ability of being online any-time and anywhere. As a consequence, the mobile games segment is one of the fastest growing fields in the gaming market [2]. In recent years, this development has also been recognized by the academic community and publications have increased [3-4].

Next to mobile gaming, mobile learning is a second trend which is accelerated by technological innovations. Supported by modern digital information and communication technologies, learning content can be prepared and structured on demand and at short notice. These technologies can be integrated in learning processes relatively easily according to situational requirements. Therefore the learning tasks should be – and so often are – structured in small learning units and short timeframes [5-6], such as for example five to ten minutes. Through m- learning, content can be accessed in a manner that is situation-specific, personalized and independent of location and time. What is more, with its technical features, m-learning offers new didactic potentials. For a considerable number of examples of mobile learning see e.g. Bachmair et al. [7]; Friedrich, Bachmair & Maren [8]; Hug [6]; Vavoula, Pachler and Kukulska-Hulme [9]. Agnes Kukulska-Hulme defines mobile learning focusing the physical mobility and mobile technology as follows: „What is new in ‚mobile learning' comes from the possibilities opened up by portable, lightweight devices that are sometimes small enough to fit in a pocket or in the palm of one's hand." [10]

When both trends of mobile gaming and mobile learning are combined, the potential of mobile game-based learning or mobile serious games becomes obvious. This trend will be discussed in the following chapter.

2   Mobile Serious Games and Mobile Game-Based Learning

Serious games appear to be an emerging, vibrant and fast-growing subject and field of research and constitute an upcoming niche market. Recent years have seen the publication of numerous works which account for this development e.g. [11-13]. Serious Games are games that aim to be more than mere entertainment [14] and game-based learning therefore refers to the process of gaming and learning. It is no longer questioned that games offer a great potential for education, however the influences, conditions and effects of game-based learning remain up to a certain extent ambiguous [15]. Despite the increasing research on the positive effects of serious games, the mobility turn of gaming devices is not taken into account. Even most serious games are developed for PC [16] or they are educational games for children aiming at improving their basics skills, for example in mathematics and English vocabulary.

As a result, mobile game-based learning is still in its initial stage and a lot of further research is needed to understand the deeper connection between mobility, gaming and learning. The few existing research papers mostly address design and development issues or present prototypes of mobile serious games. Conferences, too, seize the topic gradually (e.g. SGF 2010; Out & About: The Mobile Serious Games Conference 2010). Study results indicate better collaboration and problem solving skills in users [17], as well as a significant knowledge gain compared to the control group [18-19]. Another crucial factor is the motivation to use the game beyond school [20]. Most of the studies are conducted in formal educational settings and mostly pupils comprise the main audience. Hence, the discussion should not be limited to learning in schools and universities. Instead, the informal learning context should be taken into account and against the backdrop of life-long-learning, particularly m-learning and m-gaming are interesting for further education.

At present, however, there exists little research on the potential benefits of mobile game-based learning and especially basic research in this field is missing. In terms of basic research it is thus interesting to conduct an in-depth analysis of users' gaming and learning behavior with regard to mobile phones. Are there similarities between the trends of m-gaming and m-learning? Where do intersections emerge? Are mobile gamers also likely to be mobile game-based learners?

3   Sample and Methods

This paper presents an empirical quantitative study focusing especially on the younger generation in order to evaluate the connection between gaming and learning on mobile phones. This target group of younger people is of special interest because they are often described as the 'heavy users' of new technology. Castells et al. point out for mobile communication in general: after commercial and technological barriers break down, "young people became the drivers of mobile communication" [1]. We conducted a study which deals with the mobile and smartphone usage of students at the University of Paderborn. For this purpose the survey included 41 questions structured in five sections which were: general aspects such as information on devices (providers, brands, duration of ownership etc.), off- and online usage, costs, attitude and perception, and socio-demographic data.

A total of 597 students participated in the online-study in May 2011 (duration: four weeks). All in all, 50.4 % female and 49.6% male students were surveyed. They were invited via email, social networks such as 'facebook' and 'twitter', official university websites and flyers. On average the students took ten minutes to fill out the online questionnaire. The data were analyzed with the statistical program 'SPSS Statistics 19'. This paper aims at providing an overview and therefore focuses on bivariate analyses. Especially Cramer V which is based on Pearson chi-square statistics as well as correlations will be discussed. Their results will be presented in the following section.

4   Results

This section presents the results of the online-study and offers analyzes how mobility, gaming and learning are connected in the usage of mobile devices, especially smartphones. Different aspects will be examined: mobile gaming habits, differences in mobile gamers (m-gamer) and non mobile gamers (non m-gamers), as well as m-gamers' specific m-learning behavior.

4.1   Smartphone Usage and Mobile Gaming Behavior amongst Students

Almost all (98%) of the students surveyed own a mobile phone, so there is nearly a full supply. Furthermore, in our study the cellphone (50.4%) and the smartphone users (48.1%) are almost equally distributed. Compared to the general spread (in Germany every fifth; [21]), the smartphone possession is above average: every second student owns a smartphone. However, there is a gender gap between cellphone and smartphone users. Male students hold significantly more smartphones (63.5%) than female students (38.46%) (p<0,001; Cramer V = 0.21). This confirms the gender difference stated for all smartphone users (for further investigation and studies, see [1], [21]).

In our study two thirds (67.8%) of the students play m-games on their mobile phones (on- or offline). So for every third student mobile games are not significant; these students count to the m-gaming abstainers. In contrast to the main public and academic discourse of digital gaming the survey does not support significant gender specific differences. Although men do play more mobile games (70.4%), women engage just about as much in mobile gaming (65%). The data illustrate that gender specific differences decrease and gaming ceases to be a predominantly male phenomenon. This is an interesting finding because there is a gender gap for smartphone usage (see above), but for mobile gaming it disappears. Thus, whether someone is gaming on a mobile device or not, is more likely to be linked with personal preferences or technological issues than with gender aspects.

Yet, it is not surprising that there is a significant difference in gaming behavior between cellphone and smartphone users. Of the cellphone users 40.7% play mobile games whereas smartphone users play at a rate of 59.3% (p<0.001; Cramer V= 0.29). These findings have to be taken into account, when discussing the mobile gaming behavior of the students in the next chapter.

4.2   Mobile Gamer Profile

In the following chapter, the relationship between m-gaming and other mobile usage habits will be examined. We have titled this chapter 'The Mobile Gamer Profile' in order to study the specific mobile phone usage of m-gamers compared to non m-gamers. We contend that a playful habitus influences the way people acquire and use mobile technology. For this purpose a total of 32 items which were listed in the questionnaire and consider different mobile functions will be used for the following analyses.

To the group of the m-gamers count participants who at least play 'seldom' (off or online, these are 67.8%, see above). In this vein, figure 1 shows the nine most significant differences in a comparison between m-gamers and abstainers with respect to mobile activities. For the visualization, the categories 'frequently' and 'sometimes' were summarized according to the frequency of usage of the m-gamers.

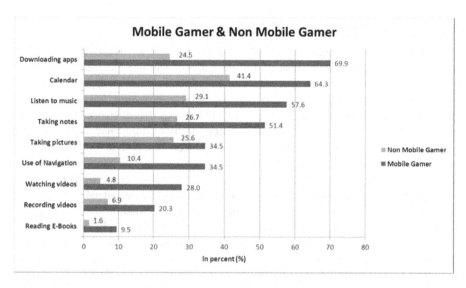

Fig. 1. Comparison of Mobile Gamers and Mobile Gaming-Abstainers (n= 287-578)

In general a higher media usage of m-gamers was observed. As figure 1 shows, there are some significant differences between m-gamers and non m-gamers concerning the use of their mobile phones. The high difference between downloading apps (p<0.001; Cramer V= 0.35) has to be mentioned, but this finding is actually not surprising, as current mobile games have to be downloaded as applications in the app- or other stores. Moreover, the m-gamer could therefore be familiar with apps, an issue which raises the affinity for using applications on a mobile phone. Furthermore, entertainment seems to be an important issue for m-gamers (listening to music and watching videos). However, especially taking pictures (p<0.001; Cramer V= 0.3) and recording videos (p<0.001; Cramer V= 0.25) reveal a creative dimension of the usage. Baacke [22] defines this as creative media figuration. This result may be significant for further research: does the playful usage of digital (mobile) media support the creative dimension of media literacy?

The significant differences in the use of the calendar function, taking notes and the navigation systems illustrate that m-gamers use their phones to structure and organize everyday life. Gamers are more technology-affine and use these tools to simplify the structuring of their lives and to save scheduled events in one device. They have a high acceptance of the mobile phone as a permanent companion as Simmel [23] illustrates it for the pocket watch at the beginning of the 20th century.

Last but not least, the gap between m-gamers and non m-gamers in their reading habits should be mentioned (p<0.001; Cramer V= 0.21). M-gamers use their smartphone to a greater extent for reading e-books than non m-gamers. This aspect is highly relevant when it comes to the point of mobile learning. Are m-gamers predestined for m-learning?

4.3   Mobile Gamer and Their Mobile Learning Behavior

This chapter aims at highlighting those aspects, which are relevant in learning contexts. As a consequence, instead of focusing on learning per se, this section concentrates on pointing out functions and possibilities, which support or can be applied in the mobile learning process. Therefore, 'browsing for information,' 'language trainer,' 'using wikis,' and 'studying' are considered. Hence, the question of how mobile applications that show connections to learning may transform and enhance learning habits of students, both m-gamers and non m-gamers, will be answered. In this context, mainly smartphone owners who use the mobile internet are taken into account because here the highest learning potential can be assumed.

When the four items which are relevant for learning are organized according to their frequency, it becomes apparent that 'browsing for information' is mentioned by most of the students and 72.5% report that they do this frequently (see figure 2). Compared to other studies it can be observed that the need for information has increased in recent years. For example a study by Accenture [24] reveals a substantial growth of mobile information programs over 31% from 2009 to 2011. These figures illustrate the potential of mobile technologies for the information society.

Second, more than half of the students doing activities related to their studies with their smartphones (52.9%; frequently and sometimes summarized), for example search in the electronic library or making arrangements for learning with other students. Strikingly, the question whether students are in general interested in using their mobile phones (in this case, cellphone and smartphone users are considered) for tasks related to their studies was affirmed by the majority of the students (61%). Yet 39% cannot imagine this kind of usage. This could be due to the fact that here all mobile phones users are taken into account and not all mobile phones feature these functions.

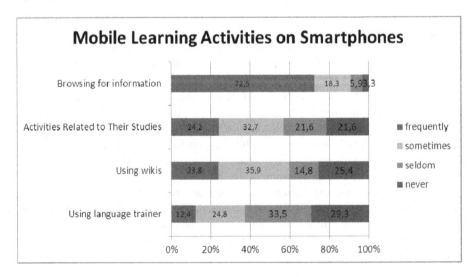

Fig. 2. Activities on the Mobile Web Regarding Mobile Learning (n= 287; Smartphone Users)

Third, using wikis connects the search for and the structuring of information. Using wikis in educational settings offers the possibility of collaborative learning through the process of searching and processing information. Only in this item, compared to the other results, a gender gap could be stated: In particular male students make use of wikis which offer a special form of communication and knowledge transfer (frequent use: 14.6% females compared to 28.5% males; $p<0.001$; Cramer $V= 0.29$).

Finally, the item 'language trainer' should be mentioned. Smartphones are used for learning languages, for example by using translation tools or vocabulary apps. This could be described as verbal mobility. Foreign languages become more and more important for both studies or career entry and private travels.

Furthermore, the question of whether there are significant differences between m-gamer and mobile gaming-abstainers regarding the selected items of learning arises. The results for this question are summarized in table1. For the search of information there are no specific differences: M-gamers browse for information (100%), just as well as non m-gamers (95%) via mobile phones.

Table 1. Comparison of Mobile Gamers and Mobile Gaming-Abstainers in Mobile Learning Activities (n= 287)

	M-GAMERS	**NON M-GAMERS**
Browsing for Information	100%	95%
Using Language Programs	94,4%	64,1%
Using Wikis	90%	67,6%
Activities Related to Their Studies	94%	71,8%

However, the other three items differ significantly in the groups of m-gamers and non m-gamers. M-gamers (94.4%) are more affine with respect to verbal mobility, because they use language trainers more often compared to game abstainers (64.1%) ($p<0.001$; Cramer $V=0.29$). This difference also applies to wikis: 90% of the m-gamers and 67.6% of the non m-gamers make use of this function ($p<0.001$; Cramer $V=0.24$). Finally, doing activities related to their studies with a smartphone is more common for m-gamers (94%) than for non m-gamers (71.8%) ($p<0.001$; Cramer $V=0.25$). These results confirm that m-gamers use a broader range of functions and that they are interested in learning activities connected to their smartphone. M-gamers use the learning capabilities of smartphones in a more intense and differentiated way than non m-gamers. They can therefore be seen as a focus group for learning programs and mobile learning.

5   Conclusion and Discussion

Our study allows for the conclusion that mobile gamers are capable of a broader and more sophisticated range of activities regarding their mobile phone usage. In this vein, significant differences can be stated for the organization of everyday life, the creative and entertaining usage, as well as the educational applications. M-gamers utilize the opportunities offered by mobile technology in an all-round way and therefore can be labeled as 'mobile all-rounders'. These findings are confirmed by the Games Online Media Monitor [25]: Gamers have diverse leisure activities and they are very communicative.

These results are also reflected in their learning behavior. M-gamers have a higher coverage rate of the learning potentials compared to non m-gamers. They use their smartphones for the search of information, for learning languages, for studying and for information exchange via wikis.

This leads to the conclusion that m-gamers are generally more capable of using mobile technologies for their own benefit. Through the use of a ubiquitous technology, communicative mobility advances to a global cultural technique [26]. One may also speak of a high mobile communication literacy. This competence also corresponds to the term 'motility.' According to Kaufman, 'motility' is defined as "the way in which an individual appropriates what is possible in the domain of mobility and puts this potential to use for his or her activities." [27]

Returning to the question of whether there are similarities and intersections between mobile gaming and mobile learning, current research on mobile serious games lacks close studies of how people use mobile game-based learning.

At this point, we can highlight two important aspects. First, most of the examined mobile serious games are quiz games [28] or games which use the mobile devices as communication tools e.g. during a paper chase (e.g. [29]). Hence, the gaming potential of mobile devices is not yet fully exhausted. The context of mobility is currently mostly used in the sense of augmented reality games and therefore in group contexts. A study of Facer et al. indicates that the mobile gamers' motivation results from game elements, such as challenges, and not just from moving around [30]. Thus, it may be doubted whether mobility is a motivational aspect, as it does not necessarily have to be part of the game itself.

Second, most mobile serious games in current studies are used in formal educational contexts like schools or universities. George and Serna [31] for example discuss the capabilities of mobile devices for class-room situations considering situated and collaborative learning. Not only spatial mobility but also temporal mobility is an important restriction. Timeframes of five minutes are reported to be suitable for mobile learning. In the sense of a 'timeless time' [1] mobile game-based learning should also be considered as being independent of time and for instance waiting periods can then be utilized for learning activities. These reflections have to be transferred to the mobile game-based learning approach by reflecting the 'anytime-anywhere' paradigm (e.g. [32]).

For this purpose, our study reveals some insights into the mobile world and its connection to m-gaming and m-learning. Based on these insights, additional and in-depth research will be necessary. For instance, the findings of this study point to a connection between a playful and creative usage of mobile devices. In this respect, further research on the correlations between mobility, playing, and creativity would be fruitful. Also, this paper follows an indirect path by exploring the potentials of mobile game-based learning. Thus the fields 'mobile gaming' and 'mobile learning' were surveyed separately in an online questionnaire and finally connected with the help of the mobile gamer profile. As a consequence, further research needs to take the direct path and study the use of mobile game-based learning offers in particular in a new survey. Due to the current lack of offers in this area, our survey was not capable of studying these offers directly. Yet in the light of the quick technological and mobile developments, especially in the field of tablets, this will constitute an inspiring field of research.

References

1. Castells, M., Fernandez-Ardevol, M., Linchuan Qiu, J., Sey, A.: Mobile communication and society: A global perspective a project of the Annenberg Research Network on international communication. MIT Press, Cambridge (2007)
2. Paul, S.A., Jensen, M., Wong, C.Y., Khong, C.W.: Socializing in mobile gaming. In: DIMEA 2008: Proceedings of the 3rd International Conference on Digital Interactive Media in Entertainment and Arts. ACM, New York (2008)
3. Soh, J., Tan, B.: Mobile gaming. Communications of the ACM 51, 35–39 (2008)
4. Liang, T.-P., Yeh, Y.-H.: Effect of use contexts on the continuous use of mobile services. Personal and Ubiquitous Computing 15, 187–196 (2011)
5. Hierdeis, H.: From Meno to Microlearning: A Historical Survey. In: Hug, T. (ed.) Didactics of Microlearning. Concepts, Discourses and Examples, pp. 35–52. Waxmann, Münster (2007)
6. Hug, T.: Mobiles Lernen. In: Hugger, K., Halber, M. (eds.) Digitale Lernwelten. Konzepte, Beispiele und Perspektiven, pp. 193–211. VS Verlag, Wiesbaden (2010)
7. Bachmair, B., Risch, M., Friedrich, K., Mayer, K.: Eckpunkte einer Didaktik des mobilen Lernens: Operationalisierung im Rahmen eines Schulversuchs. MedienPädagogik, 1–38 (2011)
8. Friedrich, K., Bachmair, B., Risch, M.: Mobiles Lernen mit dem Handy: Herausforderung und Chance für den Unterricht, 1st edn. Beltz, Weinheim (2011)
9. Vavoula, G., Pachler, N., Kukulska-Hulme, A. (eds.): Researching mobile learning: Frameworks, tools, and research designs. Peter Lang, New York (2009)
10. Kukulska-Hulme, A.: Introduction. In: Kukulska-Hulme, A., Traxler, J. (eds.) Mobile Learning: A Handbook for Educators and Trainers, pp. 1–6. Routledge, New York (2005)
11. Ganguin, S.: Computerspiele und lebenslanges Lernen: Eine Synthese von Gegensätzen. VS Verlag, Wiesbaden (2010)
12. Gee, J.P.: What video games have to teach us about learning and literacy. Palgrave Macmillan, New York (2007)
13. Prensky, M.: Digital game based learning. Paragon House, St. Paul (2007)
14. Ritterfeld, U., Cody, M., Vorderer, P. (eds.): Serious games: Mechanisms and Effects. Routledge, London (2009)
15. Egenfeldt-Nielsen, S.: Overview of research on the educational use of video games. Digital Kompetanse 1, 184–213 (2006)
16. Ratan, R., Ritterfeld, U.: Classifying Serious Games. In: Ritterfeld, U., Cody, M., Vorderer, P. (eds.) Serious Games: Mechanisms and Effects, pp. 10–24. Routledge, London (2009)
17. Sanchez, J., Mendoza, C., Salinas, A.: Mobile serious games for collaborative problem solving. Annual Review of CyberTherapy and Telemedicine 7, 193–197 (2009)

18. Huizenga, J., Admiraal, W., Akkerman, S., Dam, G.: Mobile game-based learning in secondary education: engagement, motivation and learning in a mobile city game. Journal of Computer Assisted Learning 25, 332–344 (2009)
19. Kittl, C., Edegger, F., Petrovic, O.: Learning by Pervasive Gaming. In: Ryu, H., Parsons, D. (eds.) Innovative Mobile Learning, pp. 60–82. IGI Global (2008)
20. Sandberg, J., Maris, M., de Geus, K.: Mobile English learning: An evidence-based study with fifth graders. Computers & Education 57, 1334–1347 (2011)
21. Bitkom: Jeder fünfte Handynutzer besitzt ein Smartphone (2010), http://www.bitkom.org/de/themen/54894_65506.aspx (accessed February 09, 2012)
22. Baacke, D.: Medienkompetenz als zentrales Operationsfeld von Projekten. In: Handbuch Medien: Medienkompetenz. Bpb, Bonn (1999)
23. Simmel, G.: Simmel on Culture. In: Frisby, D., Featherstone, M. (eds.). Sage, London (1997)
24. Langer, U.: Social, Local, Mobile - der neue Hoffnungsträger auf dem mobilen Internetmarkt. In: Landesanstalt für Medien Nordrhein-Westfalen (LfM) (ed.) Digitaltrends LfM: Mobile Media, pp. 8–10 (2011)
25. GOMM: Games Online Media Monitor 2012: Zielgruppe (2012), http://www.gomm-online.de/ (accessed March 27, 2012)
26. Weibel, P.: Visionen der Mediengesellschaft. In: BMW Institut für Mobilitäts-forschung (ed.) Auswirkungen der virtuellen Mobilität, pp. 57–73. Springer, Berlin (2003)
27. Kaufmann, V.: Rethinking Mobility. Contemporary Sociology. Ashgate, Aldershot (2002)
28. Petrovic, O., Brand, A. (eds.): Serious Games on the Move. Springer, Vienna (2009)
29. Schwabe, G., Göth, C.: Mobile learning with a mobile game: design and motivational effects. Journal of Computer Assisted Learning 21, 204–216 (2005)
30. Facer, K., Joiner, R., Stanton, D., Reid, J., Hull, R., Kirk, D.: Savannah: mobile gaming and learning? Journal of Computer Assisted Learning 20, 399–409 (2004)
31. George, S., Serna, A.: Introducing Mobility in Serious Games: Enhancing Situated and Collaborative Learning. In: Jacko, J.A. (ed.) HCII 2011, Part IV. LNCS, vol. 6764, pp. 12–20. Springer, Heidelberg (2011)
32. Squire, K.: Mobile media learning: multiplicities of place. On the Horizon 17, 70–80 (2009)

Science and Technology Communication Activities by Using 3D Image Projection System

Kazuya Takemata[1], Akiyuki Minamide[2], and Sumio Nakamura[1]

[1] Kanazawa Institute of Technology, Nonoichi, Japan
{takemata,junsei}@neptune.kanazawa-it.ac.jp
[2] Kanazawa Technical College, Kanazawa, Japan
minamide@ kanazawa-tc.ac.jp

Abstract. This paper describes our science and technology communication activities with a focus on the universe using Mitaka software developed by the National Astronomical Observatory of Japan. Mitaka has a stereovision mode, through which the users can show the cosmic space. It helps enhance the scientific awareness of the viewers. We developed a mobile three dimensional (3D) image projection system and carried out space science classes using Mitaka in local schools and facilities. We show the background of the 3D image projection system development and its utilization cases.

Keywords: 3D image projection, Mitaka, science communication.

1 Introduction

Since the Science and Technology Basic Act was promulgated and became effective in November 1995, Japan had been repeatedly implementing the Science and Technology Basic Plan as the first phase (1996-2000), second phase (2001-2005) and third phase (2006-2010). The purpose of the Plan was to promote the science and technology communication activities in Japan. The Plan emphasized the establishment of communication between science/technology and society [1]. For the fourth phase (2011-2015), the Plan says that it "aims to promote the science and technology communication activities by researchers as well as various science and technology activities at science museums and other museums, more than ever" [2]. Based on this Plan, we had been trying to enhance the interests in science among the people in the community near our university and enhance their science and technology literacy through the lifelong learning classes in the area of science.

2 The Universe Space Simulation Software MITAKA

Mitaka is software for visualizing the known universe with up-to-date observational data and theoretical models. It is developed by the Four Dimensional Digital Universe (4D2U) project of the National Astronomical Observatory of Japan (NAOJ) [3]. Anyone can download Mitaka from NAOJ's website for free and enjoy it. Mitaka interactively visualizes the universe on a computer. Therefore, the person who talks

S. Göbel et al. (Eds.): Edutainment 2012/GameDays 2012, LNCS 7516, pp. 121–124, 2012.

about the universe using Mitaka (a lecturer) can make an effective presentation while checking the reaction of the audience (students). Because we value the science and technology communication with the students, we thought this interactive feature of Mitaka is useful to manage our classes. Thus, we adapted Mitaka as the material for our space science classes.

To achieve the natural stereoscopic vision using the bin-ocular disparity, the images projected from each projector (image for right eye and image for left eye) to the screen needed to be accurately overlapped. To achieve it, we needed a projector rack, which had the "function to adjust the position of the projected images". We developed a ceiling type projector rack called S·O·Ra (Fig. 1). This rack has the "function to adjust the position of the projected images". We invited the students from local high schools and community people to our laboratory and showed Mitaka on a trial basis. We repeated our test runs of the "lecture on the universe using Mitaka" while observing the reactions of the audience. Finally, in August 2010, we began the public exhibition of Mitaka in our laboratory. As one of the 11 4D2U theaters in Japan, our laboratory is introduced on the web-site of NAOJ [4].

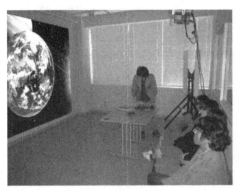 

Fig. 1. Ceiling type projector rack called S·O·Ra, which has the "function to adjust the position of the projected images"

3   Mobile 3D Projection System

Our purpose is to conduct lifelong learning classes with a focus on the space science in the community. We wanted many people to experience the Mitaka classes with the 3D projection system. Particularly, we wanted the people who were unable to visit the 4D2U theater in our laboratory to experience the Mitaka classes. So we decided to develop a mobile three dimensional (3D) projection system that could create the 4D2U theater anywhere. We developed S·O·Ra 100, a mobile rack in which 2 projectors and 2 computers with Mitaka software could be stored (Fig. 2, Upper). S·O·Ra 100 has a projector rack with a "function to adjust the position of the projected images" and has a space to store computers. It is 610 mm in width, 1170 mm in height, and 800 mm in depth. It weighs 60 kg (excluding equipment). We can move S·O·Ra 100 by using a welfare vehicle designed to transport wheel chair users.

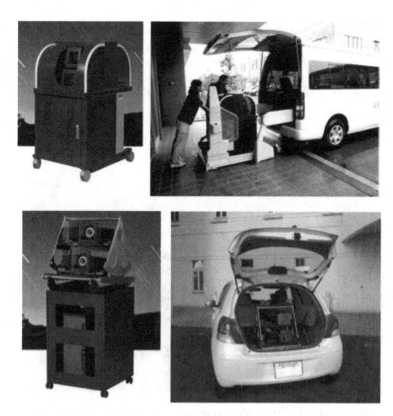

Fig. 2. 3D Projection System S·O·Ra 100 (Upper) and S·O·Ra 200 (Lower)

Then, we developed S·O·Ra 200, which had a separate projector rack and the space for computers (Fig. 2, Lower). The size of the projector rack is 505mm in width, 498mm in height, 600 mm in depth and 15 kg in weight (excluding the equipment). The size of the space for the computers is 505mm in width, 700mm in height, 500mm in depth and 21.5 kg in weight (excluding the equipment). Based on the experiences with S·O·Ra 100, S·O·Ra 200 was designed in such a way that it could be carried in a standard small vehicle, instead of a special vehicle. This design made it possible for us to carry the 3D projection system anywhere anytime without constraints and conduct the mobile lectures on the space science more flexibly. Fig. 3 shows a scene of us conducting a mobile lecture at a kindergarten on February 22. 2012.

4   Conclusion

In this paper, we described the development of the 3D projection system to promote the mobile lifelong learning classes on the universe. We adapted the universe space simulator Mitaka, as the material for our classes. In line with it, we developed an inexpensive mobile 3D image projection system to enable us to more effectively conduct mobile classes using Mitaka. Then, we visited various facilities and provided classes on the space science using the system. Conducting lifelong learning concerning science and technology communication will lead to enhancing the science and technology literacy of the community. We are planning to establish a training program to develop lectures who can conduct mobile classes on the universe using this system.

Fig. 3. Science and technology communication activities in kindergarten

Acknowledgment. We would like to express our appreciation for Dr. Hirotaka Nakayama and Ms. Yumiko Iwashita at the National Astronomical Observatory of Japan.

References

1. Minister of Education, Culture, Sports, Science and Technology – Japan, White Paper on Science and Technology (2011)
2. Minister of Education, Culture, Sports, Science and Technology – Japan, the Science and Technology Basic Plan as the forth phase, http://www.mext.go.jp/component/a_menu/science/detail/__icsFiles/afieldfile/2011/08/19/1293746_02.pdf (accessed January 02, 2012)
3. The National Astronomical Observatory of Japan, 4D2U NAVIVATOR, http://4d2u.nao.ac.jp/english/index.html (accessed January 02, 2012)
4. The National Astronomical Observatory of Japan, Four Dimensional Digital Universe Projekut, NAOJ, http://www.nao.ac.jp/cgi-bin/about/mtk/4d2u/entry.cgi (accessed January 02, 2012)

Potentials of a Low-Cost Motion Analysis System for Exergames in Rehabilitation and Sports Medicine

Loreen Pogrzeba[1], Markus Wacker[1], and Bernhard Jung[2]

[1] University of Applied Sciences Dresden, Germany
{pogrzeba@,wacker@informatik.}htw-dresden.de
[2] University of Technology and Mining Freiberg, Germany
jung@informatik.tu-freiberg.de

Abstract. This paper presents a low-cost motion analysis system consisting of the Microsoft Kinect sensor and a self-developed software for rehabilitation and sports medicine. During therapy or training sessions a person's motion is recorded through video and skeletal data. Subsequently, our software allows the analysis and comparison of all recorded motion data. The combination of motion analysis functionality, a user-friendly setup, and easy handling makes our system well-suited for the development or support of exergames.

Keywords: Motion Analysis System, Rehabilitation, Sports Medicine, Exergames.

1   Introduction

Exergames can be a powerful extension of therapy sessions to motivate patients with neuronal or muscular disorders and physical disabilities, regardless of their medical history (developmental disorder, illness, aging). While playing exergames Parkinson Disease Patients feel more engaged to do physical exercises independently at home [1]. Stroke patients enjoy training their upper limb agility [3][14] and children suffering from cerebral palsy (CP) profit from neuronal and physical improvements [4] and a grown self-efficacy [13]. According to a meta-study on exergames for patients with systemic disabling conditions, positive effects are reported in all 25 surveyed studies, "either improvements in health and function outcomes or positive reports about accessibility and usability" [12]. Detailed information about related studies can be found in a report of the American Heart Association [10].

In addition to the patients' interest in participating in exergames, the therapists have to be convinced of the feasibility and potentials of exergames in rehabilitation as well. In this context motion analysis can be an objective method to diagnose and document the therapeutic progress of patients. In daily practice, however, motion analysis is scarcely used by therapists, because they are often missing control over choice and form of the displayed motion data and rarely

S. Göbel et al. (Eds.): Edutainment 2012/GameDays 2012, LNCS 7516, pp. 125–133, 2012.

able to store it [2]. Finally the setup of the hardware should't take much preparation time, the whole analysis system should preferably be low priced and easy to be handled by patient *and* therapist alike.

Based on these various requirements our goal is to develop a motion analysis system which can be used to overcome the above mentioned drawbacks of previous exergame applications in rehabilitation and which is truly helpful to therapists. Therefore we combine a Microsoft Kinect sensor (short: Kinect) and a self-developed powerful software into a markerless motion analysis system and explore, whether it qualifies for practical use in rehabilitation and sports medicine using four selected applications. We investigate the conditions for achieving stable and robust recordings of skeletal data and aim to design a motion analysis software with a clear and straightforward graphical user interface. Since we only carried out field studies with a very limited number of subjects, our results still have to be verified under standardized conditions.

2   Related Work

The user's physical abilities and gaming experience significantly affect the usability and design of exergames. Especially in the field of rehabilitation the user input of patients is often restricted compared to healthy people due to bodily or neuronal disabilities and disorders. Therefore it is of crucial importance to choose an input technology that allows many patients with various special needs an easy and feasible way to control game interfaces.

Previous studies about exergames in rehabilitation often relied on the very popular input devices Nintendo Wii and Sony EyeToy. An overview can be found in [12]. However the introduction of the Kinect for Xbox 360 in the end of 2010 opened up many new possibilities compared to the other input devices. The Kinect contains a small 3D depth camera system which enables motion analysis based on skeletal tracking without any need of additional devices or previous preparations and is almost as easy to handle as a video camera.

Some researchers have already seized the possibilities of this new technology. An evaluation of the Kinect for clinical and in-home stroke rehabilitation tools reasoned that it offers new possibilities "as a tool for both physical therapists and stroke survivors" [9]. Research at the University of Missouri aims at using the Kinect for monitoring of the elderly to recognize in-home passive fall risks [15]. In contrast to motion analysis with a marker-based or markerless motion capturing approach (e.g. via Dynamic Athletics, Kwon3D, The MotionMonitor) the Kinect doesn't require trained personal, much maintenance or technical equipment and is often more economic. In comparison to systems which rely on video image processing (e.g. Contemplas, Dartfish, SimiMotion) the Kinect provides realtime video images *and* skeletal data with 6 degrees of freedom for up to 20 joints. In the field of exergames the Fraunhofer FIRST and project partners are developing a so called "Interactive Trainer" which uses a combination of Kinect and other sensors for fall prevention and monitoring stroke patients with the use of home-based exercises [8]. A team at Clemson University records the minimum and maximum wrist motion of stroke patients within a virtual environment application [6].

3   Implementation

Our motion analysis system consists of the Kinect and a self-developed software based on freely available open source Kinect libraries such as the Microsoft SDK or OpenNI. It runs on ordinary PCs or laptops to which the sensor is connected. The tasks of our software package can be divided into three parts:

1. **Setup and calibration.** For best capture results the sensor should be placed in front of the patient in a distance of 1.2 to 3.5 meters and the patient should be fully visible to the sensor and its embedded camera. The location should not be exposed to direct sunlight but should be well lit with artificial light. When the patient enters the field of view of the sensor, the automatic calibration phase takes only a few seconds to adjust to the patient's body, after which the realtime recording can be started.
2. **Realtime recording.** The recording of motion during a session runs simultaneously while a patient or athlete is performing the exercises. The software displays the video image (I), the detected motion on a simplified human skeleton in a freely adjustable 3d view (II), selectable motion graphs for position data of up to 20 joints (III) and a status indicator for the tracking quality (IV) in realtime (cf. Fig. 1).
3. **Analysis.** After the recording process, the therapist can evaluate the therapy sessions by replaying or scrolling through the video and motion streams with time sliders, adding comments (V), displaying motion trajectories and changing the displayed motion graphs (cf. Fig. 2).

4   Participants and Setup

Our motion analysis system has to be suitable for the needs of very different participants and various fields of applications. Our cooperation partners are therapists using the Swedish Function-oriented Music Therapy (FMT), therapists at the International Vojta Society (IVS), training theorists of the Olympic Training Center Dresden/Chemnitz (OTC), and specialists of the University Hospital Carl Gustav Carus Dresden (HCGC) at the clinic and polyclinic for orthopedy, department rehabilitation and sports medicine. We now describe our application fields in detail.

FMT deals with patients of all ages who might be suffering from CP and other birth related injuries, mental retardation, learning disabilities, muscular diseases, brain damage as a consequence of stroke, or other diseases as listed at [5]. The FMT challenges the patient to improve his physical level and to increase attention and concentration skills within individual therapy sessions. Therefore, FMT uses short melodies (music codes) in combination with a certain number of percussion instruments which the patient is requested to play in a defined sequence. Due to the fact that the therapy is nonverbal the patient has to discover the demanded sequence via trial and error by himself. For recording tests we used the OpenNI framework and positioned the Kinect in a distance of 2.5 m and 1.6 m in height in front of the sitting person.

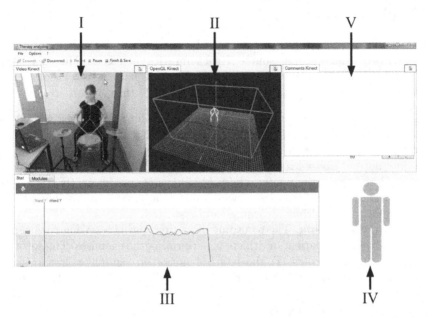

Fig. 1. Realtime recording. Realtime view of video image (I), 3d view (II) and motion graphs (III). Green status indication (IV) signals realtime skeletal tracking.

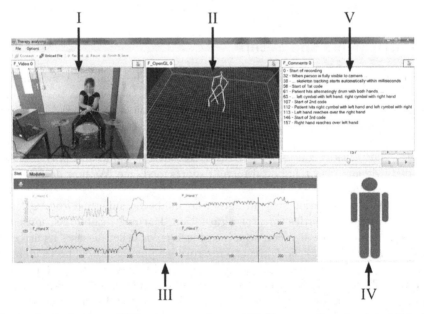

Fig. 2. Analysis phase. Video image at frame 157 (I), zoomed and rotated 3d view (II), motion graphs (III) of vertical (Y) and horizontal translation (X) of left and right hand and a list of comments (V). Red status indication signals offline recording (IV).

IVS therapists attend to patients of all ages potentially suffering from CP, multiple sclerosis, stroke and other disorders as a result of damages to the central nervous system [17]. The therapist invokes body reactions (reflex locomotion) by performing physical pressure on defined places of the patient's body in defined postures and as a consequence can (re)activate and restore bodily functions. The patient is predominantly treated in a horizontal body position. First recording tests with IVS were carried out in May 2012 using the Microsoft SDK. The Kinect was placed in a distance of 2.3 m and 1.45 m in height in front of the standing patient, who performed a defined set of movements before and after the treatment.

Our research partners at the HCGC have specialized in rehabilitation, training methodology, sports biochemistry, and diagnostics. Additionally they want to offer training support for professional and ambitious nonprofessional runners. On that account the setup for recordings focuses on gait analysis on a treadmill.

The OTC offers advice, guidance and coordination in various fields in professional sports, e.g. sports medicine, training theory and performance diagnostics. We are planning various test recordings but the setups highly vary depending on the examined sport, e.g. skiing, swimming and bobsleighing. First recordings dealt with the jump height during a volleyball session. We connected two Kinect sensors to different PCs with either OpenNI framework or Microsoft SDK. Then we tracked the athlete simultaneously in a height of 1.7 m from behind and from the left side in a distance of 2.9 m and 4.0 m respectively.

5 Discussion

We now discuss our results of test sessions with FMT, IVS, HCGC and OTC. Concerning the realtime recording phase, the recording speed, accuracy, and stability were completely satisfactory for the tested applications. All tests took place indoor with artificial lighting to avoid disturbances of the Kinect infrared technology. Even when exceeding the recommended distance between Kinect and subject, it still detected a running athlete fast enough, when he entered the field of the Kinect. During the FMT test recordings a person handed over a different set of drum sticks to the patient from outside the Kinect's field of view, which had no negative impact on the recording of the motion data.

In the areas of FMT and IVS our motion analysis system enabled the therapists to objectively evaluate the therapeutic progress for the first time. Before that, the FMT therapists had worked with sporadic video recordings and had no experience with motion analysis systems or software. Thus, there is a vast awareness about its potential to track the progress of their patients and the possibility to verify the efficacy of the whole therapeutic approach.

The sport scientists of HCGC and OTC are familiar with motion analysis systems, yet appreciated the realtime visualization and immediate availability of video and motion data after the exercises. The instant motion feedback enabled them to point out suboptimally performed movements in the video images and 3d view. Additionally the trainers were able to observe improvements in the performance of the athlete with the help of the motion graphs.

FMT, HCGC and OTC were very enthusiastic about the straightforward and quick setup, which integrated seamlessly in their therapy or training sessions. Finally they can completely concentrate on the patient or athlete without the need for a long preparation time or learning phase to use the system. They found it easy to detect irregular or asymmetric motion, e.g. limping or asymmetric body postures while playing drums (cf. Fig. 3). Furthermore they considered the low price of the Kinect a major advantage, because during therapeutic or training sessions, the hardware might get damaged or even destroyed and must be repurchased. Due to the ease of operability and the robust realtime recording of the system the FMT and HCGC project partners were very eager to get a private version for independent use and offered their service as beta testers.

However our motion analysis system has some limitations which arise from the use of the Kinect. Due to the high sensitivity to direct sunlight it is not suited for outdoor activities. Thus many sports can not be tracked unless they can be practiced indoors under similar conditions. As a consequence of a maximal sample rate of 30 frames per second, fast motion cannot be detected accurately and restricts the applicability in the field of sports medicine to actions with a moderate motion speed. These disadvantages do not have a strong influence on applications in the area of rehabilitation, because therapy sessions are predominantly practiced indoors and, depending on the disorders of the patient, do not require extreme motion speed. However, the limited field of view of the Kinect can have a negative impact on the practical use of our motion analysis system in therapy sessions. If the therapist stands between the Kinect and the patient and masks him partially or completely with his own body, the skeletal tracking of the patient cannot proceed. Finally it is recommended to use the Kinect with sitting or standing persons facing the Kinect.

The last mentioned drawback coincides with our experiences at the test recordings with the IVS. It was not possible to track the patient from a position horizontally or obliquely above. In addition the therapy required close physical contact and thus would have provoked lots of masking problems. During FMT sessions we sometimes encountered problems with the legs' motion data being hidden by the musical instruments, but this was of no importance for the therapists who mainly focused on the upper body. And we had difficulties to record robust motion data when the Kinect tracked the motion of an athlete *through* a volleyball net as soon as the athlete came closer than 0.5 m to the net and therefore decided to record the athlete from behind.

Concerning the test recordings with our cooperation partners a markerbased or markerless motion capture system could overcome some drawbacks of the Kinect but the user would have to accept the already mentioned disadvantages. The IVS preferred our motion analysis module and decided to record a sequence of movements before and after the treatment to analyze the improvements in disordered joints by comparison.

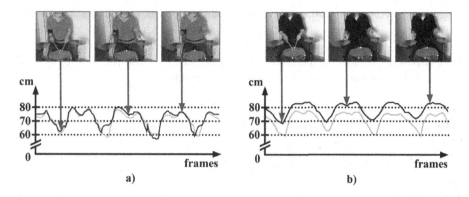

Fig. 3. Symmetric (a) and asymmetric (b) motion while performing a FMT code. Right participant shows an abnormal mismatch of 8 cm between his left (dark gray) and right (light gray) hand. Video images and motion graphs (with subsequently adapted axes) taken from our motion analysis system.

6   Conclusion and Future Work

With the support of our low-cost motion analysis system a new quality of treatment in rehabilitation can be achieved. It is a versatile tool for the evaluation of therapy and training sessions and thus is well suited for extending already existing exergames with the possibility of motion analysis operations or developing new games. Where some exergames are offering a simple score at the end of the game, our motion analysis package presents an additional benefit for therapists, because they can store the recorded motion and evaluate it in more detail. Due to the low-cost Kinect sensor the motion analysis system and derived exergames are easily affordable for rehabilitation and physiotherapy clinics and self-employed therapists. The system works in nearly invisible manner, that means without markers, suits or other necessary preparations and therefore is ideally suited for patients with fear of contact, athetosis, twitches, tremors, autism and dementia. However, the underlying software has to be carefully designed for the users to be of maximum use.

Our field studies indicate that our motion capture system is well suited for practical use in individual therapy, especially for the evaluation of stationary performed motion (e.g. drumming, standing and sitting, walking on a treadmill). Non-stationary sports (e.g. sports with inrun and over longer distances) require a longer testing period to find the optimal recording setup. Long-term studies with a large group of participants (e.g. in combination with an already existing exergame) have to show whether our results are reproducible and transferable to other areas of application.

We have discussed our system with the FMT therapists and established a research and development plan for the analysis tool. In the future our project partners will use the motion analysis system independently for long-term studies. FMT studies with a larger number of participants will most likely follow this

August in Sweden. For that reason, we are planning to extend the features of the motion analysis system, so that it detects and tags comparable motion patterns automatically using mathematical methods like dynamic time warping [11]. The next hardware version of the Kinect sensor might also raise the quality level of the camera image as well as the precision of the data.

Acknowledgments. We would like to thank our project partners for organizing personnel and equipment for test recordings as well as for their interest, and enthusiasm. Thank to European Commision (Europian Social Fund) for funding this research project.

References

1. Assad, O., Hermann, R., Lilla, D., Mellies, B., Meyer, R., Shevach, L., Siegel, S., Springer, M., Tiemkeo, S., Voges, J., Wieferich, J., Herrlich, M., Krause, M., Malaka, R.: WuppDi! – Supporting Physiotherapy of Parkinson's Disease Patients via Motion-based Gaming. In: Proc. Mensch und Computer 2011 (Entertainment Interfaces), pp. 469–478. Universitätsverlag der TU Chemnitz, Chemnitz (2011)
2. Annema, J.-H., Verstraete, M., Abeele, V.V., Desmet, S., Geerts, D.: Videogames in Therapy: A Therapist's Perspective. In: Proc. of the 3rd International Conf. on Fun and Games, pp. 95–98. ACM, New York (2010)
3. Burke, J.W., McNeill, M.D.J., Charles, D.K., Morrow, P.J., Crosbie, J.H., McDonough, S.M.: Optimising Engagement for Stroke Rehabilitation using Serious Games. J. The Visual Computer 25(12), 1085–1099 (2009)
4. Deutsch, J.E., Borbely, M., Filler, J., Huhn, K., Guarrera-Bowlby, P.: Use of a Low-Cost, Commercially Available Gaming Console (Wii) for Rehabilitation of an Adolescent With Cerebral Palsy. J. Physical Therapy 88(10), 1196–1207 (2008)
5. Functionally oriented music therapy,
   http://www.fmt-metoden.se/fmtsiteng/index.html
6. Hayes, A., Dukes, P., Hodges, L.F.: A Virtual Environment for Post-Stroke Motor Rehabilitation, http://www.cs.clemson.edu/reu/documents/
   stroke_rehab_abstract.pdf
7. Hanneton, S., Varenne, A., Hanneton, S.: Coaching the Wii: Evaluation of a Physical Training Experiment Assisted by a Video Game. In: Proc. of the Haptic, Audio, Visual Environments and Games Conf., pp. 54–57. IEEE, New York (2009)
8. John, M., Klose, S., Kock, G., Jendreck, M., Feichtinger, R., Hennig, B., Reithinger, N., Kiselev, J., Gvercin, M., Steinhagen-Thiessen, E., Kausch, S., Polak, M., Irmscher, B.: SmartSenior Interactive Trainer - Development of an Interactive System for a Home-Based Fall-Prevention Training for Elderly People. In: Ambient Assisted Living – Advanced Technologies and Societal Change, Part 7, pp. 305–316. Springer, Heidelberg (2012)
9. LaBelle, K.: Evaluation of Kinect Joint Tracking for Clinical and In-Home Stroke Rehabilitation Tools. Thesis, Indiana (2011)
10. Lieberman, D.A., Chamberlin, B., Medina Jr., E., Franklin, B.A., Sanner, B.M., Vafiadis, D.K.: The Power of Play: Innovations in Getting Active Summit 2011: A Science Panel Proceedings Report From the American Heart Association. J. Circulation 123(21), 2507–2516 (2011)
11. Müller, M.: Information Retrieval for Music and Motion. Springer, Heidelberg (2007)

12. Plow, M.A., McDaniel, C., Linder, S., Alberts, J.L.: A Scoping Review of Exergaming for Adults with Systemic Disabling Conditions. J. Bioengineering & Biomedical Sci., 1–11 (2011)
13. Reid, D.T.: Benefits of a Virtual Play Rehabilitation Environment for Children with Cerebral Palsy on Perceptions of Self-Efficacy: A Pilot Study. J. Pediatric Rehabilitation 5(3), 141–148 (2002)
14. Rand, D., Kizony, R., Weiss, P.L.: Virtual reality rehabilitation for all: Vivid GX versus Sony PlayStation II EyeToy. In: Proc. 5th Intl. Conf. on Disability, VR & Assoc. Tech. 2004, pp. 87–94 (2004)
15. Stone, E.E., Skubic, M.: Evaluation of an Inexpensive Depth Camera for Passive In-Home Fall Risk Assessment. In: Proc. 5th Int. Conf. on Pervasive Computing Technologies for Healthcare (PervasiveHealth) and Workshops, pp. 71–77 (2011)
16. Tanaka, K., Parker, J., Baradoy, G., Sheehan, D., Holash, J.R., Katz, L.: A Comparison of Exergaming Interfaces for Use in Rehabilitation Programs and Research. J. Loading 6(9), 69–81 (2012)
17. Vojta Therapy, http://www.vojta.com/index.php

Puzzle-it: An HTML5 Serious Games Platform for Education

Puzzle Based Serious Games for Education

Danu Pranantha, Francesco Bellotti, Ricardo Berta, and Alessandro De Gloria

Department of Naval, Electrical, and Information Technology Engineering (Dynatech),
University of Genoa,
Genoa, Italy
{danu,franz,berta,adg}@elios.unige.it

Abstract. Serious games as learning medium have advanced in the past few years. They have been applied to support learning in various fields such as security, health-care, and education. Serious games can scale from low budget games up to high budget games depends on the games' objectives and features. For instance, military may utilize games with 3D simulation, live characters, and extensive scenario for combat training due to its critical mission. Nonetheless, in a classroom or remote set-up learning environment, most of these high level games are impractical to be adopted due to the amount of costs they may induce. This is most of the case in educational games which main objective is to motivate the student to learn. However, a game development remains as a time consuming, complex, and laborious process. In order to simplify and shorten this process, it is highly attractive to create a platform to produce educational games. Therefore, this paper, based on our previous work, proposes a platform for authoring HTML5 serious games intended in particular, but not limited to create lightweight serious games for educational purpose using the upcoming HTML5 standard playable in common web browsers. This platform, puzzle-it, divides the work of game development into two distinct layers i.e. contents authoring and core engine development. Both readily and work in progress components of the platform are presented and discussed.

Keywords: serious games, game development, puzzle game, HTML5, JavaScript, game engine, game content authoring, social networks.

1   Introduction

The advancement of information technology has revolutionized how people work, live, and learns. Learning has changed in various forms from conventional teaching in the classroom, the advent of distance learning and cyber classroom, and the use of e-learning system. One of appealing approaches is the use of serious games. Educational serious games (SGs) – games that use pedagogy to infuse instruction into the game play, in particular fostering situated cognition [1] – have acknowledged educational potential shown by their ability to induce motivation in learning and

S. Göbel et al. (Eds.): Edutainment 2012/GameDays 2012, LNCS 7516, pp. 134–143, 2012.

improve academic performance [2]. SGs are not only adopted in academic curriculum [2], but also they are adopted in military training [3]. While commercial games can be purposely shifted for learning, most of them can be difficult to adjust or expensive to acquire. On the other hand, developing a full extensive game for a certain purpose consumes a lot of time and budget. Certainly, in critical purposes such as warfare simulation which results are the matter of life and death, it will be valuable to have very powerful games using 3D living world, non playable characters (NPC), and simulation to induce real experiences to the military soldiers. However, it is hardly necessary in schools to have such systems in the classroom. It is more likely to be simple, flexible, and ease to create contents.

Therefore, this paper proposes puzzle-it, a platform to create HTML5 SGs for educational purpose. This platform exploits the state of the art web technologies and social networks which offer open platform and ease dissemination. The most compelling feature is that it offers loose coupled between contents and the core components of the game i.e. game engine. Furthermore, this platform, based on our previous work in [4], supports three types of interaction modalities to provide amusing game mechanics via common web browser and connection to social networks for user profiling and to intrinsically encourage collaboration and competition.

This paper is organized as follows. Section 2 discusses related work about games development, gaming platform, and their related technologies. The platform which encompasses the system architecture, game engine, gaming data, contents authoring, and social networks are described in Section 3. Section 4 shows some examples of games developed using the platform. Finally, conclusion and future work are presented in Section 5.

2   Related Works On Developing SGs for Education

According to [5], there are two types of approaches in having games for educational purposes: 1) use commercial off-the-shelf games, or 2) use ad-hoc designed games. The first requires purpose shifting of the games since their nature were not intended for educational purposes, whereas the later is more direct. Nonetheless, there are two identifiable obstacles that are commonly met in adopting ad-hoc designed games. Firstly, developing a game is a complex and laborious task which requires detailed elicitation and programming on, for example, game props and mechanics, story line, game world, and characters. Secondly, a game is commonly developed under a very specific purpose which means the reuse of the game components, e.g. game objects/props, is somewhat limited.

Therefore, several game engines are both commercially and freely available to facilitate and to ease game development, such as Torque Game Engine (TGE), Quark, Unity 3D, and Unreal Engine [6, 7] along with their game props. Albeit their abilities to support any game genre development, they still require complex modeling, in particular 3D modeling, and programming experts which are not economical. Moreover, these game engines rely on plug-in which related to cross platforms issues discussed in [7]. This leads to two particular research focuses for educational games:

1) the development of platform for ease to use game creation using pre-created game props 2) the use of advanced web technologies to develop browser games which offers cross platform capability. The first focuses on creating a platform that enables, for instance, instructor to create a specific educational game suits to his objectives by utilizing some pre-created game props such as game objects and characters. An outstanding example on this work is e-Adventure, a game development platform to create a point-&-click adventure game [8, 9] developed using Java technologies. Hence, it can be deployed as standalone application or as an applet for online use. Similar but slightly different application is StoryTec [10], a digital storytelling platform for authoring and experiencing of Interactive and Non-linear Stories. It has compelling potential to be extended as a game platform which offers an insight for this work. The second tries to overcome cross platforms issues by using web technologies playable via common web browsers. Oxyblood developed in [7] is a good example for this case. Oxyblood is a 3D Real Time Strategy (RTS) game for learning how human respiratory system works developed using WebGL, a JavaScript API for rendering 3D graphics. This work highlighted the power of web technologies in constructing a more complex and interactive application which should be exploited for more extensive gaming platform.

One of utmost important works on web technologies is the upcoming HTML5 standard. The work on HTML5 is a joint cooperation between the World Wide Web Consortium (W3C) and the Web Hypertext Application Technology Working Group (WHATWG). According to W3C, this will be the new standard for HTML, XHTML (Extensible Hypertext Markup Language), and the HTML DOM (Document Object Model) [11]. Though HTML5 is still a work in progress, most modern browsers e.g. Safari, Chrome, Firefox, Opera, Internet Explorer have some HTML5 support. A major advantage of HTML5 is that it reduces the need for scripting and the need of external plugins which unlike, for instance, Flash and Java applet. HTML5 create a much richer web applications comparable to desktop applications. Other web technology which has to be noted is Asynchronous JavaScript and XML (AJAX) which contributes to the rise of Web 2.0. One of applications which heavily rely on this technology is the social networks. For instance, Facebook system introduces APIs called Javascript Standard Development Kits (SDK) [12] to connect to their system and to utilize their data.

Those three technologies (WebGL, HTML5, and JavaScript) have grown remarkably with one of notable applications is Google Maps [13]. Moreover, games that are available in Google Play [14] exploit those technologies by combining HTML5, JavaScript, and several images all together [15]. In other words, richly interactive cross platform web applications comparable to desktop applications are already on the way to reality. Thus, we are strongly convinced that such an increasing capability of web technologies in delivering rich interactions should be fully exploited not just for playing casual games, but also for more serious objectives, such as learning and education. The work on this paper tries to fuse both research focuses together. To this end, we create a platform to facilitate ease educational HTML5 SGs construction, i.e. puzzle-it, by exploiting the state of the arts web technologies. We choose to focus on puzzle game since puzzle based learning is extensively studied in [16] for their ability to enhance general development such as logic, memory, problem solving.

3   Platform Development

Puzzle-it, our platform which is still work in progress, comprises of four major components: 1) Game Engine (GE), 2) Gaming Data Management and Interface (GDMI), 3) Game Authoring Tool (GAT), 4) User Profiling and Personalized Learning (UPPL), and Add-Ons. It uses client-server architecture (Fig. 1).

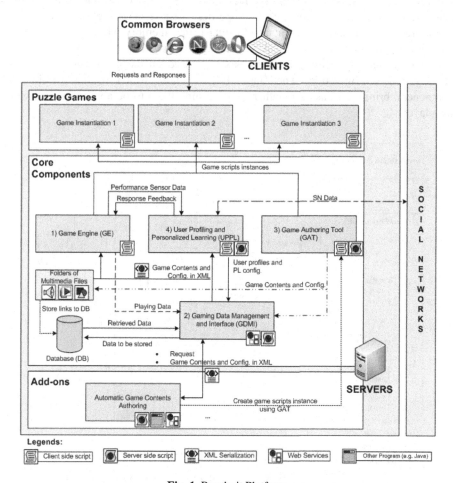

Fig. 1. Puzzle-it Platform

3.1   Game Engine (GE)

The constructed platform exploits the use of images and audio (multimedia files) as game assets to be rendered to the display, an HTML5 Canvas on the common web browser. To this end, a GE was created in JavaScript to regulate the rendering of the game assets. The GE renders the game assets based on their configuration which are provided by GDMI (Fig. 1).

Fig. 2 shows the structure of the GE which consists of 10 main classes as follows. Asset Manager class plays a role in managing game assets by performing assets listing and assets caching, whereas Timer class and Header class are responsible in managing gaming time and gaming information, respectively. Entity class is an abstraction used to represent each individual asset having coordinates as class properties for rendering purpose. This class is then further extended into three different subclasses, i.e. Game Entity class, Feedback Entity class, and Adhoc Entity class having different additional class properties. Case Generator class retrieves the configuration of the game contents by loading it into memory which then the assets are uploaded into the memory by Asset Manager class. Performance Manager class manages the scoring rules and computes score based on the given rules set in the gaming data configuration. The Game Engine class, which resides within GE component, brings all classes together by governing them to be able to interact with the players.

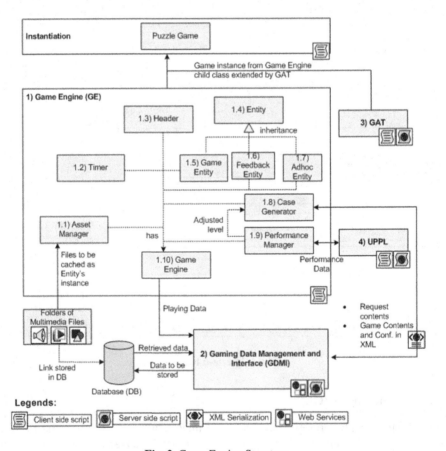

Fig. 2. Game Engine Structure

The Puzzle-it platform supports three different types of interactions i.e. click and play, draw lines, and drag and drop. Click-&-play requires players to click on an object (the correct or the wrong one, according to the problem). Draw lines demands players to draw a line between two objects that are considered as matching between each other. Drag-&-drop asks players to take an object and put it on its right position in a target space. The interaction listeners are implemented as methods within the Game Engine class. The work on these interaction modalities is discussed in [4].

3.2   Gaming Data Management and Interface (GDMI)

GDMI separates GE from the gaming data in the sense that the modification of the database structure and the data does not affect the GE codes. There are three types of gaming data managed by GDMI: 1) game configuration, 2) game contents, and 3) playing data. Game configuration provides the basis game setup which GE needs to follow such as playing rules, type of interaction, etc. Game contents store the list of game assets used and how they should be used within the game. Those data should be created via game authoring tool (GAT). On the other hand, playing data, i.e. playing sessions such as playing score, are produced upon players completing the game. Fig. 3 shows the implementation of GDMI. GDMI was implemented using server-side scripting which one of tasks is to serialize data from the database into XML type. This enables GE to read the game contents and configuration which was implemented in client-side scripting using JavaScript.

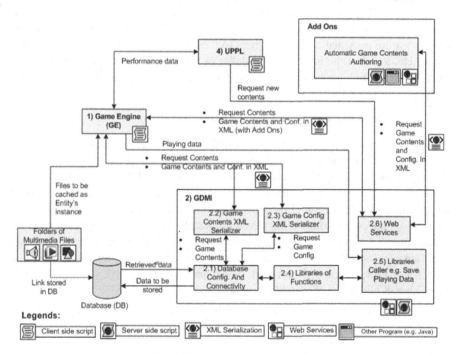

Fig. 3. Implementation of GDMI

Moreover, GDMI provides a list of functions in its libraries to be used to retrieve game information, such as storing playing data, displaying top ten players, displaying the ten best attempts of a player, etc. In order to enable communication with the Add-Ons e.g. automatic game contents authoring implemented in different platforms, a module in form of web service is provided. For instance, in Fig. 3 the web service may request the automatic game contents authoring to provide contents which then it gives response in form of XML format of game contents and configuration. The XML format produced by the automatic game contents authoring should standardized to conform to XML format produces by GDMI modules.

3.3   Game Authoring Tools (GAT)

Albeit this work is still under progress, GAT is essential part of the platform. There are two types of authoring tools which will be constructed i.e. Automatic Content Generator (ACG), as Add-ons, and Manual Contents Generator (MCG). The idea of having ACG derived from the fact that some game assets can be created automatically by providing modules whose outputs comply with XML formats defined by the GDMI specification. This enables third parties to extend GAT which suit to their objectives. On the other hand, MCG is provided to facilitate instructors to create game assets, define scenario and rules according to their didactic plan. An important thing that authors should be aware in creating an engaging game is that they have to follow Malone principles (i.e. provide challenge, curiosity, and fantasy) [17] as well as the flow principle [18]. Hence, the players will be always in the flow by, for instance, giving them adequate challenges according to their skills or inducing their curiosity. Another feature provided by GAT is that GAT enables authors, i.e. course instructors in any field, to select the interaction modality of the created game given the available options of interaction modalities aforementioned.

3.4   Users Profiling and Personalized Learning (UPPL)

Another work in progress besides GAT is UPPL. We divide this component into two modules: 1) User Profiling (UP), 2) Personalized Learning (PL). UP is constructed using available data captured from the social networks platform which is one of contributions of Puzzle-it which currently not available in the state of the arts of serious games for education (Fig. 1). The prolific player's data available in social networks should be exploited alongside with the player's playing data to form a PL module intended specifically for his learning style. To this end, task model and user model are developed to represent the task complexity and the player ability shown in Table 1 and Table 2, respectively. Task model and user model will serve as inputs to PL which will output list of suitable contents presented to a player.

Table 1. Task Model

Metrics	Description of Metrics
Game Level	Difficulty level of the tasks presented (judged by expert or author)
Expected Playing Duration	Expected duration of play
Difficulty Adaptation Range	Range for difficulty level adjustment in order to allow the personalization engine to decrease or increase difficulty level in acceptable range
Entertainment Value	Entertainment value of the task
Educational Value	Educational value of the task
Acquired Knowledge	Knowledge acquired given the content/task
Acquired Skills	Skill acquired given the content/task

Table 2. User Model

Metrics	Description of Metrics
User Level	Knowledge and skill level of a player
Learned Knowledge	Knowledge mastered by a player
Learned Skills	Skills mastered by a player
Average Score	Average score achieved by a player
Average Playing Time	Average playing time consumed by a player to play a game
Misconceptions	Misconceptions of a player deduced from the playing data
Incomplete Tasks	Contents that are not completed by a player

4   Game Samples

In this section, we provide two instances of games developed using Puzzle-it platform. Since GAT is not yet available, we directly inserted game contents and configuration into the database. The first game is being used in Biomedical Engineering BSc course for first year students in University of Genoa. The objective of this game is to support students in learning timing diagram of digital circuit, in particular Flip-Flop circuit.

Fig. 4a shows the presented problem (on the left side) as two images: 1) the image of the circuit (top), 2) the timing diagram which has to be solved (bottom). The list of possible answers is given on the right side of the display which should be dragged and dropped into the empty zones of the timing diagram. Hence, this game categorized as a drag-&-drop puzzle game. The game is available online in [19]. The top-left part in

Fig. 4a shows the title of the game, whereas the top-right part shows the time consumes by a player in playing the game. Bottom-left part shows the number of mistakes the player made during the game progresses and the volume of the background sound, whereas the bottom-right part shows several clickable links which correspond to top ten scores, a player's best score, and top ten players of the game. All of these game assets (i.e. the images, the title text, the timer) were rendered on top of HTML5 canvas.

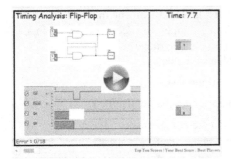 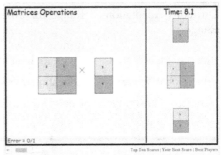

Fig. 4. a) Timing Analysis Game (left), b) Matrices Operation Game (right)

5   Conclusion

This paper presents our work in progress, i.e., a platform for developing educational HTML5 serious games, Puzzle-it. This platform divides the work of game development into two distinct layers i.e. contents authoring and core engine development. Hence, this enables instructors to create contents whereas core engine are provided by the game engine developers. There are four main components of the core engine of Puzzle-it platform: 1) Game Engine (GE), 2) Gaming Data Management and Interface (GDMI), 3) Game Authoring Tool (GAT), and 4) User Profile and Personalized Learning (UPPL). Furthermore, Puzzle-it platform enables game developers to develop add-ons, for instance, automatic content authoring tool, yet they have to comply with communication format in form of XML stated by GDMI. Based on the preliminary use in Biomedical Engineering BSc course, in which we tested out alongside Moodle e-learning platform, there was a necessity to integrate our platform into the e-learning platform. Hence, we will try to elaborate this in the future as part of UPPL component.

Future works will revolve around the implementation of GAT and UPPL. To this end, a mathematical model for personalized learning will be constructed to be attached into UPPL. Moreover, since this work can be viewed as a component based development, Intelligent Tutoring System (ITS) architecture proposed by Clancey's [20] will be used as a benchmark in refining our work.

Acknowledgment. This work was supported in part by the Erasmus Mundus Joint Doctorate in Interactive and Cognitive Environments, which is funded by the EACEA Agency of the European Commission under EMJD ICE FPA n 2010-0012. This work also has been co-funded by the EU under the FP7, in the Games and Learning Alliance (GaLA) Network of Excellence, Grant Agreement nr. 258169.

References

1. Van Eck, R.: Digital game-based learning: It's not just the digital natives who are restless. EDUCAUSE Review 41(2) (2006)
2. Blunt, R.: Does Game-Based Learning Work? Results from Three Recent Studies. In: The Interservice/Industry Training, Simulation & Education Conference (I/ITSEC), NTSA, Orlando, Florida, USA, pp. 945–954 (2007)
3. Zielke, M.A., Evans, M.J., Dufour, F., Christopher, T.V., Donahue, J.K., Johnson, P., Jennings, E.B., Friedman, B.S., Ounekeo, P.L., Flores, R.: Serious Games for immersive cultural training: creating a living world. IEEE Transaction on Computer Graphics and Applications 29(2), 49–60 (2009)
4. Pranantha, D., Bellotti, F., Berta, R., De Gloria, A.: A Format of Serious Games for Higher Technology Education Topics. In: Proceedings of IEEE Conference on Advanced Learning Technologies (ICALT 2012), Rome, Italy (2012)
5. Djaout, D., Alvarez, J., Jessel, J.P.: Classifying Serious Games: the G/P/S model. Medicine (2008)
6. Ritzhaupt, A.D.: Creating a Game Development Course with Limited Resources: An Evaluation Study. Computing 9(1) (2009)
7. Barbosa, A.F.S., Silva, F.G.M.: Serious Games - Design and Development of OxyBlood. In: Proceedings of the 8th International ACM Conference on Advances in Computer Entertainment Technology, ACE (2011)
8. Torrente, J., Blanco, Á., Moreno-ger, P., Martínez-ortiz, I.: Implementing Accessibility in Educational Videogames with <e-Adventure>. In: Proceedings of the First ACM International Workshop on Multimedia Technologies for Distance Learning (MDTL 2009), pp. 57–66 (2009)
9. e-Adventure, e-Learning Group of Universidad Complutense de Madrid, http://e-adventure.e-ucm.es (last accessed in April 2012)
10. Göbel, S., Salvatore, L., Konrad, R.A., Mehm, F.: StoryTec: A Digital Storytelling Platform for the Authoring and Experiencing of Interactive and Non-linear Stories. In: Spierling, U., Szilas, N. (eds.) ICIDS 2008. LNCS, vol. 5334, pp. 325–328. Springer, Heidelberg (2008)
11. HTML 5, W3C, http://www.w3schools.com/html5/html5_intro.asp (last accessed in April 2012)
12. Facebook developers, Facebook, http://developers.facebook.com/docs/sdks/ (last accessed in April 2012)
13. Google Maps, Google, http://maps.google.com (last accessed in April 2012)
14. Google Play, Google, https://play.google.com/store?hl=en&tab=w8 (last accessed in April 2012)
15. Cut the Rope: behind the scene, Zeptolab, http://www.cuttherope.ie/dev/ (last accessed in April 2012)
16. Falkner, N., Sooriamurthi, R., Michalewicz, Z.: Puzzle-based learning for engineering and computer science. IEEE Computer 43(4), 20–28 (2010)
17. Malone, T.W.: What makes computer games fun? Byte 6, 258–277 (1981)
18. Csikszentmihalyi, M.: Flow: The psychology of optimal experience. Harper Perennial, New York (1990)
19. Serious games for learning Elios Lab. UNIGE, http://www.elios.dibe.unige.it/sglearning/ (last accessed in April 2012)
20. Maciuszek, D., Ruddeck, G., Martens, A.: Component-based development of educational games: The case of the user interface. In: Proceedings of the 4th European Conference on Games-based Learning (ECGBL 2010), Reading, UK, pp. 208–217 (2010)

Authoring of Serious Adventure Games in StoryTec

Florian Mehm, Stefan Göbel, and Ralf Steinmetz

Multimedia Communications Lab (KOM), Technische Universität Darmstadt, Germany
{florian.mehm,stefan.goebel,ralf.steinmetz}@kom.tu-darmstadt.de

Abstract. Adventure games, being characterized by a strong focus on narrative, interaction with virtual characters and solving puzzles, are a genre that can be used for Serious Games, especially those in the domain of educational games. However, the creation of a serious adventure game, similar to other game genres when being used for serious purposes, leads to a set of new problems. As new team members (such as domain experts and pedagogues) are added to teams, the common vision of the game can get lost, communication overhead is added and collaboration is harder to achieve. We propose that an authoring tool that integrates the tasks of the various groups found in serious adventure game development into one tool can help in mitigating these problems. We demonstrate this with the authoring Tool StoryTec that was used in re-authoring an existing commercial educational adventure game in StoryTec. Additionally, the integration of an open-source engine for third person adventure games in the authoring tool is shown.

In order to achieve this fully integrated authoring tool, we analyze the current game development processes of adventure games and the state of the art of adventure game authoring tools or editors. These processes are mirrored in the workflows that are captured in StoryTec, structuring the interaction and communication especially between game programmers and designers as well as domain experts. Based on a model for game content, the authoring tool StoryTec is described. The results of one usability and one focus group study show the applicability of the presented approach.

Keywords: Authoring Tool, Digital Educational Game, Adventure Game.

1   Introduction

Serious Adventure Games strive to combine the positive aspects of adventure games with a serious purpose such as education. The adventure game genre is defined by the focus on slow gameplay with comparably few action-laden or timed sequences as compared to other game genres. A strong narrative is used to embed puzzles [6]. Gros [7] established the adventure game as one of seven game genres for educational games. Using this genre for Serious Games has several beneficial aspects. For example, educational content (in the case of educational games) can be transported by means of the strong narrative. It can be embedded in the game world and puzzles by means of the game design and players can take their time in assimilating the presented knowledge due to the absence of time limits. On the other hand, gamers have lower

S. Göbel et al. (Eds.): Edutainment 2012/GameDays 2012, LNCS 7516, pp. 144–154, 2012.
© Springer-Verlag Berlin Heidelberg 2012

expectations on the graphics or effects of adventure games as compared to other genres in which games have to push the limits of current hardware to be accepted, resulting in lower costs for assets and technology. Furthermore, adventure games follow a very common interaction structure and are similar to another concerning gameplay (while content can vary between realistic and fantastical and all literary genres). Therefore, tools for their production exist (see section 2) which aids in the production of the game.

The main field of application of serious adventure games has been in the educational sector, however, several adventure games have also been developed for other purposes, for example advertisement. The genre has received the attention of educators for building educational games both during their initial era of commercial success (see [5]) as well as in recent times [9].

The addition of a serious purpose to a game incurs higher production costs compared to non-educational/purely entertainment-focused games. This results from the additional team members with specialized backgrounds who augment a regular game development team involving game designers, artists and programmers. For an educational game, domain experts as well as pedagogues are added. This addition of team members and roles can then lead to communication problems involving different tools and processes, differing nomenclature or expectations.

We propose to offer a unified authoring tool, integrating the roles sketched here and identified in the following section in one authoring tool. This allows processes to be visible to all team members and collaboration to take place.

In the remainder of this paper we describe our approach to authoring serious adventure games. Sections 2 focuses on the current state of the art of (serious) adventure game production and section 3 on authoring tools for this genre. The concept and implementation of the authoring tool, StoryTec, are described in Section 4, followed by the results of two evaluations of the tool in Section 5.

2   Serious Adventure Games

First examples of serious adventure games stem from the early days of the genre, see for example [5]. In the following, we provide an analysis of the production process of adventure games. For this purpose, the authors interacted with a German developer of educational adventure games and carried out a literature survey, including [1], [8] and [13].

The production of an adventure game is initiated with a phase of game design. During this phase, the game's narrative as the means of binding the puzzles of the game together is written and fleshed out with the help of concept artists. Apart from the story, the main work at this stage is the definition of puzzles the player has to solve and their placement in the game. Since the adventure genre has strong standards concerning gameplay, game designers need not define completely new interaction methods but rather follow the existing conventions. For example, the way in which the player's inventory is managed is very similar in most adventure games, as is the navigation of characters (e.g. via pointing and clicking a mouse cursor).

During the design stage, domain experts for the domain of the Serious Game to be developed should be included, since the game's narrative and puzzles should conform with the serious purpose it is developed for. For example, the narrative could already embed domain knowledge, e.g. by making it historically accurate in the case of an educational game. Puzzles as the main form of interaction for the player should be linked to the purpose of the game, e.g. by reflecting real-world practices that a player should internalize while playing the game.

After this first phase of game development, the actual production of the game is carried out. During this stage, the game's engine is either created or re-used from another source (a previous project, a commercial or freely available engine). Using the engine, programmers implement the game mechanics as specified during the game design phase. Assets (such as virtual character models, images, GUI elements or sounds) are produced based on concept art and the game design and the integrated in the game. This step can involve programmers again, since content has to be integrated with the logic of the game. Adventure game engines commonly use scripting languages for programming at this level. This calls for a user trained in the tools necessary who is able to program in the scripting language of them.

Quality Assurance (QA) is carried out in parallel to the development of the game, with the goal of reducing technical and logical or content-related problems. For serious games, QA also involves assuring that the game is suitable for the serious purpose for the chosen target audience.

3   Authoring Tools for Adventure Games

Authoring tools are used for editing and composing content in various fields, including multimedia computing [4] and e-learning ([3]). They provide simple and customized interfaces that allow authors to work with content and publish it in various forms without author intervention (e.g. when publishing an e-Learning course as an interactive web site).

Several general-purpose authoring tools or game editors for adventure games are available. The free Adventure Game Studio (AGS)[1] has generated a large community of independent adventure game developers. The Visionaire Studio[2] was used in the development of the educational adventure game Winterfest [9].

Authoring tools for adventure games with a serious purpose that include functionalities specifically for this purpose are not found often in the literature. The e-Adventure authoring tool [15] provides the possibility to export a game created with the tool to a Learning Management System [2] and allows authors to create in-game books to transport knowledge textually.

---

[1] http://www.adventuregamestudio.co.uk
[2] http://www.visionaire-studio.net/cms/
adventure-game-engine.html

4   Authoring Adventure Games Using StoryTec

Two versions of StoryTec are described in this paper. One version was used to re-author an existing first-person commercial educational adventure game, using original assets and providing all interaction templates (including a puzzle, see figure 2) used in the original game. The second version recently integrated the Wintermute[3] adventure game engine, allowing the creation of 2D third person adventure games (see figure 4). Therefore, these two variants cover the most common variations of 2D adventure games.

4.1   Game Model

In this section, the model we use for capturing the content of serious adventure games is described. This model is based on the atomic unit of scenes, which are connected via links referred to as transitions. Objects are placed inside scenes to realize scenery, characters or logical objects such as variables, and parameters used to control properties of scenes and objects. Game logic is be configured by high-level commands, referred to as actions, which can be organized sequentially or branching and be conditionally executed. The execution of a sequence of actions is triggered by an event from the game environment, termed a stimulus.

The concept of a scene is chosen as the atomic unit of a game's structure in the model established here. In theater or movies, a scene comprises a small part of the overall narrative, delimited in space by the set or the theatrical scenery, with a set of fixed scene items (props) and a set of actors. Similarly, in this concept, a scene is intended to model a small part of the overall game, containing all objects and logic to capture the interaction of the player while the scene is experienced by the player.

"Object" is the umbrella term for all objects that are visible to the player in the game (images, 3D models, virtual characters, …), other media elements (e.g. sounds) or interactive elements (buttons, text fields, …). Apart from these objects the player interacts with directly, we have chosen to add also logical and control objects under the term "object". These objects include mainly variables (for keeping track of information about the game state) and other objects not directly perceivable by the player such as 3D cameras for a 3D game environment.

In order to model the connections between scenes, the concept of a transition is introduced. A transition is a directional relation between two scenes, indicating that the game can jump from the scene at which the transition starts to the scene at which it ends. Therefore, by adding transitions to the hierarchically organized scene structures, we arrive at a story model that is realized as a directed graph structure.

Game logic is handled by the concepts of stimuli (high-level events that are triggered in the game) and actions that the author specifies to occur when the event is triggered. Actions are aligned sequentially and can be made to be executed conditionally based on the state of the game world or variables.

The intricacies of interaction with the player are handled by the concept of interaction templates (described in section 4.2)

---

[3] http://dead-code.org/home/

For establishing a layer of abstraction above the actual target system (game engine), a "Story Engine" component is used. This engine parses files in which games are encoded according to the model presented here and sends high-level commands based on them to the actual game running on the game engine. Therefore, the technical development of the game is carried out in the game engine, whereas the content production for the game is carried out in the authoring tool by filling configurable game templates. In the case of integrating the Wintermute engine, the Story Engine was connected as a component to the engine, implementing details of actions in terms of Wintermute objects.

4.2   StoryTec

StoryTec integrates the work of the game development roles as described in section 2 into one unified authoring tool. Two possibilities for collaboration in game development teams [16] are acknowledged by this concept. It provides the possibility of a team-wide uniform vision of the game as all members of the team are able to see the whole structure of the game as it evolves and work directly on the game. Furthermore, it removes the bottleneck introduced by the need for programmers to be closely involved in most parts of the game development. The problem created by a plethora of tools being used is alleviated by using only one tool. Figure 1 shows the mapping of tasks from several groups into components of the authoring tool.

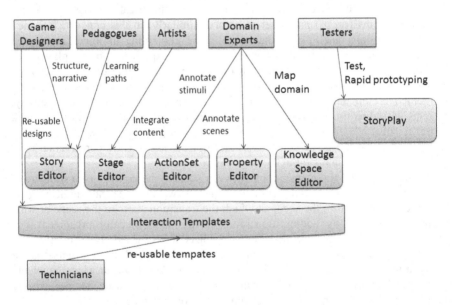

Fig. 1. Some of the possible mappings between user groups and the components of the described authoring tool. Note that not all combinations are shown, for example, game designers could also use StoryTec and StoryPlay in conjunction for storyboarding and rapid prototyping.

By mapping all users into the authoring tool and its components, the authors all share a common work environment and work with the same version of the game instead of everyone working in different tools (text editors, spreadsheets, programming IDEs etc.). The authoring tool then resembles a "virtual blackboard" on which all team members can see their activity along with that of other authors.

The modular authoring tool is composed of several interlinked editors. The first editor to be used commonly by authors is the Story Editor. This editor is used to configure the high-level structure of the game, by breaking down the whole game into a set of scene and defining the transitions between scenes. Figures 2 and 4 show two instances of the StoryTec GUI including the Story Editor.

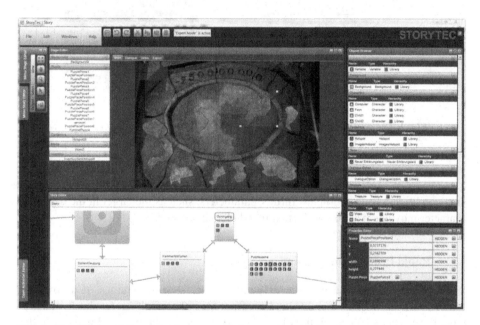

Fig. 2. StoryTec used for authoring a puzzle in an educational adventure game. The editors shown in this figure and figure 4: Stage Editor (upper left), Story Editor (lower left), Objects Browser (upper right) and Property Editor (lower right).

In the Stage Editor, authors work on one specific scene's content in a WYSIWYG fashion. By dragging and dropping, objects from the Objects Browser are instantiated. The central concept behind the Stage Editor is that of interaction templates. Interaction templates are used to encapsulate the actual interaction of the player with the game, in essence the gameplay of the game. An example is a puzzle game, in which the interaction lies in the user dragging puzzle pieces to their correct location and the game signaling whenever the task is completed. An interaction template is programmed by game programmers and then provided in the authoring tool to be filled with arbitrary content by authors. A fitting counterpart from the world of analogue games are "frame games" [14].

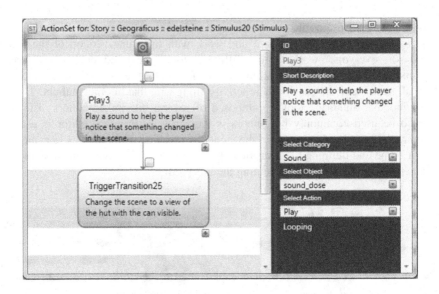

Fig. 3. The ActionSet Editor for configuration of control flow during the game

Actions as described in the previous section are configured in the ActionSet Editor (see Figure 3). Actions are aligned sequentially as well as branching based on run-time conditions. Each action has further parameters, such as the target in the case of a character movement action or the text in a dialogue action.

4.3   Rapid Prototyping, Testing

Rapid Prototyping is the practice of iterating over several versions of a software project such as a game quickly and incorporating the resulting feedback quickly. StoryTec is accompanied by the player application StoryPlay [10], which allows the simultaneous play of a StoryTec created game and the analysis of context information about the game flow and the internal data of algorithms (e.g. concerning adaptation) as well as the creation of log data, which can be evaluated later on. Authors can test game prototypes quickly and react to feedback. Musil et al. [11] call for such an agile approach in order to improve the production of games.

StoryPlay is split into a player aspect and an evaluation aspect. In the player aspect, the game's current state is shown in a playable version with which an evaluator or game tester can interact with. During play, log data and visualizations are created, which can be displayed in the evaluation aspect. Visualizations include the state of variables, the history of previous player choices and the state of internal variables such as the player model.

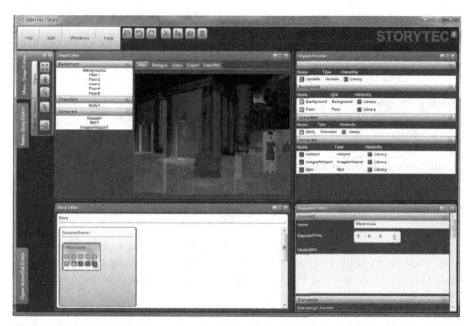

Fig. 4. StoryTec version targeting the Wintermute adventure engine. Red areas indicate interactive areas and the main character, green areas are walkable by the character.

5   Evaluation

In the following, we describe the methodologies and results of two evaluation studies performed on StoryTec.

5.1   Usability Study

The first study was carried out in the form of a usability study involving students recruited from a lecture on Serious Games (N=26, one female). The mean age of the participants was 25.2 years with a standard deviation of 3.71 years. 13 participants stated to have previous experience with authoring tools. The tools that participants referred to included Unity 3D, Blender, 3ds Max, Audacity, Novelty, RPG Maker and Photoshop. The participants' rating of their knowledge of these tools varied strongly, on a scale from 1 to 7 a questionnaire resulted in a mean value of 3.69 (higher values indicate more perceived knowledge) with a high standard deviation of 1.70.

The test was carried out with groups of three participants. In order to motivate the participants to talk about their experience with the software in the style of the "Thinking Aloud"-method, they were given one of three roles, separating the tasks of reading and communicating the instructions ("reader"), executing them on the PC used ("performer") and observing the task and giving input ("observer"). The task consisted of restoring missing elements from a part of an educational adventure game modeled in StoryTec. By design, the users could look up missing elements in the remaining parts of the game and understand concepts based on this.

A questionnaire based on the usability standard ISO 9241-10 was used to allow the participants to rate their experience with the tool. Table 1 shows the mean values and standard deviation of answers grouped in the seven basic principles of the standard.

Table 1. Results of the usability questionnaire (Values range from 1 to 7)

Basic principle	Mean value	Standard deviation
Suitability to the task	4.74	0.88
Self-description	3.51	0.93
Controllability	5.48	0.77
Conformity with user expectations	4.55	1.06
Error tolerance	3.42	0.80
Suitability for individualization	4.42	0.72
Suitability for learning	5.14	0.78

For the purpose of comparing StoryTec with other software tools, measurements from a test on 41 software tools with 1265 users [12]. Comparing the results of the study presented here and that by [12], StoryTec is rated average in all but two criteria (Self-description and Error tolerance).

Participants were asked to rate their perceived knowledge of StoryTec based on their experience in the test. This resulted in a mean value of 2.64 (SD = 1.44), lower than their knowledge of other authoring tools. However, this perception resulted from the very short initial exposure of less than one hour to StoryTec.

5.2   Focus Group Study

Subsequently, a focus group study of StoryTec with the goal of ascertaining whether StoryTec could be used in the context of a game development studio was carried out at a German development studio of educational adventure games. Three participants (aged 31, 37, 46, one female, three male) involved in the game development at the studio took part in this study. The participants were given similar tasks as during the first evaluation, adapted for only one person. Afterwards, the participants took part in individual guided interviews, including questions about the applicability of StoryTec in their fields of work (including game design, graphics and programming). The interview was based on a set of 15 questions, again drawn from and categorized into the criteria of ISO 9241-10. As a result, it can be noted that the experts were interested to hear about the development of StoryTec and, keeping the prototypical state of the system shown to them, they noted that a full version might be used for game development. In the state it was demonstrated to them, they regarded it as suitable for storyboarding and prototyping.

One question of the guided interview asked the participants to judge the applicability of StoryTec in the use case of a teacher using it for the creation of an educational game for class use and for game designers. All participants proposed that StoryTec in the state it was shown to them in was more suitable in the first use case that the second. One participant noted that the simple programming approach and the choice of the genre point and click-adventure were beneficial for this user group, another pointed out the necessity of a German translation for use in Germany. For game designers, the common judgment of the participants was that the present possibilities in StoryTec were yet too limiting on game designers. They noted that they perceived it as a good tool for creating game storyboards (requiring note and text capabilities, as one participant stated) and that it could be well suited in the presented state for hobbyist game designers.

A second question concerned the time that the participants estimated they would require to fully understand and use StoryTec. The answers to this question ("two hours" in two cases, "several days spent building more complex games") indicate that the participants' insight during their short initial exposure to StoryTec allowed them to understand the main concepts of the authoring tool.

Areas that required improvement as indicated by all test participants were the intended usage of the Story and ActionSet Editors, the details of which appeared unclear to the participants. Specific feedback on these editors has been incorporated in newer versions of StoryTec, for example offering more functionality in context menus for authors searching context-related commands there.

6   Conclusion

In this paper, we have described the genre of adventure games as a possible genre to be used for Serious Games. On the one hand, adventure games have very positive properties, especially when used in the educational sector. On the other hand, adventure games, just as other genres of games, lead to a set of typical game development problems.

The basic game model on which StoryTec is constructed was shown, followed by a description of the authoring tool itself. It maps the tasks of the typical members of adventure game development into one unified authoring tool, allowing collaboration and a project-wide uniform vision of the game by using the same interface for all involved users. The practical implementation of two versions of StoryTec has been shown, covering the two major strands of 2D adventure games (first and third person games). For the development of third person games, an existing engine (Wintermute) has been leveraged, thereby extending the reach of StoryTec on the one hand and demonstrating the viability of the software engineering approach of a Story Engine working on a structured game content model on the other hand.

Compared to existing tools (especially intended for serious adventure games as in the case of e-Adventure [15]), StoryTec allows a wider range of game tasks to be added due to the extensibility provided by the interaction template concept. Therefore, a workflow for adding tasks such as the puzzle shown in Figure 3 exists.

The results of two studies were shown, indicating the usability of StoryTec[4] in the domain of educational adventure games.

---

[4] Available for an open community at http://www.storytec.de

References

1. Amory, A.: Building an Educational Adventure Game: Theory, Design and Lessons. Journal of Interactive Learning Research 12(2/3), 249–263 (2001)
2. Del Blanco, A., et al.: Easing Assessment of Game-based Learning with e-Adventure and LAMS. In: ACM Multimedia Workshop, pp. 25–30 (2010)
3. Brusilovsky, P.: Developing adaptive educational hypermedia systems: From design models to authoring tools. Information Sciences, 377–409 (2003)
4. Bulterman, D.C.A., Hardman, L.: Structured multimedia authoring. ACM Transactions on Multimedia Computing Communications and Applications 1(1), 89–109 (2005)
5. Cavallari, B., et al.: Adventure games in education: A review. Australian Journal of Educational Technology 8(2), 172–184 (1992)
6. Dickey, M.D.: Game Design Narrative for Learning: Appropriating Adventure Game Design Narrative Devices and Techniques for the Design of Interactive Learning Environments. Educational Technology Research & Development 54(3), 245–263 (2006)
7. Gros, B.: Digital Games in Education: The Design of Games-Based Learning Environments. Journal of Research on Technology in Education 40(1), 23–38 (2007)
8. Hodgson, P., et al.: Managing the Development of Digital Educational Games. In: Third IEEE International Conference on Digital Game and Intelligent Toy Enhanced Learning, DIGITEL 2010, pp. 191–193. IEEE (2010)
9. Malo, S., Müsebeck, P.: Winterfest - An Adventure Game for Basic Education. In: Workshop-Proceedings Informatik 2: 3rd Workshop on Inclusive E-Learning, pp. 61–65. Franzbecker, Hildesheim (2010)
10. Mehm, F., et al.: Bat Cave: A Testing and Evaluation Platform for Digital Educational Games. In: Proceedings of the 3rd European Conference on Games Based Learning. Academic Conferences International, Reading, UK (2010)
11. Musil, J., Schweda, A., Winkler, D., Biffl, S.: Improving Video Game Development: Facilitating Heterogeneous Team Collaboration through Flexible Software Processes. In: Riel, A., O'Connor, R., Tichkiewitch, S., Messnarz, R. (eds.) EuroSPI 2010. CCIS, vol. 99, pp. 83–94. Springer, Heidelberg (2010)
12. Prümper, J.: Der Benutzungsfragebogen ISONORM 9241/10: Ergebnisse zur Reabilität und Validität. Software-Ergonomie 1997 – Usability Engineering: Integration von Mensch-Computer-Interatkion und Software-Entwicklung, Teubner, Stuttgart, pp. 253–262 (1997)
13. Sommeregger, P., Kellner, G.: Brief Guidelines for Educational Adventure Games Creation (EAGC). In: Sugimoto, M., et al. (eds.) Fourth IEEE International Conference on Digital Game and Intelligent Toy Enhanced Learning, pp. 120–22. IEEE Computer Society (2012)
14. Stolovitch, H.D., Thiagarajan, S.: Frame Games. Educational Technology Publications, Englewood Cliffs (1980)
15. Torrente, J., et al.: Introducing Accessibility Features in an Educational Game Authoring Tool: The <e-Adventure> Experience. In: 2011 IEEE 11th International Conference on Advanced Learning Technologies, pp. 341–343. IEEE (2011)
16. Tran, M.Q., Biddle, R.: Collaboration in serious game development. In: Kapralos, B., et al. (eds.) Proceedings of the 2008 Conference on Future Play Research Play Share, Future Play 2008, pp. 49–56. ACM Press, New York (2008)

Designing an Interactive Storytelling Game

Chun-Tsai Wu[1,2], Szu-Ming Chung[1], and Shao-Shiun Chang[2]

[1] Department of Digital Content Design, Ling Tung University, 1, Ling Tung Rd., Taichung, Taiwan, R.O.C.
[2] Department and Graduate Institute of Industrial Education & Technology, National Changhua University of Education, No.1, Jin-De Road, Changhua, Taiwan, R.O.C.
{ltctht53,smc2006312}@teamail.ltu.edu.tw, chess1@ms8.hinet.net

Abstract. This paper presents a teaching strategy that engages deep learning in game design. The learning objectives include brain storming, researching, setting goals, integrating game structure and storytelling, creating artistic style, and programming. Two students choose a true story—Jack the Ripper—to base their interactive storytelling game. In the meantime, the authors adopt mind mapping tool to help students develop their concept map. Through analyzing the concept map, the authors trace how they work on their project and discover the entire learning process involves problem solving, cooperating, self-challenging, self-exploring, and self-asserting. The authors thus conclude that "Learning by doing" is a significantly effective way of deep learning.

Keywords: Interactive storytelling, Project-based learning, Game design.

1 Introduction

1.1 Graduate Project—Project Based Learning

Project based learning is designed to integrate the deep learning by collaborative learning. Within the department of digital content design of Ling Tung University, all students have to create a production to complete their bachelor degree. This motivates them to have a learning plan from the beginning of their four year university education. In the second semester of the third year, they have to organize a team (from 1 up to 6 members) and come up with a project. In midterm and final weeks, they are required to present the progress to all faculties of this department and the evaluation will be recorded as their midterm and final grades. In their senior year, the project has to be accomplished and displayed in the Young Designers Exhibition held in Taipei. The projects are expected to be digital content design integrating all their designing knowledge and skills learned along with required or selective courses. These project contents categorize as digital film making, web design, 2D/3D animation, and 2D/3D games. This paper intends to present a 3D interactive storytelling game guided by the authors and which is also accomplished within the timeline.

1.2 Concept Map Authoring Tool

A team of two female students decide to create a 3D interactive storytelling game, in which they would apply their knowledge of theory and programming skills. In the

S. Göbel et al. (Eds.): Edutainment 2012/GameDays 2012, LNCS 7516, pp. 155–160, 2012.

beginning, they compare the true story and fiction, and then they realize "Jack the Ripper" can be an unsolved mystery to create a non-linear game. The authors adopt the concept map authoring tool to guide students creating a script and then a major plotline with interrelated sub-plotlines. These two students will be the imagined narrators to create a game that can be replayed and lead to different endings. Through teamwork, all members have to communicate their ideas, discuss possibilities, contribute knowledge and skills, recycle this process, and evolve the ideas until the goal has accomplished.

2   Game Design Project

The entire thinking process of designing a game progresses in two parts as game design and programming. Game design includes game type, development tool, artistic style, and game story script. Programming follows the logic of Giro game and RPG puzzles game. The following section explains in detail.

2.1   Interactive Storytelling and Giro Game

Storytelling is an activity to motivate learning and creativity. The narrator has to use his/her own voice [1] to organize, communicate, and evaluate and transform life experiences [2]. As technology progresses, it changes our lives, learning, and education. Integration of narrative and technology—the digital storytelling—brings a powerful force for educational practice. Integrating digital storytelling in curriculum offers a creative and open environment for students to express views and ideas. Lukosch and et al [1] propose a cooperative storytelling. The concept map assist students to organize knowledge and information [3,4], to increase structural awareness of interleaved information, to help students assess the structure of facts, and potentially to promote storytelling abilities. Interactive storytelling does not depend on a pre-defined story but on related facts and events narrated by users and their interaction with narration. In interactive storytelling game project, the main focus is not on the gameplay but on the interactive applications of interesting narration input.

Giro game is a strategy game, such as the Monopoly. The players possess some investment money, through dicing they get luck cards and earn profits by using trading strategy. Integrating the above ideas, this project has developed a new interactive storytelling game played by a strategy and rules as a giro game. One of the projects is game design. From overall point of view, this interactive storytelling game is plotted as a linear story. The game levels unfold a story. But, based on the random chosen poker cards, the sequential order of the story is actually decided by the players. Equipped by the tool box, the players choose which level they explore first, which gives non-linear story flexibility. The following sections present a case study of developing a non-linear interactive storytelling game.

2.2   Game Story and Structure

The story background is about 19 century (Victorian era) London and its people and culture. In this society, the lowest social rung was full of hypocrisy, poverty, and unjustness. It was a dangerous city for common citizens to live in. The notorious Jack the Ripper made many horrific killings in 1888. London was frightened by this serial killer. Based on historical facts and emotional factors, the player can solve the criminal case (fiction) by playing an interactive storytelling game.

The game is structured by a major plotline and four sub plotlines (Fig. 1). The players must learn about Victorian people and culture in order to win money from mini games to buy needs. The tool shop offers cooking materials and a direction map. After taking care of basic needs, the player can move on by following the direction map to reach the final destination. The dialogs with a bartender reveal knowledge about Victorian people and culture. A non-linear section (free zone) is divided into two areas for collecting clues.

2.3   Interface Design

Start Page. Double clicks to open the selection icon and then six cards will appear. Player can select any card and move step(s) by card number. Each step triggers different events (direction, normal event, sub-event, mission, tool, free zone, and major event).

Gameplay Interface. On the bottom left side of the gameplay interface (Fig. 2) displays a help desk with buttons for the backpack, notebook, map, system menu, main menu, and explanations. The notebook is used to collect all the clues. The map shows the present location. Players can set the volume on the system menu and load, save, close the game. The explanations are also on the main menu.

Gameplay Flowchart. After the beginning animation and drawing cards on the Start Page, the game begins. Depending on different triggered events, the game will bring out scenes. Every mission's results will be recorded and reported. Transitional animations show story development and connect every game scene. The mini game of different levels is for exploring and disclosing directions.

2.4   Artistic Style

Students use 3D and 2D software to present the spectacles of the game. The logo, interface, and NPC are created by 2D software. 3D software is used to create characters, scenes, and animations (Fig. 2). The realistic style is based on British people and culture of the 19th century. Students must possess good drawing skills to reach such a visual style. The amount of drawing parts is extensive. Students continue striving for their own project. Repetitive communication and revising are not hardships for them. Learning is active. They confront the challenges with courage and positive attitudes.

2.5   Programs

The new type of the game combines the unexpectedness and variability of Giro and the logic of a puzzle game. Students choose Flash to integrate and develop the game, and use 3D Max to create characters and backgrounds. Zbrush is used to sculpt and texture. The sound design is achieved by using Nuendo and Adobe Audition. Adobe Photoshop and Illustrator are used to create 2D objects. Post-production is integrated by After Effects. The game is developed by Action Script.

These programs develop Giro game and RPG puzzles. In Giro, the position of the protagonist triggers the five different events—mini game, tool shop, bar, free zone, and major stage. By following the path on Giro, each step triggers different events. The dialogs of NPC module start by the player. Scene module is in charge of changes of scenes.

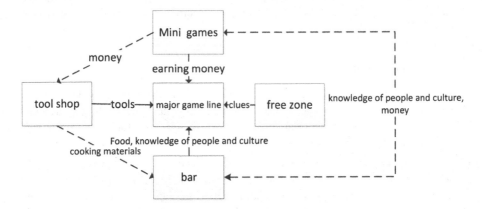

Fig. 1. Game Structure

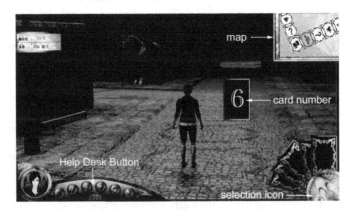

Fig. 2. Gameplay Interface

3   Evaluation

The evaluation process follows the semester schedule. Students are required to finish one thirds of the project in the first semester, to complete the whole project in the second semester, and to display their projects in the graduate exhibition and Young

Designers Exhibition. The grades are divided as project (60% contributed by all faculties), participation (20% contributed by group advising teacher), exhibition preparation (collaborative works distributed to each student, 20% contributed by the elected director of graduate project).

4   Results and Discussions

Before gravitating into theoretical discussions, the authors explain the nature of graduate project required for students majoring in digital content design, which is a deep learning strategy based on the following educational theories.

4.1   The Project Based Learning

Project based learning consist the following features: (1) Project is a complicated mission to challenge problem solving skills, which engages students to design, solve problems, make decisions or research activities; (2) Project based learning provides students with self-motivated works which lasts longer; (3) the final result is to display the products in exhibitions; (4) project based learning provides a simulation of real job situations, solving problems, and practical evaluation through the collaborative learning and reflections [5].

The collaborative learning promotes students' involvement and engagement of learning. The observant should attend to five strategies to promote more effective collaborative learning as follows: participation and contribution, listening and reflecting, explaining and clarifying, discussion and consensus, understanding and non-offending [6]. Even opinion differentiate, effort should be focus on solving problems instead of personal disagreements.

4.2   The Thinking Process

The concept map offers students an opportunity of understanding their own thinking [5,6]. This software can support students' learning. Utilizing related items establishes the learning mission, supporting the plan and execution, and aiding students to understand the mission and learning effects [7]. Through analyzing the concept map of game design project by students, the problems solving process motivates students' creativity and critical thinking. Students experience a repeating process of practicing, discovering problems, and solving them until they accomplish the project.

4.3   The Deep Learning

Learning strategy influences the students' decision making. The individual student would monitor and adjust self perception, motivation, and behavior. Students use different cognitive and metacognitive strategy and resource management to control their learning. Learning strategy, according to knowledge level, divides into deep, surface, and strategic learning. Deep learning strategy links relevant knowledge unit to previous knowledge and tests empirical evidence to support theoretical hypothesis, which is applied to involve related concepts, such as critical thinking and stating feedbacks. Collaborative learning advances individual student's achievement in academy, which motivates more dedication of time and effort in schooling and problem solving than individual learning [8]. Students can identify problems and use their knowledge to find a suitable method to solve problems. From students' feedback on their own project, the authors observe how students face their problems and solve them actively. They face challenges, integrate new knowledge with their own, seek help from teachers, and take time and effort to achieve goals.

4.4   Learning by Doing

The development of creativity requires certain elements, including challenges, resources, and environment. The core of a creative course is an exciting challenge. The teacher should provide students with challenging questions, encourage creative methods, and stimulate their motivation to study. Sufficient resources and collecting related knowledge and information of problems, providing tools and materials for testing, sufficient time for thinking, are factors for creative problem solving. Positive learning environment enlighten a student's new perspective of new concepts and collaborating with others to create.

The graduate project adopts project based learning strategy to motivate students' use of knowledge, skills, and creative power. From observing the case study of these two students, it can be deduced: "learning by doing" is the best way of realizing the true meaning of theory. It lets the students take charge of their own learning, and eventually succeed in accomplishing their project and displaying it in exhibitions.

References

1. Lukosch, S., Klebl, M., Buttler, T.: Facilitating Audio-Based Collaborative Storytelling for Informal Knowledge Management. In: Briggs, R.O., Antunes, P., de Vreede, G.-J., Read, A.S. (eds.) CRIWG 2008. LNCS, vol. 5411, pp. 289–304. Springer, Heidelberg (2008)
2. Liu, C.-C., Liu, K.-P., Wang, P.-H., Chen, G.-D., Su, M.-C.: Applying tangible story avatars to enhance children's collaborative storytelling. British Journal of Educational Technology 43(1), 39–51 (2012)
3. Kwon, S.Y., Cifuentes, L.: The comparative effect of individually-constructed vs. collaboratively-constructed computer-based concept maps. Computers & Education 52(2), 365–375 (2009)
4. Nuutinen, J., Sutinen, E., Botha, A., Kommers, P.: From mindtools to social mindtools: Collaborative writing with woven stories. British Journal of Educational Technology 41(5), 753–775 (2010)
5. Lightner, S., Bober, M.J., Willi, C.: Team-based activities to promote engaged learning. College Teaching 55(1), 5–18 (2007)
6. Reiser, B.J.: Scaffolding complex learning: the mechanisms of structuring and problematizing student work. Journal of the Learning Sciences 13, 273–304 (2004)
7. Jadin, T., Gruber, A., Batinic, B.: Learning with E-lectures: The meaning of learning strategies. Journal of Educational Technology & Society 12(3), 282–288 (2009)
8. Kolfschoten, G., Lukosch, S., Verbraeck, A., Valentin, E., Vreede, G.J.: Cognitive learning efficiency through the use of design patterns in teaching. Computers & Education 54(3), 652–660 (2010)

Towards Puzzle Templates for Multiplayer Adventures

Christian Reuter, Viktor Wendel, Stefan Göbel, and Ralf Steinmetz

TU Darmstadt, Darmstadt, Germany
{christian.reuter,viktor.wendel,stefan.goebel,
ralf.steinmetz}@kom.tu-darmstadt.de

Abstract. Serious Games combine motivating game elements with serious applications like learning, with the genre of Adventure Games being particular suited for this kind of application. Multiplayer Games are also promising for this domain since they allow collaborative learning. This leads to the idea of combining these two elements into Multiplayer Adventures. However, there are hardly any examples of this kind of game, mainly because of the difficulty in designing appropriate puzzles. We therefore developed some ideas on how established puzzle types can be adapted for multiple players, serving as a template for designers who are only familiar with traditional Adventure Games.

Keywords: serious games, multiplayer games, adventure games.

1 Introduction

The idea of Serious Games has been researched for quite some time now. Since puzzles offer a natural way to include learning content, Point-and-Click Adventure Games are especially suited for this purpose [1]. Their slower pace also allows consolidation and rethinking.

Multiplayer Games on the other hand can help to enhance social skills and promote collaborative learning [2]. This leads to the question if it is possible to enrich Adventures with multiplayer-mechanics to further enhance their learning potential.

2 Related Work

There is literature available regarding the design of Adventures [3], Multiplayer Games in the context of collaborative learning [4] or multiplayer puzzles general [5]. However there are hardly any approaches that combine these elements into a Multiplayer Adventure Game. We could only find one example where traditional Adventure gameplay was combined with collaborative puzzles [6]. A major reason for this might be that designing collaborative puzzles is more difficult, as noted during the creation of this game.

S. Göbel et al. (Eds.): Edutainment 2012/GameDays 2012, LNCS 7516, pp. 161–163, 2012.

3   Concepts

As a first approach towards puzzle design for Multiplayer Adventure Games, we took the standard puzzle types described by Grünwald [7] and discussed how each type has to be modified in order to work in a multiplayer setting. We included two more types, physics-based puzzles and quizzes. Since this approach builds on established conventions, it offers developers of traditional Adventures a familiar starting point. These ideas use the previously described concept of player separation and are meant to fulfill the requirements we already extracted from related work [8].

Combination puzzles require the usage of an item from the player's inventory on a specific spot in the game world. In a multiplayer setting items can be bound to one player, creating some kind of skill-based player separation. Another possibility would let the players collect / exchange the items themselves, but constrain the number of items they can carry so they have to distribute them amongst each other. It is important whether the players can see the objects of their partner. If this is not the case, they will have to talk more often. A shared inventory in contrast reduces the need for collaboration.

Inventory puzzles require the combination of two items inside the players' inventories. Therefore they require similar considerations, with the additional constraint that the involved items cannot be bound to different players if exchange is impossible.

For exploration puzzles the player has to find objects or clues in the game world. This search offers a natural reason for collaboration, since splitting up is faster. The game may also uses different movement skills for the player characters to encourage this.

In this dialog puzzles the players have to talk to a non-playable character, often to get an object or information. This is also a good opportunity to introduce skill-based separation, e.g. based on charisma. A puzzle where the players have to take different roles, like the good-cop-bad-cop-principle, is also possible.

Puzzles in which the players have to understand a complicated machine are called machine puzzles. They are a good way to insert learning content for physics, for example about electricity. When multiple players are involved, the machines can become more complex and it is possible to operate different parts simultaneously.

Action sequences, often based on reaction time, are no puzzles in a narrow sense. However, some games use them to add variety. When they are based on other genres, the designer is able to use the multiplayer mechanics already implemented there.

The term classic puzzle describes puzzles from other domains like jigsaw puzzles. Their applicability for multiplayer therefore depends on the original. Jigsaw puzzles for example can already be solved by multiple people solving different sections.

Physics-based puzzle exploits natural phenomena like weight or magnetism and is therefore a good fit for learning content. It can be combined with skill bases player separation, when the characters differ regarding their weight. This kind of puzzle does not only require knowledge, it also offers its application in practical situations.

Quizzes are commonly used to assess the learner's progress. They however threaten to break the immersion and should therefore be used sparsely. In a multiplayer setting this can be done individually or as a group. Voting requires less coordination effort but consensus requires the players to accept a common answer through discussion, which benefits learning.

4   Conclusion

In this paper we presented first concepts on how traditional (singleplayer) puzzle types of Adventure Games can be adapted for multiple players. We believe that these ideas can serve as a foundation for further research on Multiplayer Adventure Games, which seem promising in regards to collaborative learning in Serious Games.

Further work in this direction may include the implementation of concrete puzzles, which then can be evaluated by user studies in comparison to their singleplayer forms. It is also possible to implement them as abstract templates for authoring platforms or game engines, which then can be filled with content by designers.

References

1. Frazer, A., Argles, D., Wills, G.: The Same but Different: The Educational Affordances of Different Gaming Genres. In: Proceedings of the 2008 Eighth IEEE International Conference on Advanced Learning Technologies, pp. 891–893. IEEE Computer Society, Washington, DC (2008) ISBN 978-0-7695-3167-0
2. Voulgari, I., Komis, V.: Massively Multi-User Online Games: The Emergence of Effective Collaborative Activities for Learning. In: 2008 2nd IEEE International Conference on Digital Games and Intelligent Toys Based Education, pp. 132–134 (November 2008)
3. Nelson, G.: The Craft of Adventure (1995)
4. Zea, N.P., Sánchez, J.L.G., Gutiérrez, F.L., Cabrera, M.J., Paderewski, P.: Design of Educational Multiplayer Videogames: A Vision from Collaborative Learning. Adv. Eng. Softw. 40, 1251–1260 (2009) ISSN 0965-9978
5. Kim, S.: Multiplayer Puzzles (2005), http://www.scottkim.com/thinkinggames/multiplayerpuzzles/index.html
6. Manninen, T., Korva, T.: Designing Puzzles for Collaborative Gaming Experience - CASE: eScape. In: Proceedings of the 2005 Digital Games Research Association Conference, p. 15. University of Vancouver, Vancouver (2005)
7. Grünwald, S.: Methoden Interaktivem Storytellings, 1st edn. (2007)
8. Reuter, C., Wendel, V., Göbel, S., Steinmetz, R.: Multiplayer Adventures for Collaborative Learning With Serious Games. Accepted at: 6th European Conference on Games Based Learning (ECGBL 2012) (2012)

Context-Sensitive User-Centered Scalability: An Introduction Focusing on Exergames and Assistive Systems in Work Contexts

Oliver Korn[1], Michael Brach[2], Albrecht Schmidt[3],
Thomas Hörz[1], and Robert Konrad[4]

[1] University of Applied Sciences Esslingen, Esslingen, Germany
`{oliver.korn,thomas.hoerz}@hs-esslingen.de`
[2] University of Muenster, Institute of Sport and Exercise Sciences, Muenster, Germany
`michael.brach@wwu.de`
[3] University of Stuttgart, VIS, Stuttgart, Germany
`albrecht.schmidt@vis.uni-stuttgart.de`
[4] KTX Software Development, Egelsbach, Germany
`robert@ktx-software.com`

Abstract. This paper introduces an approach for implementing context-sensitive user-centered scalability (CSUCS) into interactive applications using motion recognition. With scalability we refer to a system's ability to adapt to the physical and cognitive abilities of a specific user. We discuss an adapted HAAT-model (Human Activity Assistive Technology Model) and the flow concept and show their use in two prototypical implementations: An "exergame" enriching sports exercises for the elderly and an assistive system using gamification elements to enrich the working experience of impaired and elderly persons.

Both systems have in common that they use motion detection and mechanics from game design (gamification). They transparently adapt to and visualize the users' performance. The real-time analysis of the users' movements is a prerequisite for the successful implementations of CSUCS.

Keywords: Assistive technology, User-Centered Design, Human Computer Interaction (HCI), Human Machine Interaction (HMI), Elderly, Gamification, Exergame, Serious Games, Augmented Reality.

1 Introduction

Many sensor-based systems are able to adapt to changing contexts. A good example is the dynamic route finding of navigational systems in cars. However, these systems often fail to integrate the user – most navigation systems will not detect if the user is tired and recommend a pause. Systems being able to take into account both the context and the user in real time offer better assistance, more security and potentially more fun. The main aim of the present paper is to introduce a conceptual approach called "context-sensitive user-centered scalability" (CSUCS). We illustrate the coverage of this concept by presenting two example applications.

S. Göbel et al. (Eds.): Edutainment 2012/GameDays 2012, LNCS 7516, pp. 164–176, 2012.
© Springer-Verlag Berlin Heidelberg 2012

In order to create games or assistive systems that challenge or support users adequately, these solutions have to scale with the users' abilities and dispositions. The system should adapt to changes both in performance and skill. To achieve this scalability, our approach uses "gamification", i.e. elements and mechanisms typically used in game design are integrated into "serious" applications.

A system that offers user-centered scalability needs to assess the actions of the users in real-time. This requirement is an essential part of traditional games where the game creates a virtual context and the user interacts with it by using a controller. At the same time assessment in real-time is an open research question for computer-supported exercises and work experiences, where the real world is the context and the users' interaction with a computer is peripheral to the key activity. Hence we apply our conceptual approach to the following examples which reflect this research question:

1. an "exergame" combining play and exercise to enrich preventive exercises for the elderly (see Bogost 2005 for a historical review of exergames). The main feature of this application is to implement modern principles of exercise science without a human instructor present. Thus high-quality exercises can be performed by users who are not able or willing to join typical group-based exercises.
2. an assistive system using gamification elements to enrich the working experience of impaired and elderly persons. In this field, the challenge is to utilize the potential of the user who faces impairments or handicaps.

Main characteristics of the example applications are to adapt feedback and assistance in order to enable and maintain a given performance in the working environment, and to adapt task difficulties in order to meet the user's abilities and goals in the exercise environment. In both fields of application, human-computer interaction (HCI) is realized as natural interaction (NI), so that the user's body becomes the "controller". This choice was made because consciously using a controller does cause distraction from the correct performance of the required actions (i.e. balance exercises or manual assembly work). Using NI as the primary mode of interaction is a new option – it draws strongly from advances in motion recognition (summarized amongst others by Shotton et al. 2011) allowing permanently tracking and interpreting human body movements.

After describing the motivation and the requirements we introduce an adapted HAAT-model (Human Activity Assistive Technology Model) and the concept of flow used for designing the gamification elements. Then we portray two prototypical implementations of context-sensitive user-centered scaling (CSUCS) as announced above.

2   Motivation

We consider the CSUCS approach a general concept which can be used for persons of all ages and skill levels. In this paper, however, we exemplarily apply it to two groups who are in special need of individualized assistance: elderly and impaired persons.

With "impaired" we refer not only to elderly persons showing typical age-related problems but also to strongly impaired and disabled persons who require special support by caretakers. To some extent these groups share common problems which are due to three reasons:

1. the general reduction of physical health in older age, especially the loss of muscle, power balance and cardio-respiratory abilities   (Nelson 2007)
2. the gradual reduction of short term memory first shown by Anders (1972)
3. defined problems in sensorimotor control (Goble et al 2009), caused by morbidities, degeneration (Freiberger et al. 2011) or accidents (Farrow & Reynolds 2012)

The groups do not only share members, their members also share common interests: It is their aim, as well as the aim of their caretakers and society as a whole, that they lead a life as autonomous and independent as possible (Betz 2010). Goals as staying independent, prevention from falls and the need of care are not imaginable without personal movement and physical activity as well as an assistive environment. Although these requirements are becoming well established, another important aspect of life is currently underrepresented: workplaces (Brach & Korn 2012).

Meanwhile, elderly workers are considered to be valuable due to their experience and accountability. As a consequence of their health problems, however, many elderly workers retire earlier than they legally are obliged to and often also earlier than they want to (Steg 2006). They suffer from health impairments and frequently also from slight cognitive impairments like reduced short term memory. These impairments increase the effects, repetitive and potentially dull work processes already have: they are prone to human errors and mistakes. We argue that using games and gamification thus has a great potential for the targeted users in both contexts (sports and work). Without a motivating approach these user groups may have great difficulties:

- they may resign to perform the required actions at all (skipped sports exercises, early work retirement)
- they may perform poorly and suffer accidents and injuries or produce errors in production

By utilizing the potential of games, meaning and purpose can be added to potentially dull activities. However in order to succeed, gamification of sport and work contexts does not suffice: the systems have to adapt or scale to meet the competences of individual users.

3   Requirements

Context-sensitive user-centered scaling (CSUSCS) is a method to adapt challenges in sports and work to the individual level of competence. Although this user-specific adaptation sounds natural, it actually differs from most systems currently used: if the user can alter the challenge a system poses at all, he or she has to deliberately choose a difficulty setting (games) or a support level (assistive systems).

However the main philosophy behind user-centered design is to build software "around" the users' needs,   limitations and intentions instead of forcing them to adapt their behavior to the software or assess their personal strengths by selecting a difficulty. Especially with seniors and impaired persons the physical and mental state can vary considerably from one day to the next or even within a few hours. Often they are not consciously aware of these sudden changes. Thus it is an essential requirement that the systems scale accordingly and measure the user's actual behavior in real-time (versus his or her self-perceived competence).

A second requirement is that the changes in difficulty (and thus challenge) level resulting from this scaling are both transparent and motivating or at least unobtrusive. Especially the reduction of challenge due to a context where the user repeatedly fails to reach the targets (by making errors in the sports exercises or in the assembly sequence) has to be communicated in a way that does not add to the frustration caused by the mistakes but support and mentally bolster the user. Meeting these requirements can help to utilize potentials for individual improvements.

4   Model

4.1   Human Activity Assistive Technology Model

When designing the appropriate interventions for the users in both contexts (motivating elements in sports and work), we assumed that both applications, i.e. the exergames and the production wizard can be interpreted as assistive systems. For this reason we used the Human Activity Assistive Technology Model (HAAT, Cook & Hussey 1995) based on the basic Human Performance Model (Bailey 1989). The HAAT-model (figure 1) describes four basic components: activity (areas of performance, e.g. work, play, school), human ("intrinsic enabler", including skills), assistive technology ("extrinsic enabler") consisting of human-technology interface (HTI), activity output, processer and environmental interface, and context (setting, social, cultural, physical).

These components have been mapped to the current approach (figure 2). The assistive technology of the work and the training contexts share several sub-components as follows.

While the HTI and the processor are realized by the traditional combination of a computer with a display and audio output, the new approach focuses on (a) the environmental interface (realized by natural interaction NI, i.e. human body tracking) and (b) the activity output, which is enriched by gamification. The use of NI allows continuous movement analysis and thus almost real-time intervention – an important requirement in both the work and the training context, where errors can lead to accidents. NI also led to an addition to the model (figure 2, green dashed arrow): Since the user's body becomes the direct controller without the need of purposeful or even conscious interaction, the environmental interface directly interacts with the user. This implicit interaction is helpful in both contexts, because errors will also often be performed unconsciously and without notice.

At the same time NI allows to meet the requirement that the system scales to meet the user's current competence level – even if the self-assessment was different or the performance level changes within a single day and unnoticed by the user due to the strong variation of physical and mental states.

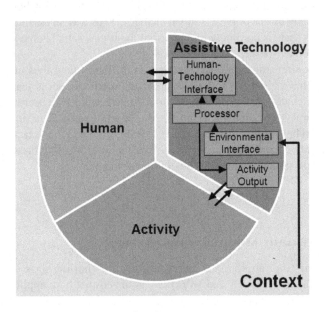

Fig. 1. The Human Activity Assistive Technology Model (HAAT, Cook & Hussey 1995)

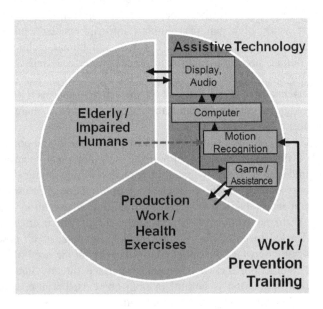

Fig. 2. The adapted and enhanced HAAT-model used in the CSUCS approach

4.2   Flow

In the context of this paper gamification is seen as a means to achieve "flow" – a mental state in which a person feels fully immersed in an activity, experiencing energized focus and believing in the success of the activity. It is an area where high skill and adequate challenge converge, first proposed by Csíkszentmihályi in 1975. According to a model presented by Csíkszentmihályi et al. (2005) there are four conditions necessary to achieve the flow state:

- One must be involved in an activity with a clear set of goals. This adds direction and structure to the task.
- One must have a good balance between the perceived challenges of the task and the own perceived skills. One must have confidence to be capable to do the task.
- The task at hand must have clear and immediate feedback. This helps negotiate changing demands and allows adjusting performance to maintain the flow state.
- The activity is intrinsically rewarding, so there is a perceived effortlessness of action.

The use of NI allows the immediate feedback required for the flow state. The concept of flow and its implications when applied to work environments are described in more detail by Korn (2012). In the context of this paper, user centered scaling can be interpreted as a means to sustain the flow state even if the performance in work or sports drops suddenly.

5   An Exergame for the Elderly

In the first of the two prototypical implementations context-sensitive user-centered scalability (CSUCS) was applied in an exergame for the elderly which is part of a research project called "motivotion60+" (www.motivotion.org). The project and the corresponding program AAL (Ambient Assisted Living) is described in more detail in Brach & Korn 2012. The project aims to integrate prevention exercises into the everyday lives of senior citizens (figure 3, for an overview see Wiemeyer & Kliem 2012). In order to meet the large heterogeneity of interests and capabilities between users as well as their change over time, the system should be extremely flexible.

To make the prevention exercises motivating, they were integrated in seven mini-games, linked by a virtual journey to interesting cities like Rio or Rome. The mini-games are based on exercises for improving balance and strength – areas helping to prevent the elderly from falls. Details on the exercise conception and training configuration are discussed by Brach et al. (2012).

The environmental interface (HAAT-model) is realized by sensor-based body tracking. Thus within the exergames the seniors' do not have to focus on using interfaces or controllers – the body becomes the controller in natural interaction (NI).

Fig. 3. Users from the target group of the elderly performing exercises during an evaluation of the prototype

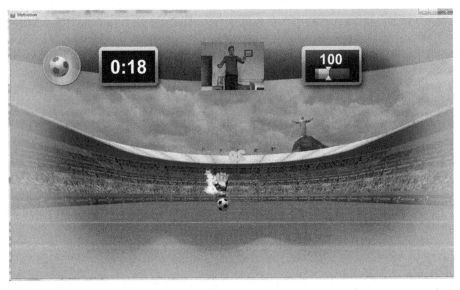

Fig. 4. Currently the user successfully prevented a goal in the soccer game situated in Rio. For this reason the screen receives a temporary green overlay.

When a user starts the game for the first time, the training parameters can either be a standard set or have been individually adapted to the user before. However the difficulty is always set to the lowest level to prevent early frustration. During the exergame the user receives points for successful activities (like catching a ball or grabbing a coin) and sometimes lose points (e.g. by failing to catch a ball or by ramming opponents). These points are the product of the user's level and a constant. Obvious and motivating visual feedback guides the seniors:

- right actions trigger a green screen overlay, wrong actions trigger a red one
- accordingly points are represented as rotating numbers in green or red
- a progress meter on the top right screen (fig. 4) always shows if the current performance will reduce (red), retain (yellow) or increase the level (green)

This consistent visualization keeps the scaling process transparent and motivates the user. Apart from this dynamic visualization there is a results screen after each exercise, where substantial improvements or degradations of the performance are commented in a friendly and humorous manner and recorded in the database immediately. The difficulty level then scales according to the user's current performance to prevent underchallenge or overexertion.

Although the user is informed about these changes in level, their swiftness in both ways makes it easier to accept degradation on a bad day and thus the auto-adjustment prevents declines in motivation. Rather than comparing performances between different users via highscores as in regular entertainment games, the system highlights the individual progress and motivates the users by positive feedback like achievements represented in decorative medals or cups.

The soccer game is a good example for context-sensitive user-centered scalability. The following parameters can be adapted to change the exercise's difficulty:

- size of the goal area: extent of movement the user has to perform in order to catch or to ward off a ball
- frequency of shots: ability to focus attention quickly to the new situation
- ball velocity: user's reaction speed
- flight characteristics – although all balls are shot in a random angle, both the height of the flight path and the option to bounce are parameterized: user's reaction speed and cognitive ability in anticipating the flight path

The logic rules and boundaries for changing levels are stored externally from the source code in Lua-files. Lua is a "lightweight" programming language mostly used as a scripting language. The code fragment (figure 3) shows how the LUA is integrated into the code of the soccer game and how the ball's speed is regulated there:

```
void kickBall() {
    speed.x() = config().soccerSpeed();
    speed.y() = Random::get(20, 60) / 1000.0f;
    speed.z() = Random::get(-20, 20) / 1000.0f;
}

void checkFloorCollision() {
    if (position.y() < floorHeight) {
        position.y() = floorHeight;
        speed.y() = -speed.y();
    }
}

void moveBall() {
    speed.y() -= 0.001f;
    position += speed;
    rotation += speed.getLength();
    checkFloorCollision();
}
```

Fig. 5. The C++ code fragment integrating LUA-code. It initializes the ball's speed (kickBall), correspondingly adjusts the ball's speed and rotation (moveBall) and adds momentum on collisions with the ground level (checkFloorCollision).

Within the realized prototype, the variations between the exercises manifest in only three difficulty levels – a more granular implementation of context-sensitive user-centered scalability (CSUCS) is subject of future research and would strongly benefit from higher resolution depth cameras.

6   Work-Related Gamification for the Impaired and the Elderly

The second of the two CSUCS implementations portrayed is a new kind of assistive system for production workplaces. Most users of this new system are employed in sheltered work organizations – i.e. their age varies, but they suffer from cognitive and physical impairments. Currently many of them cannot assess their full potential because working in more demanding tasks would require almost permanent observation. This is due to the enormous variation in workers' physical and mental state from day to day or even from hour to hour. However, a one-to-one ration of caretakers and workers cannot be financed.

At this point autonomous assistive systems come into play. Current assistive systems only show instructions and check if the "picks" (picking components from boxes, figure 6) are correct. They cannot assess the tasks in more detail and focus on controlling the results at the end of a work sequence. Our experience shows that providing continuous and context-sensitive feedback in real-time within the tasks is much more helpful especially to impaired and elderly users. The assistance has to change from a summary to a process-oriented approach.

Fig. 6. An assembly worker in an experiment designed to test the creation of context-sensitive interventions by using motion recognition

When designing for impaired and elderly persons, HCI has to become more natural and user-centered. Like the exergame the assistive system realizes the environmental interface (HAAT-model) by directly tracking the user's movements. This is pre-requisite for the process-oriented assistive systems in production environments (ASiPE, cf. also Korn et al. 2012, Brach & Korn 2012) which use motion sensors to allow permanent assistance.

Our design goal is that, like the anti-lock braking system in cars, the system should stay in the background most of the time and intervene only if an error occurs – however in that case the intervention needs to be triggered as soon as possible. This requires the system to permanently check the user's performance compared to previous tasks and to the average performance. Only this permanent comparison allows the flexibility to scale down or scale up if a worker's physical or mental state undergoes a change, like an impaired worker suddenly producing twice as fast as usually. The system then should still be able to guide him through the assembly process.

The benefits of process-orientation and real-time interventions come with ethical questions (which are not the focus of this paper). The motion data generated cannot only be used for the assistance – potentially it allows a very detailed analysis of the individual performance. For our research the system was developed as a black box only focused on assisting a single user and not comparing users or reporting mistakes.

Like in the exergame, the process of scaling is made transparent by gamification elements. Based on the predetermined assembly sequence, each work process is visually represented by a brick in a puzzle game resembling Alexey Pajitnov's classic Tetris (figure 7). Motion tracking allows to compare the pre-recorded work process with the user's actual movements in real-time and adjust the brick's downward movement speed accordingly, so a slow performance of a work process results in a slowly descending brick. The user's average process speed is represented by a grey brick, so he or she can check anytime how the process completed so far compares to the personal average. The "shadow brick" parallels the exergame's progress meter thus enabling users to compare their current performance to previous ones.

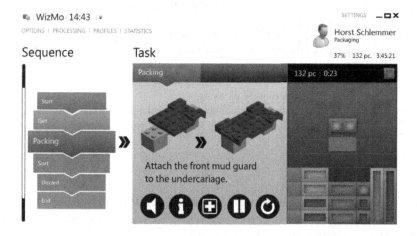

Fig. 7. Metro-oriented Design of the gamification element "WizMo"

After a certain number of sequences are completed, the build-up brick rows disintegrate. Both the intensity of this visual feedback and the number of resulting points are based on the number of green bricks, i.e. the performance. If the resulting daily and weekly high scores exceed certain values for a longer period, the assistive system allows to "raise the bar" by reducing the underlying process durations. This increase of aspiration effort effectively motivates the user, since underutilization leads to boredom and a feeling of lacking appreciation (McGonigal 2011: 29). The change will be made transparent and has to be accepted by the worker – but since the "level-up" is a direct result of good work performance it should also result in monetary or other adequate compensations.

The changes in performance and the resulting trends can help to find hidden strengths: especially impaired workers are often assigned processes which do not adequately access their potential. Here the system increases transparency, e.g. if a certain type of work process is dark green while the others are red. Thus a hidden strength (previously hidden in an average result) is revealed, helping the worker to get access to new challenges (i.e. more demanding tasks) and better wages.

Since a motivating implementation is considered essential for both user acceptance and performance improvement, the approach meticulously addresses the conditions for achieving the flow state:

Table 1. Flow: Condition and implementation

Condition	Implementation
being involved in an activity with a clear set of goals	(i) macro level: complete a (flawless) assembly sequence (ii) micro level: complete the active process (brick movement) as quick (green) as possible
good balance between perceived challenges and perceived skills	(i) starting difficulty level based on average user competence (ii) adjustable process durations (e.g. shorter durations / more demanding sequences)
task must have clear and immediate feedback	(i) color changes and shadowing dual-code visual feedback (ii) (optional) sound integrates another sensory channel
the activity is intrinsically rewarding	(i) on the micro level "getting a brick down" quickly is immediately pleasing (ii) the final disintegration of the built brick sequence appeals to the basic human desire for order and completion

7   Conclusion

In this paper we introduced an approach for context-sensitive user-centered scalability (CSUCS). It is based on an adapted and enhanced HAAT-model and the concept of flow. Two implementations have been described:

1. an exergame enriching sports exercises for the elderly
2. an assistive system enriching assembly work for impaired and elderly persons

Both prototypes share the use of mechanics adapted from game design (gamification) and the use of motion detection systems. Interpreting the user's movements in real-time allows implicit and natural interaction (NI). NI enables an almost immediate scaling of the challenge according to the users' actual performance without demanding conscious interaction on the side of the user. This "unconscious" or implicit interaction is essential in both implementations, because errors will often be performed unconsciously and without notice.

Both the exergame and the assistive system transparently adapt to and visualize the users' performance. Our results strongly suggest that in spite of the real world contexts, the CSUCS approach creates an immersive and game-like experience.

The next research steps include elaborate empirical tests to evaluate the user's acceptance level and the systems' robustness with respect to quick variations in context and user performance. Another line of research is the generalization of the approach for other contexts and target groups.

References

1. Anders, T.R., Fozard, J.L., Lillyquist, T.D.: Effects of Age Upon Retrieval from Short-term Memory. Developmental Psychology 6(2), 214–217 (1972)
2. Bailey, R.W.: Human Performance Engineering Using Human Factors/Ergonomics to Achieve Computer System Usability, 2nd edn. Prentice Hall, Englewood Cliffs (1989)
3. Betz, D., Cieslik, S., Dinkelacker, P., Glende, S., et al.: Grundlegende Anforderungen an AAL-Technologien und -Systeme. In: Meyer, S., Mollenkopf, H. (Hrsg.) AAL in der alternden Gesellschaft. Anforderungen, Akzeptanz und Perspektiven, Berlin, pp. 63–108 (2010)
4. Bogost, I.: The Rhetoric of Exergaming (2005), http://www.exergamefitness.com/pdf/The%20Rhetoric%20of%20Exergaming.pdf
5. Brach, M., Korn, O.: Assistive Technologies at Home and in the Workplace – A Field of Research for Exercise Science and Human Movement Science. EURAPA (European Review of Aging and Physical Activity) 9 (2012), doi:10.1007/s11556-012-0099-z
6. Brach, M., Hauer, K., Rotter, L., Werres, C., Korn, O., Konrad, R., Göbel, S.: Modern Principles of Training in Exergames for Sedentary Seniors: Requirements and Approaches for Sport and Exercise Science. International Journal of Computer Science in Sport (IJCSS) 11, 86–99 (2012)
7. Csikszentmihalyi, M., Abuhamdeh, S., Nakamura, J.: Flow. In: Elliot, A. (ed.) Handbook of Competence and Motivation, New York, USA, pp. 598–669 (2005)
8. Cook, A.M., Hussey, S.M.: Assistive Technologies: Principles and Practice. Mosby, St. Louis (1995)
9. Farrow, A., Reynolds, F.: Health and Safety of the Older Worker. Occupational Medicine 62(1), 4–11 (2012)
10. Freiberger, E., Sieber, C., Pfeifer, K.: Physical Activity, Exercise, and Sarcopenia - Future Challenges. Wiener Medizinische Wochenschrift 161(17-18), 416–425 (2011)
11. Goble, D.J., Coxon, J.P., Wenderoth, N., Van Impe, A., Swinnen, S.P.: Proprioceptive Sensibility in the Elderly: Degeneration, Functional Consequences and Plastic-adaptive Processes. Neuroscience & Biobehavioral Reviews 33(3), 271–278 (2009)
12. Korn, O., Schmidt, A., Hörz, T.: Assistive Systems in Production Environments: Exploring Motion Recognition and Gamification. In: Proceedings of the ACM PETRA 2012 (2012)
13. Korn, O.: Industrial Playgrounds. How Gamification Helps to Enrich Work for Elderly or Impaired Persons in Production. In: Proceedings of the ACM EICS 2012 (2012)

14. McGonigal, J.: Reality is Broken: Why Games Make Us Better and How They Can Change the World. Random House, London (2011)
15. Nelson, M.E., Rejeski, W.J., Blair, S.N., Duncan, P.W., Judge, J.O., King, A.C., Macera, C.A., Castanda-Sceppa, C.: Physical Activity and Public Health in Older Adults. Recommendation from the American College of Sports Medicine and the American Heart Association. Circulation 116, 1094–1105 (2007)
16. Shotton, J., Fitzgibbon, A., Cook, M., Sharp, T., Finocchio, M., Moore, R., Kipman, A., Blake, A.: Real-Time Human Pose Recognition in Parts from Single Depth Images. In: Proceedings of the IEEE Computer Vision and Pattern Recognition, CVPR (2011)
17. Steg, H., Strese, H., Loroff, C., Hull, J., Schmidt, S.: Europe is Facing a Demographic Challenge. Ambient assisted living offers solutions. Report compiled within the Specific Support Action "Ambient Assisted Living", Berlin (2006)
18. Wiemeyer, J., Kliem, A.: Serious Games in Prevention and Rehabilitation – A New Panacea for Elderly People? European Review of Aging and Physical Activity 9, 41–50 (2012)

The Impact of Different Gaming Interfaces on Spatial Experience and Spatial Presence – A Pilot Study

Anna Lisa Martin[1] and Josef Wiemeyer[2,*]

[1] Graduate School Topology of Technology, Technical University of Darmstadt, Germany
martin@ifs.tu-darmstadt.de
[2] Institute of Sport Science, Technical University of Darmstadt, Germany
wiemeyer@sport.tu-darmstadt.de

Abstract. The general aim of the pilot study was to analyze and compare the impact of different game interfaces on spatial experience and spatial presence in digital games. The study is based on a generic framework integrating different theories and empirical results of the first pilot study of the research project. In the pilot study selected questionnaires were completed after playing two digital beach-volleyball games. Results show that there are differential influences of game interfaces on spatial experience and presence (self-location). Furthermore, we found an impact of different interfaces on flow experience.

Keywords: Digital Sports Games, Technology-mediated Game Experience, Spatial Experience, Spatial Presence.

1   Introduction

The proposed paper focuses on the recently published interaction devices in digital games and their impact on spatial presence and experiences of space while playing digital beach-volleyball games on two different consoles. Several approaches address the game experience ([4],[9]) and the experience with digital sports games in general. Nacke [8] compared two different controllers (Sony gamepad vs. Wiimote) in a third person shooter. He found a higher level of self-location in the Wiimote condition but no difference concerning game experience. Furthermore, he found relations between selected EEG parameters and spatial presence both in the Sony and the Wiimote conditions. Whereas EEG was related to possible actions in the Sony condition, EEG was related to self-location in the Wiimote condition. Limperos et al. [5] compared two different consoles (Sony Playstation 2 vs. Wiimote) in a football game. The authors found significantly higher feelings of enjoyment and control with the PS2 controller. Gerling et al. [2] compared the impact of different controllers (PC mouse and keyboard vs. analog stick controls) on game experience in first person shooter games. Whereas the authors found no differences between the controllers, preference for controllers had a significant impact on game experience. Regardless of the controller the participants reported a greater challenge, more engagement and more usability issues when playing with their non-preferred controller.

---

[*] We'd like to thank G. Kollegger and Th. Eckhardt for their support in this study.

S. Göbel et al. (Eds.): Edutainment 2012/GameDays 2012, LNCS 7516, pp. 177–182, 2012.
© Springer-Verlag Berlin Heidelberg 2012

The reported studies address the issue of game experience in a broad way. Space, spatial experience and the experience of spatial presence have only rarely been addressed in game research yet. In this pilot study a space-based theoretical background and a new methodological instrument is used in combination with existing research instruments. The complex interactions of the player, the technology (interface) and the game are illustrated by the following generic framework (Figure 1).

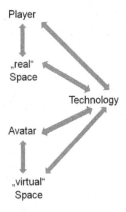

Fig. 1. Generic framework of interactions between player, technology and gameplay in digital games (Source: Martin & Wiemeyer, 2012, p. 136)

While playing digital games the player experiences a technology-mediated environment ('virtual' space) in addition to her directly perceived environment ('real' space). The technical device as a mediator makes it possible for the player to influence the 'virtual' world by her actions in 'real' space. The transformation rules of the player's own movements to movements of the avatar and the resulting virtual feedback need to be experienced to control the game. With the introduction of new controllers allowing a more intuitive whole-body interaction with the game the general question arises how the complex interactions illustrated in Figure 1 are experienced by the player.

2   Theoretical Background

Several theoretical approaches from cognitive psychology, computer science, and movement science are relevant to the generic framework. In this paper only those approaches are discussed in more detail that are relevant for the pilot study.

Game experience is a complex concept comprising immersion, tension, competence, flow, emotions or affects, and challenge [9]. The "Game Experience Questionnaire" (GEQ) has been developed to assess these components [9]. 'Flow' means the experience of total absorption by an activity [1]. The focus of attention is centered in this activity. Flow happens within a corridor of an optimal combination of challenge and skill, i.e., between boredom and anxiety and is experienced very individually. Sweetser and Wyeth [11] established the concept of game flow. According to this approach, the game flow comprises eight elements: concentration, challenge, skills, control, clear goals, feedback, immersion and social interaction [11]. Because these factors are not stable during a game session, the flow experience can change. For exergames, Sinclair, Hingston, and Masek [10] suggested a dual-flow model taking into consideration a skill-challenge and a fitness-intensity relationship. Flow is also coupled to the spatial presence [12]. Presence denotes the subjective feeling of 'being there' in an environment (overview: [6]). Wirth et al. [12] proposed a two-level Process Model of Spatial Presence (PMSP) which addresses antecedents and dimensions of spatial presence. The PMSP is the basis of the so called "Measurement, Effects, Condition - Spatial Presence Questionnaire" (MEC-SPQ). The MEC-SPQ consists of 8 dimensions: Focus of attention, spatial situation model, spatial presence/ self-location, spatial presence/ possible actions, suspension of disbelief, involvement, domain-specific interest, and visual-spatial imagery [12]. The short version of the MEC-SPQ, i.e., 'Spatial Presence Experience Scale [3], focuses on two dimensions (self-location and possible actions) with 4 items per dimension.

Based on this theoretical background several questions were addressed in the study:

- Do different interfaces elicit different experiences of spatial presence?
- Does the use of the technical devices influence the experience of flow differentially?
- Do sports and game experience moderate the differential experience of spatial presence and flow?

Due to the reported evidence significant differences of spatial and game experience in favor of the less-constraining interface (i.e., the Kinect interface) were expected.

3   Method

As first step, a pilot study was performed to test the feasibility of the research design. Therefore a small group of only 8 students of sport science (4 males, 4 females) with ($N_1 = 4$) and without ($N_2 = 4$) specific experience in volleyball and playing digital games on consoles and computers (age: Range = 22 to 28 years; $M = 25.1$ years) volunteered to participate in the study. The participants played the volleyball games 'Sports Champions-Beach volleyball' on the Sony PS3 including the Interface 'Move' and 'kinect sports' on the Microsoft Xbox 360 including the interface 'kinect' (Figure 2). None of them had any previous experience with the interfaces of the two systems.

One male and one female of each group started with the Xbox 360 and the other two male and female group members started with the PS3. In the second session the console was switched. Playing each single game took between 4-7 minutes and playing the tutorial about 5 minutes. Two cameras, one in the front and one in the back of the player, recorded each session to get objective data in addition to the verbal reports of the participants. Both games played are similar to each other but not equal. They differ in the following categories: Interface, graphic representation, instruction, perspectives, sound, game session and avatar (Table 1). At the time of measurement no completely identical volleyball games were available for the two different consoles.

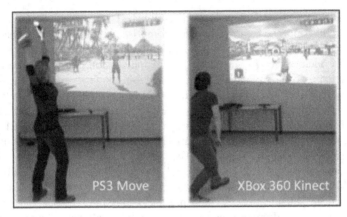

Fig. 2. Beachvolleyball games on PS3 and Xbox 360 (Source: Martin)

Table 1. Comparison of PS3 Move 'Sports Champions' vs. Xbox 360 kinect 'kinect sports'

	PS3 ‚Move' - ‚Sports Champions'	Xbox 360 ‚kinect' - ‚kinect sports'
Interface	• 1 or 2 PlayStation Move controller(s) with haptic feedback • PlayStation Eye • Direct kinematic Interface	• No controller, no haptic feedback • Kinect-Sensor (3D, Infrared, Prime Sense) • Indirect kinematic Interface
Graphic representation	• Better animation • More realistic style • Effect of an 'open space' (no boundary) surrounding the player	• Very 'unreal' style • Effect of a 'endemic space' (being surrounded by the audience, etc.)
Instructions	• Player learns complete moves • Player can choose different levels • Instructions during the match	• Player learns single basic moves • Only one level • No in-match instructions
Perspectives	• Bird's-eye view or third person view • Slow changes of perspective • Replay with first person and worm's-eye view	• Low third person view/worm's-eye view and rare switches to bird's-eye view • Quick changes of perspective • The players' avatar can turn around and stand face to face with the player
Sound	• Natural sound of the sea, birds and environment • Heroic music after every complete move	• Fast-paced music all the time • Enthusiastic audience (competition simulation)
Game Session	• Win by 8 points • No rotating serve within the team	• Win by 5 points • Rotating serve within the team
Avatar	• Avatar moves very accurately and dynamically • It's possible to control the avatar in many different ways and moves	• Avatar moves delayed and not very dynamic • Avatar imitates all movements of the player during the short breaks • Options for movement are very limited

Between and after playing two match sessions with each console, respectively, all participants completed two questionnaires: the SPES and the modified GEQ (based on [11]). For the statistical analysis SPSS 20 was used. ANOVAs and non-parametric follow-up tests (U test, Wilcoxon test) were applied. ANOVA was choosen because it is very solid despite the small N.

4   Quantitative Results, Discussion and Outlook

Significant differences between the two groups of non-athletes without game experience (N_1 = 4) and athletes with game experience (N_2 = 4) concerning frequency of sports activities (N=8, z=-2.37, $2p$= .018), playing with the Nintendo Wii (N=8, z=-2.25, $2p$=.025) and playing computer games (N=8, z=-2.000, $2p$=.046) were found.

A 2 (groups) x 2 (consoles) x 4 (items) Analysis of variance (ANOVA) with repeated measures on the last factor revealed significant main effects of groups ($F_{1,6}$ = 13.84, $p < .05$, partial η^2 = .70) and console ($F_{1,6}$ = 9.52, $p < .05$, partial η^2 = .63) and a significant interaction of consoles and items ($F_{3,18}$ = 3.31, $p < .05$, partial η^2 = .36) for the feeling of self-location (example item: 'I felt like I was actually there in the environment of the presentation') . For possible actions (example item: 'I had the impression that I could be active in the environment of the presentation') the main effect of groups missed the significance level of 0.05 ($F_{1,6}$ = 5.21, p = .06). Concerning flow (8 Items) ANOVA revealed a significant main effect of consoles ($F_{1,6}$ = 20.74, $p < .01$, partial η^2 = .78) and a significant interaction of consoles and items ($F_{7,42}$ = 6.17, $p < .01$, partial η^2 = .51). The participants reported a greater feeling of self-location and flow experience with the PS3, compared with the Xbox 360. This surprising result of great practical relevance as indicated by the large effect size seems to be due to the low degree of control in the Xbox volleyball game. The 3D technology did not recognize movements correctly and therefore disruptions in the gaming experience occurred. The results for possible actions support this explanation.

Due to the fact that the interface was not the only difference between the two consoles, other reasons like graphics, perspectives, sound, session and avatar (Table 1) could explain the results. Therefore, the results cannot clearly confirm the expectations that different game interfaces alone elicit different game experiences, particularly experience and perception of space. However in this game (genre), the relation of interface and control of the avatar is the key issue. Regardless of graphics, perspective, session, and sound, an avatar has to be controlled in real-time to solve motor tasks in sport. Therefore, it seems reasonable to assume that the superiority of the 'move' interface is due to the fact that feedback was both more accurate and less delayed than the feedback provided by the 'kinect' system. This explanation is confirmed by the verbal reports of all participants.

Further research must show whether the effects are really due to different interfaces or if there is an additional impact of graphics, perspectives, sound, session and avatar.

An additional question is whether effects are specific to particular game genres. Currently differences have been found in first person shooter games and sport games.

Furthermore it would be interesting to investigate which influence the players' comfort platform has on the measured spatial experience [2]. In the current pilot study the players did not have any experience with both interfaces.

Currently the main experiment is performed using a similar method with more detailed questionnaires (MEC-SPQ, SPES and GEQ) and a more detailed interview guideline. The optimal sample size is 20 participants (ES=0.7; $\alpha = 0.05$; 1-$\beta = 0.80$).

References

1. Csikszentmihalyi, M.: Flow: The psychology of optimal experience. Harper Perennial, New York (1990)
2. Gerling, K.M., Klauser, M., Niesenhaus, J.: Measuring the impact of game controllers on player experience. FPS games. In: MindTrek 2011, Tampere, Finnland, September 28-30 (2011)
3. Hartmann, T.: The Spatial Presence Experience Scale (SPES): A Short Self-Report Measure for Diverse Media Settings. University Amsterdam (2009) (unpublished manuscript)
4. Ijsselsteijn, W.A., Poels, K., de Kort, Y.A.W.: The game experience questionnaire: Development of a self-report measure to assess player experiences of digital games. FUGA technical report, Deliverable 3.3, TU Eindhoven, Eindhoven, Netherlands (2008)
5. Limperos, A.M., Schmierbach, M.G., Kegerise, A.D., Dardis, F.E.: Gaming Across Different Consoles: Exploring the Influence of Control Scheme on Game-Player Enjoyment. Cyberpsychology, Behavior, and Social Networking 14(6), 345–350 (2011)
6. Lombard, M., Ditton, T.: At the heart of it all: The concept of presence. Journal of Computer-Mediated Communication 3(2) (1997)
7. Martin, A.L., Wiemeyer, J.: Technology-mediated experience of space while playing digital sports games. International Journal of Computer Science in Sport 11(Special Edition 1: Serious Games - Theory, Technology & Practice), 135–146 (2012)
8. Nacke, L.E.: Wiimote vs. Controller: Electroencephalographic Measurement of Affective Gameplay Interaction. In: FuturePlay @ Vancouver Digital Week 2010, Vancouver, Canada, May 6-7 (2010)
9. Poels, K., de Kort, Y.A.W., Ijsselsteijn, W.A.: Game Experience Questionnaire. In: FUGA - The Fun of Gaming: Measuring the Human Experience of Media Enjoyment. Deliverable 3.3, TU Eindhoven, Eindhoven, The Netherlands (2008)
10. Sinclair, J., Hingston, P., Masek, M.: Considerations for the design of exergames. In: Proceedings of the 5th International Conference on Computer Graphics and Interactive Techniques in Australia and Southeast Asia, pp. 289–295. ACM, New York (2007)
11. Sweetser, P., Wyeth, P.: GameFlow: A model for evaluating player enjoyment in games. ACM Computers in Entertainment 3(3) (2005)
12. Wirth, W., Hartmann, T., Böcking, S., Vorderer, P., Klimmt, C., Schramm, H., Saari, T., Laarni, J., Ravaja, N., Gouveia, F.R., Biocca, F., Sacau, A., Jäncke, L., Baumgartner, T., Jäncke, P.: A Process Model of the Formation of Spatial Presence Experience. Media Psychology 9, 493–525 (2007)

Perceptual and Computational Time Models in Game Design for Time Orientation in Learning Disabilities

Geert Langereis, Jun Hu, Pongpanote Gongsook, and Matthias Rauterberg

Department of Industrial Design, Eindhoven University of Technology
{g.r.langereis,j.hu,p.gongsook,g.w.m.rauterberg}@tue.nl

Abstract. Several empirical studies confirm the importance of time-awareness in learning disabilities. Designed tools and environments to interact with time are essential for the training and diagnosis of an impaired notion of time. Training which improves sense of time may improve learning, daily functioning and quality of life. This paper reviews perceptual and computational time models in literature and present briefly our first attempts in applying the knowledge in the design of playful tools for children to orient their time.

Keywords: time models, time perception, learning disability, game design.

1 Introduction

Time perception is an abstract capability that facilitates the ability to predict, anticipate, and respond efficiently to coming events. For example, the preparation of fast responses benefit from the ability to predict precisely the point in time when an impending event requires a response. Also, precise representation of temporal information is required for the ability to organize and plan sequences of actions, particularly when sequences of novel or unskilled movements are required [1-3].

Several empirical studies confirm the importance of time orientation of children with learning disabilities [4]. The difficulty for processing time in its different dimensions has been shown to be an interesting universal characteristic of the dyslexic individual with reading problems. Furthermore, other conditions like Attention Deficit Disorders with hyperactivity (ADHD) appear to be characterized by comparable dysfunctions in time orientation.

Efforts in improving the time concepts of children in game design can already be found in many commercial or free products. Using a clock is a straightforward approach, such as the 24 Hour Analog Clock app for Android platforms [5]. TimeBuddy [6] from GoLearn International Inc tries to teach children about their daily routines and rhythms by using flash cards and stickers. Many interactive games are also available, for example Clockworks by BBC [7], teaching children how to tell time from a clock. On the website of free-training-tutorial.com, there are many similar "telling time" online games, most of which are using clocks as indicators of time or a time span [8]. Searching on Google with the keyword "time games for kids" returns a huge amount of hits, many of which are online games. A similar search using

S. Göbel et al. (Eds.): Edutainment 2012/GameDays 2012, LNCS 7516, pp. 183–188, 2012.

keywords "time games" and "learning disabilities" returns almost no links to products but concerns. A further investigation on these games discovers that most of these games are aims at teaching normal children using a straightforward clock concept without referring to or being based on clear and solid learning and time perception theories. Hardly any of them are designed for children with learning disabilities.

In interactive computer games for time orientation, instance and interval based computational computer models are applied in these games, either explicitly or implicitly. However while the goal of the games is to work on the mental models of the perceptual time, the computational models work at a lower level for the need of driving the games with time computation. Next we first review in the literature the concepts of the perceptual time models, followed by computational models. We then present three design cases where these time models are taken into account, as the first attempts in applying the knowledge in game design for children to orient their time to deal with learning disabilities.

2   Perceptual Models

Perceptual time models try to explain how time perception operates. In the literature, there are basically two categories of perceptual time models, depending on whether timing is seen as the output of a dedicated system. Grondin   provides a good overview of these models in his literature review about timing and time perception [9], as summarized in Table 1.

Table 1. Perceptual time models [9]

No Central Clock	intrinsic models	Timing is dependent specifically on a modality or a coordination-dependent system
	state-dependent network	Timing does not depend on a clock, but on time-dependent changes in the state of neural networks
With Internal Clock	Oscillators	There are temporal intervals embedded in sequences of signals.
	Pacemaker-counter models	The pacemaker emits pulses that are accumulated in a counter, and the number of pulses counted determines the perceived length of an interval.

The purpose of time perception in human beings is to become adaptive in behavior, because it facilitates the ability to predict, anticipate, and respond efficiently to future events. The first thing children learn in primary school is what day it is, what month and what year. This is preceded by the notion of day and night. This all includes the ability of time orientation. At a shorter timescale, the ability of time estimation is needed. To prepare for a fast response we have to develop the ability to predict the point in time when an event requires a response. A third time perception aspect helps us to perform executive tasks and to have a social life. Precise representation of temporal information is required for the ability to organize and plan a series of actions, particularly when such a sequence exists out of new or fairly-new actions. These three aspects of time are summarized in Table 2. The three categories differ in how the brain has to process the concept of time and differ in the time span.

Table 2. Methods to study timing and time

	Perception aspect	Methods
1	Time orientation (day, hour)	Zimbardo Time Perspective Inventory (ZTPI)
2	Time estimation (duration) or retrospective timing	Temporal order judgements related to auditory functions and temporal tasks
3	Planning or prospective timing	Short intervals (sec): prospective timing Long intervals: prospective memory and executive tasks

This overview provides a mapping for referencing to the different ways we interpret time perception. The orientation in time (absolute time) is described by the Zimbardo Time Perception Inventory (ZTPI) which provides an overview of how people remember and refer to time concepts [10].

Time estimation with respect to duration is a relative time concept. It involves the ability of retrospective timing and focuses on the estimation of past actions based on temporal judgement. This is based on short momentum in seconds or minutes [9].

Planning, or prospective timing, is orientated towards the future and can be discriminated in short and long term prospective timing. Short-term focuses on the timing itself while long-term prospective timing relates to memory [9].

Time perception has been assumed to be impaired in children with learning disabilities and some developmental impairment. Also, the occurrence of sleep disturbances in children with learning disabilities might be related to time concepts. For example, time orientation deficits have been studied with children with dyslexia, dyscalculia, autism, ADHD [4], and Duchenne Syndrome. However, the causal relation between training (the lack of) time perception and the impairment remains unclear.

3   Computational Models

Having looked into the perceptual models, we try to get an overview how timing and time are modeled in in multimedia systems, since most of the interactive games designed to improve children's time orientation are multi-modal by using multimedia content. Hu provides an extensive overview [11] based on the literature.

A multimedia system is characterized by integrated computer-controlled content generation, storage, communication, manipulation and presentation of independent time-dependent and time-independent media objects. Timing sits at the heart of multimedia systems, describing and managing the temporal relations between these media objects [12]. In multimedia systems, two representations of temporal relations can be indicated. These are based on *instants* and *intervals*. A time instant is a zero-length moment in time, such as "9:30am". By contrast, a time interval is defined by two time instants and therefore, their duration (e.g., "10s" or "9:30am to 9:40am").

Both instant and interval based models rely explicitly or implicitly on a timeline, which is often driven by a discrete computer clock. Comparing to the conceptual models in Table 1, one can easily conclude that these computational models work well with the perceptual models that do assume an internal clock. The perceptual models do not assume a central clock. They can therefore be implemented into state machine models or event driven models in computation. Although they are not necessarily described in the documentations of multimedia systems as basic timing mechanisms, these models are well supported by most of the computation platforms.

4   Design Cases

In the previous sections, we have seen there are indications of a link between time perception and some classes of learning and developmental disorders, and the perceptual time models are well supported by time models in multimedia systems. We have also seen that the concept of "time" plays a crucial role in computer architectures. This yields the assumption that there are design opportunities to create environments or products to interact with time. For example, in Virtual Reality environments, there are options to deviate from a linear progress of time [13]. We can switch in minutes from day to night or from summer to winter, or even reverse time. In addition, by using the multiple forms of product semantics, we may be able to interact with time by means of tangible products. In the following design cases, we show some examples of projects where products were designed with the aim to interact with time.

4.1   Retrospective Timing

The designed time interaction tool consists of a three-button input device and a software program (Fig. 1). The user has to memorize tone patterns of no more than three sounds that are supported by colored blocks on a screen. After a few seconds of pause, the sound has to be reproduced by pushing the buttons. The assumption is that children with dyslexia perform worse on the task, and show a slower learning curve for the accuracy of the task. An instant based time model is used to implement the program, but the intervals are derived from the time instants for the children to estimate the time span of the sound.

Fig. 1. Time interaction tool

4.2   A Timer for Parent-Child Interaction

When the parents tell their children to go to bed within five minutes, the concept of "five minutes" is hard to understand for a young child. A product is developed that visualizes time in an abstract way such that time becomes less tight and strict (Fig. 2).

The goal of this product is to introduce more structure in the daily life of parents with their baby/child. Through this product, the child learns to understand and deal with the concept of time, especially the time intervals which are essential for planning.

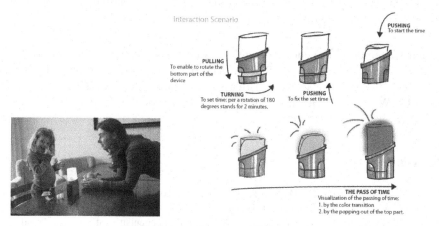

Fig. 2. A timer for parent-child interaction

4.3   Management of ADHD in Classrooms

In another project, we developed an interactive tool that helps children with Attention Deficit Hyperactivity Disorder (ADHD) to make fruitful use of breaks. Children with ADHD have concentration problems, but also problems with planning (so timing) of executive tasks. The interaction tool uses power breaks in a classroom to reflect and to plan the executive task in a playful way (Fig. 3). In this design, both time instants and intervals are important for the children to make proper planning.

Fig. 3. Management of ADHD in classrooms

5   Conclusions

According to literature, there are basically two types of perceptual timing models in humans, with or without a central clock. We think all these timing models shall play an important role in improving time orientation of children with learning disabilities. When designing interactive multimedia games, designers shall pay attention to not only the clock based time perceptual models, but also the models that do not necessarily require a clock. Technically speaking, all these perceptual models are well supported by the computational time models in multimedia systems in one way or the other. It is more a design challenge than a technical one. Three design cases are presented, to show our first attempts in developing interaction, training and diagnostic tools for children with time orientation problems, taking into account the problems in different perceptual time models that relate to the learning disabilities.

Acknowledgements. The authors would like to thank the students who designed the tools and games, among others, Rens Brankaert for retrospective timing, Teun van Roessel for ADHD management in classrooms, and Alice van Beukering, Kyra Frederiks, Wouter van Geesink and Bas van Hoeve for the timer for parent-child interaction.

References

1. Gibbon, J., Malapani, C., Dale, C.L., Gallistel, C.: Toward a neurobiology of temporal cognition: advances and challenges. Current Opinion in Neurobiology 7, 170–184 (1997)
2. Hazeltine, E., Helmuth, L.L., Ivry, R.B.: Neural mechanisms of timing. Trends in Cognitive Sciences 1, 163–169 (1997)
3. Ivry, R.: Cerebellar timing systems. International Review of Neurobiology 41,555 (1997)
4. Hurksa, P.P.M., Hendriksenbc, J.G.M.: Retrospective and Prospective Time Deficits in Childhood ADHD: The Effects of Task Modality, Duration, and Symptom Dimensions. Child Neuropsychology 17, 34–50 (2010)
5. Pomeroy, S.: 24h Analog Clock Widget (2011, May 1, 2012)
   https://play.google.com/store/apps/
   details?id=info.staticfree.android.twentyfourhour
6. GoLearn International Inc. TimeBuddy (May 1, 2012), http://timebuddy.com
7. BBC. Clockworks, A fun activity to help children at KS1 learn about telling the time (May 1, 2012), http://www.bbc.co.uk/bitesize/ks1/maths/telling_the_time/play/
8. FreeTrainingTutorial.com. Telling Time Games (May 1, 2012),
   http://www.free-training-tutorial.com/telling-time-games.html
9. Grondin, S.: Timing and time perception: a review of recent behavioral and neuroscience findings and theoretical directions. Attention, Perception, & Psychophysics 72, 561–582 (2010)
10. Zimbardo, P.G., Boyd, J.N.: Putting time in perspective: A valid, reliable individual-differences metric. Journal of Personality and Social Psychology 77, 1271 (1999)
11. Hu, J.: Design of a Distributed Architecture for Enriching Media Experience in Home Theaters, PhD Thesis, Department of Industrial Design, Eindhoven University of Technology, Eindhoven (2006)
12. Hu, J., Feijs, L.: IPML: Structuring Distributed Multimedia Presentations in Ambient Intelligent Environments. International Journal of Cognitive Informatics & Natural Intelligence (IJCiNi) 3, 37–60 (2009)
13. Bartneck, C., Hu, J., Salem, B., Cristescu, R., Rauterberg, M.: Applying Virtual and Augmented Reality in Cultural Computing. International Joural of Virtual Reality 7, 11–18 (2008)

StoryTec: Authoring Adaptive Cross-Platform Games

Florian Mehm and Christian Reuter

TU Darmstadt, Darmstadt, Germany
{florian.mehm,christian.reuter}@kom.tu-darmstadt.de

Abstract. In this workshop we will present the Authoring Tool StoryTec, which allows subject-matter-experts without programming experience to create games based on their domain knowledge. With one possible application being teachers who want to present their lecture in a novel way, it offers the possibility to create games which adapt themselves according to the player's knowledge or preferred style of play. In order to maintain ease of use StoryTec contains predefined templates, which the author can fill with his own content without needing to create the underlying structure himself. A recent update added minigames such as memory or puzzles and the ability to export the created game to multiple platforms like Windows, Mac, Android and Websites. The Workshop will include hands-on-exercises for which participants are encouraged to bring their own content like texts and images. We will also gather feedback and suggestions regarding new features, which will be considered for further versions of the Authoring Tool.

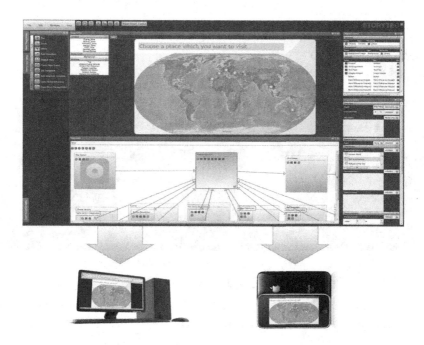

Fig. 1. Main window of StoryTec and export platforms

S. Göbel et al. (Eds.): Edutainment 2012/GameDays 2012, LNCS 7516, p. 189, 2012.
© Springer-Verlag Berlin Heidelberg 2012

Veni, Vidi, VICERO – But Where to Start?

Kai Erenli

University of Applied Sciences bfi Vienna/Film, TV & Media Production, Vienna, Austria
kai.erenli@fh-vie.ac.at

Abstract. To help educators pick the right Virtual World platform we have developed a Scoring Model and Criteria Catalogue which support choosing the most suitable platform for teaching purposes. Educators can use the Scoring Model to rate the criteria based on their respective demand. The Scoring Model will then suggest a Virtual World platform and instruct the educator how to install/use/maintain the platform. Which virtual world is most suitable for my needs? What are the first steps? What must be considered? Exactly these questions should be answered with the following Scoring Model, which we developed to solve the problems you will be encountered with. Workshop participants will be able to get a hands-on demonstration and to test Virtual Worlds and Environments on their own but under supervision. They will also get the story behind VICERO and be able to give input for further development of the scoring model.

Project VICERO

Fig. 1. VICERO

S. Göbel et al. (Eds.): Edutainment 2012/GameDays 2012, LNCS 7516, p. 190, 2012.

Author Index